CHICAGO RAGTIME

Chicago Ragtime
Another Look at Chicago 1880–1920

Richard Lindberg

Icarus Press
South Bend, Indiana
1985

CHICAGO RAGTIME: ANOTHER LOOK
AT CHICAGO, 1880–1920 Copyright
© 1985 by Richard Lindberg

*All rights reserved. No part of this book
may be used or reproduced in any manner whatsoever
without the written permission of the publisher,
except in the case of brief quotations
embodied in critical articles and reviews.*

Manufactured in the United States of America.

1   2   3   4   5   88   87   86   85

Icarus Press, Inc.
Post Office Box 1225
South Bend, Indiana 46624

Library of Congress Cataloging in Publication Data

Lindberg, Richard, 1953–
   Chicago ragtime.

   Bibliography: p.
   Includes index.
   1. Chicago (Ill.)--History--1875-
2. Chicago (Ill.)--Social conditions. 3. Chicago
(Ill.)--Social life and customs. I. Title.
F548.45.L56   1985   977.3'11041   85-4318
ISBN 0-89651-103-0

To Shoeless, Happy, Chick, and Swede. To Buck, Fred, Cicotte, and Lefty, who paid the price.
" . . . nothing to look backward to with pride, and nothing to look forward to with hope."
—Robert Frost

Contents

"What a Young Man Ought to Know" ix
Foreword: This Is *Not* a Book about the
    Chicago World's Fair xi
1. Chicago's Labor Pains: Cops, Anarchists,
    and Haymarket 1
2. Close-up on the 1880s: The Boodler's Bathroom Escape 45
3. A Summer of Gold: Chicago in 1896 74
4. Close-up on the 1890s: Dawn of a New Century 114
5. Levee Low Life 119
6. Close-up on Chicago in the 1900s: Virtue and Betrayal 169
7. ... Of Bombs, Gamblers, Racing Wires,
    Newspaper Wars, & Mont Tennes 177
8. A Summer of Lost Innocence, May to August 1919 214
Sources and Notes 257
Index 268

"What a Young Man Ought to Know"

"No Young Man or young woman can afford to read fiction before they [sic] are twenty five years of age. There is too much that is indispensable for intelligence, for laying of foundation principles for study, for business, health and morals, that need to be read first. If fiction is begun before a correct taste is formed and foundation principles laid, the best books will never be read at all. The habit of reading rapidly for the simple sake of the story will destroy the power, and even the wish, to read thoughtfully and seriously. The power to concentrate thought will, as a consequence, never be acquired. A vitiated taste is the inevitable result. If it is important that the body should be fed upon the most nourishing food, the same is also true of that upon which the mind is to be fed.

"Read only the best. There are but few books that have enough of merit to enable their publishers to sell the first edition. The book that lives five years has some merit; those that live ten have more; but many of the best books are twenty-five and fifty years old or more. The books which start a young man aright, which impart the right principles, inspire with high and holy ambition, and give a dauntless and undying purpose, are the best books."

—Sylvanus Stall, D.D.,
Purity & Truth: Self and
Sex Series: What a Young
Man Ought to Know

FOREWORD
This Is *Not* a Book about the Chicago World's Fair

SOME YEARS AGO, I READ A MARVELOUS BOOK CALLED *Time and Again* BY A New York-based writer named Jack Finney. It was the hard-to-put-down kind of book, concerning a secret government plan to send an average 1970s man back in time to New York of 1882. The hero sees the sights, solves a ninety-year-old mystery, and falls in love. When the time comes to return to his own age, he weighs his options and decides to remain. I think many of us have shared this fantasy at some point in our lives.

Jack Finney wanted to live his character's life, and during his research time, he *did*. Each day Finney visited the New York Public library's reading room piecing his story together and reveling in every new discovery. He found a strange, long-lost world that seemed better than his own. On the outside, there was the din of 42nd Street traffic and the presence of steel-and-glass towers choking out the sunlight. Inside, Finney could hear horse-drawn carriages briskly trotting down cobblestone streets. I never met Jack Finney, but I think I understand how he felt when he was putting his book together. Sometimes you need a little Walter Mitty in you to get through the present, which at times seems like an impossible mess.

This book is not a fantasy, but it could be. Everything really happened—proving to me, at least, that history is stranger than fiction. Like Finney, I wanted to write a book about the years between the Civil War and the war that changed everything. At all times, Chicago provided the backdrop for the stories. What was Chicago then? It was brawling, totally corrupt, but always wonderful. The town sprung from the ashes of the 1871 fire because the financiers, immigrants, cops, trade unionists, reformers, and even the "low life" forged their talents to the task before them. As Robert Casey observed, Chicago "is an independent miracle—vigorous, powerful and uninhibited. It takes the risks and it needs no advice."

In 1893, Chicago paused to pay homage to its growth and, coincidentally, the founding of America by Christopher Columbus. The result of their months of planning was the World's Columbian Exposition, which convinced the provincial eastern critics that the ugly frontier town had become a thriving metropolis. This book is *not* about the World's Fair, however.

Other writers have described the singular miracles of the "White City" better than I could. It is a fact that no other single aspect of Chicago history (with the exception of Al Capone and the Great Fire) has been studied as much as the 1893 Fair.

As Chicago approached the twentieth century, it was a city struggling to establish its own identity. The new industrial age brought with it a changed value system and new temptations. As Ray Ginger described it in his book *Altgeld's America*, it was the "Lincoln Ideal Versus the Changing Realities." Victorian ideas about chastity and morality continued to hold sway in the popular media, as well as from the church pulpit. Yet the city recognized that man was an imperfect being and therefore entitled to his vices. But only in the context of a segregated two-mile district where every libidinous desire known to man was indulged.

They created the levee . . . and then tried for twenty years to close it. Vice and reform earned Chicago its lusty reputation. It's the only city in America where the reformers were in it for an angle.

I've always wanted to write a book about those changing turbulent years. When I started, I was unsure of what directions to take, but like driving south on Halsted, I knew I would find something along the way. Some of the stories are obscure; others are not.

There are incidents of crime, scandal, and mayhem in the streets. The *real* history of this town cannot be written any other way. Chicago is a brutal city; a world apart from Beacon Hill, Greenwich Village, and New York's Lower East Side. Reality exists in the neighborhoods of Studs Lonigan, Ruth Younger, and Sister Carrie. The spirit of the city is captured in its literature—sometimes gloomy, but honest and direct.

Foreword

I have not intentionally avoided the city's cultural achievements. Louis Sullivan's architecture, the music of Theodore Thomas, and the sculpturing of Augustus Saint-Gaudens are timeless examples of Chicago's creative vision. They will always stand by themselves, but somehow they belong to another Chicago. Artistry is born from inspiration. After inspiration . . . New York. This city will break your heart if you remain too long. No one knew this better than Theodore Dreiser, but the mood of the city left its mark in his writing, as it has every Chicago artist.

The millionaries, the immigrants, the politicians, and the crooks remained. Their lives are profiled here.

Offered for your consideration in this volume are Mont Tennes, Professor Holmes, Brownie, King of the Bums; Mossie Enright; the terrible Gentlemen brothers; Hinky Dink Kenna; and the boss of them all, Mike McDonald. This book also remembers the glittering world of the Chicago wealthy. Their lives are contrasted to some of the little people, the unknowns, who through one single desperate act of their lives put their names in the papers and, years later, my book.

People. Were they so different back then? We can look at the old tintypes and stiffly posed family portraits and see grim, determined faces that never smiled. We conclude that they must have worked dawn to dusk and beat their children for the sport of it. But sometimes you have to look at the picture *within* the picture. Look closely at some of the downtown street scenes at the turn of the century. The cameraman captured a *moment*, a frozen second of time when a young woman is admiring a new dress in Field's display window or the man crossing the street commenting on the Chicago Colts' tough loss. Caught off guard, they are showing the same emotions and motivations that people have since time began.

But they were different from us because Chicago was quite a different place. There were houses on Michigan Avenue and celery farms on Ashland Avenue, when the "country" was still Lakeview and Norwood Park. People lived closer to downtown and traveled only as far as the streetcar ran.

Intolerance to blacks and the foreign born was tacitly encouraged by the media. Corruption in the city government and within the police force was more widespread than it is now, due in part to ethnic cronyism. The saloon became the focal point of the city neighborhood, and within its walls, the alliance with the city council was cemented. First a barkeep, then an alderman, or so the story goes.

They didn't have the pervasive media influence, so people attended theatre, went to lectures, and spent more time with their families and neighbors. They formed neighborhood organizations and belonged to fraternal brotherhoods, where they shared common experiences with other newly arrived immigrants from their homeland. The fraternal orders have somehow survived the second and third generations, but their numbers continue to dwindle because assimilation has been achieved.

The key to their world for me were the newspapers, for the newspapers provide as accurate a portrayal as any of a past age. Traditional historians will argue that newspapers cannot be trusted. Their research time is devoted to the study of diaries and letters left behind. Average people rarely kept a diary, and the noted men of letters had little contact with the flow of American life.

The *Chicago Tribune* served as my guide because (with apologies to Melville Stone and Wilbur Storey) no other paper of that time reported the news as thoroughly and consistently. The *Tribune* postured, preached, and at times was downright unfair in its political views, but it was truly a great paper for the time. Opposing points-of-view were provided by the sensational Hearst newspapers, always the sliver in the skin of the conservative *Tribune*. As a writer and observer of the period, it was my job to evaluate the sometimes conflicting data and *then* interpret. Too often, the political current in the city room clouded the real picture.

I returned to the neighborhoods and street corners where these people once lived and worked. The pleasant tree-lined streets of the 1880s and 1890s have been replaced by squalid slums, impersonal high rises, or, in some cases, vacant lots. The Chicago Coliseum, sight of the colorful First Ward Ball and William Jennings Bryan's "cross of gold" speech, stands in ruins on Wabash Avenue. The wooden doors have caved in, but the front façade remains. Prairie Avenue mansions, the stockyard district, and the beautiful old train stations are vanished symbols of Chicago's industrial might. Some of the photographs in this book show the modern realities of the city. Chicago has selfconsciously destroyed the historic reminders of its raw adolescence—all destroyed in the name of progress and the lingering embarrassment because of its reputation. To the historian and preservationist who mourns the passing of Burnham's and Root's Masonic Temple, *progress* is just a buzz word for "carelessness."

It can be no other way in Chicago because there is just no time to

Foreword

stop and evaluate where we have been. Always building, ever growing, the city remains vibrant and alive. In the summer time, Chicago emerges from its winter blues. Baseball. Yes, baseball! Boat rides in the Lincoln Park Lagoon. Bicycling and ice cream sundaes with real cream. Is there anyone still alive who remembers legal fireworks ("Have a Sane Fourth!"), jackstraws, and the little books whose silhouetted pages *moved* when they were flipped rapidly? This is the idyllic city before the Great War and before the race riot.

This was the Chicago without fault, the city that the older generation prefers to remember. In their rejection of the troubled present, they forget that summer was many other things also.

Summer killed. Summer was a time for renewal. The simple joys of urban existence were often just a contrast to the ugly and grotesque slice of life—seen through a broken, dirty pane of glass by a small child living on Maxwell Street. To stay alive in this town you had to be tough and mean, especially during the summer months when the streets were an angry, dusty, sweating stew.

I'd like to acknowledge the assistance and inspiration provided by some special people. Again, Bruce Fingerhut and his wife Laila transcended the usual author-publisher relationship. The staff at the Chicago Historical Society and the Chicago Public Library Microfilm Reading Room were always cooperative, and so was Phil Sander of Kenosha and Mrs. Spicknell at St. Elizabeth's Hospital.

The Chicago writing tradition is being kept alive in the coffee houses, public libraries, and other places where artists gather to critique and offer encouragement to one another. The Grassfield Writer's Collective has provided that outlet to myself and others, and I am grateful.

Thanks to Bob Deckert of Fort Walton Beach, Florida, an unrecognized talent whose illustrations for this book are greatly appreciated. My parents, Oscar and Helen Lindberg, wanted only the best things for me, while Jim Janda, Denise Lindberg, and little Anna Deckert provided moral support during the down times. And to Joyce Pelc, an old college friend who saw a book or two in my future, thanks belatedly.

Richard Lindberg
Fall 1984

1
Chicago's Labor Pains: Cops, Anarchists, and Haymarket

PROLOGUE: June 27, 1885

AT LAST DERBY DAY HAD ARRIVED—A DAY FOR HANDSOME LIVERIES, beautiful ladies, and stalwart men. The summer social season would commence with the running of the famed American Derby at the Washington Park Grounds located at 61st and Cottage Grove Avenue.

For one brief afternoon, the fashionable and well-heeled ladies of the south side would put aside their notions about the vulgar sport of horse racing and the wagering that accompanied it. Summer! The skies were a radiant azure blue this particular morning, as the stone castles up and down Grand Boulevard and Prairie Avenue stirred to life. Inside the great houses of the Ryersons, Catons, Chauncey Blairs, and Armours, the domestics worked furiously to make this day special for their lords.

Much of the parlor talk concerned Mary Leiter's debut in Washington society. She attended Grover Cleveland's inaugural the previous March, and surely she would find a man of good position to bring honor to the old Chicago name of Leiter. Levi's daughter would do well for herself. Dazzling them in her black silk gown of scarlet and gold, she would soon become Lady Curzon and be off to India with her husband as the viceroy and vicereine for Queen Victoria.

Had Chicago at last taken its rightful place in American society? Is it proper for a lady to be seen alone in a hansom cab? Was progressive euchre (a card game that was the rage that summer) a bad thing for one's character? The questions were surely asked that morning by women who had little knowledge of the deep changes that were swirling about them and would change the course of their lives. The answers to these serious dilemmas were to be found in the little volume entitled *Don't* by Oliver Bellbunce, popularly known by his pen name, the "Censor." Bellbunce patiently outlined proper manners for the cretins who did not know better. Well-bred people *don't* eat with a knife, you know.

It was a steaming hot day, but at least a lady could wear a cooling white gown over her bustle and hip pads. To achieve the desired "shapely" look, a woman need only employ a whalebone tied together in the casings to create the "hump." If expensive whalebone could not be secured, then a coiled spring would do. (Foreign-born shop girls who also coveted the current fashion tied old newspapers together and placed them in their underskirt.) The skirts were multi-layered and lined with muslin. Sleeves were drawn skin tight, and a lady required a button hook to undo the numerous buttons that ran up to the elbow. The hump and the bustle remained in vogue until 1890, when Worth of Paris decided he was tired of the look and announced that he would make no more.

So with petticoats rustling and her bonnet secure milady stepped into the sunshine and her awaiting cab, and Derby Day *really* began.

The true measure of a man's worth was his carriage. For weeks the C.P. Kimball Company had feverishly manufactured carriages of all makes for the Derby. Twenty-six hand-crafted rigs had been sold to Chicago millionaires in just twenty-one days. Double suspension Victorias Demi-Landaus, Tally-Ho coaches, Langhams, English White Chapel Dog Carts, Stanhope Phaetons, drawn four-in-the-hand led one social observer to rave about how far Chicago society had progressed since the bleak period following the great fire of 1871.

The true display of regal ostentation was the promenade down Grand Boulevard and across to Drexel with its tree-lined parkways and elegant stone mansions. To show off one's dog cart on Derby Day was becoming a Chicago tradition. The first derby was held just a year earlier, but already some things were established.

It was a leisurely southward drive to the racetrack, a half hour if anyone bothered to count the minutes. The boulevards were alive with people this fair afternoon. A brief shower at noon gave way to sunshine so the carriage tops were lowered and the society belles twirled their summer parasols while graciously acknowledging old friends along the way.

"Such a gathering of thoroughbred animals, such a meeting of the highest social elements, such a display of fashion, elegance and wealth, and beauty has never been seen upon any race course in the country," exclaimed the *Chicago Inter-Ocean* the next day. The owners must have been proud; this was what Washington Park had been created for in the winter of 1882–83. The Chicago Driving Park on the western edge of the city had proven to be inadequate. The club was officially chartered on February 10, 1883, "to promote good fellowship among its members by providing a clubhouse and pleasure grounds for their entertainment where at all times they may meet for social intercourse, and further, to encourage by providing the proper facilities, raising, improving, breeding, training, and exhibiting horses at meetings to be held at stated times each year." One-hundred-seventy-four stockholders contributed the funds to pay architect Solon Beman to design a place where the rough element—the Swedes, Poles, Irish, Jews, and Germans—might be kept at a safe distance from the clubhouse.

Seating inside the Washington Park Clubhouse was limited to the "best" 800—families of Anglo-Saxon vintage, whose wealth and esteem extended back to the early Chicago era of John Kinzie and Mark Beaubien. To be listed in clubhouse membership? Well, there was simply no finer honor. Unless, of course, one belonged to the Commercial Club, whose membership numbered just sixty. The Commercial Club was for the prime movers of Chicago business and industry, the captains of trade who gathered together the last Saturday of each month at varying locations to discuss the "topic." It could be the fixing of railroad rates, deals in the pit, or the tinkering with the destiny of the city. Over cigars and brandy, the sixty members were notified of the evening's subject of discussion from a courier sent out by the club secretary several weeks before the meeting.

The best and the brightest were clubmen, whether it be the Union League Club, the Union Club, the Iroquois Club, or the Calumet Club, where an imposing 8' x 13' oil portrait of General Ulysses Grant inspired John Wentworth to donate a 10' x 15' portrait of himself. It was a world of privilege.

On Derby Day, the clubmen brought along their bored wives. "Toilets of unusual elegance worn by ladies of position, grace, and beauty were seen on every side," the *Inter-Ocean* continued. They moved easily through the clubhouse, enjoying the luncheon music of Austin & Rosenbecker's First Regiment Band playing Offenbach, while boys were sent downstairs to lay "Paris mutual" bets for them. To stand in a line of betting men was unthinkable.

Outside, dark clouds gathered. Carriage tops were raised by those who could only be content with positions by the guard rails. The lucky ones succeeded in raising their carriage tops before the first drop fell. And then it poured for almost two hours, and there was nowhere to go. The track, which had been pronounced "fast," suddenly became a muddy quagmire with standing pools of water. Small boys dashed between the carriages selling programs to people who were suddenly in no mood to make merry.

With heads held high and determined looks on their proud faces, Mr. and Mrs. Arthur Caton appeared in their carriage with Charles Schwartz lashing his "four in the hand" into the grounds. Proud people they were, these Catons. Their landau was splashed with mud and muck. Their summer finery was soaked and ruined, for they rode in a topless carriage that they had purchased for the event. Nevertheless, they were Catons, and no singular act of God would stop Derby Day . . . or the chuckles of Mrs. Potter Palmer, secure and dry in the clubhouse.

At three o'clock the skies broke, and cheers were heard from the grandstand. The jockeys appeared from the stables to inspect the track. Their feet sank in the mud. This sent the high rollers back to the odds boards while Secretary John E. Brewster navigated his way across a makeshift sidewalk that had been constructed for him. After conferring with the judges, Brewster rang the bell. Let the races begin!

The American Derby was the featured event of a five-race card and the richest stakes in the west. Nobody seemed to care that Kosciusko won the first race in 1:49 flat or that the second event, known as the Lakeside Stakes, went to a two-year old named Trance. The American Derby was the third event, and the men in the clubhouse decided to move close to the rail to get a better look. The young ladies who stood by the rail found themselves outnumbered by men, but wasn't it grand! They flirted, they chatted, they bet their candy, gloves, and glasses of lemonade, and somehow never lost!

The American Derby was for three-year-olds, the finest horse flesh in America. The favorite was Ten Stone, owned by Edward Corrigan, a Chicago racing promoter who also ran the West Side grounds. In 1891, he went into direct competition with Washington Park by founding the Hawthorne Track in suburban Cicero.

Just before race time, Ten Stone was scratched. The odds were upset because Isaac Murphy, known in racing circles as the "Colored Archer," who was the most successful jockey in America, was not riding.

The new favorite was Volante, owned by the Baldwin Stables of California. "Plunger" Walton, big-time New York investor, rushed to the post to attend to this matter. Gambler, speculator, and rogue, Walton transacted a last-minute deal with Corrigan. Five hundred dollars to the "Colored Archer" if he agreed to ride, and $1,000 to Corrigan if the horse won. It took ten seconds to decide. Murphy, who won the 1884 Derby riding Modesty, mounted Volante.

This upset the odds again, but Walton already had $2,000 riding on Volante. The horse was magnificent, appearing at the gate wearing the Baldwin colors of black and red with a Maltese Cross. They left the gate with Alta Favor and Alf Estell breaking into an early lead. But Murphy urged his steed on with whip and spur. As they entered the final turn, Volante took over the lead. Alta Favor finished second, a full two lengths behind. Plunger Walton was given a marker good for $8,000.

There were two more races, but Chicago society departed after the derby. An estimated crowd of 20,000 (which would swell to 40,000 in the following years) dwindled to a mere 2,000 souls, as the broughams and landaus made their way out of the gates.

The afternoon waned. Gas lamps on Michigan Avenue flickered on to greet the approaching night. The great thoroughfare was still residential in 1885 and was still known as Pine Street north of the Chicago River. Everyone wanted to live on these streets, thought by many to be lined with gold.

"Those were leisurely days," recalled Mrs. Carter Harrison, Jr., in her memoirs of Chicago society, *Strange to Say*, when life seemed easy and there was plenty of time to spare. We had the telephone and the electric light, and to us it seemed that there was nothing more to be dreamed of. But we had much to learn."

It was a doomed, but enchanted world those rich and prominent Chicagoans lived in. All about them was disease and poverty, but they did not hear the voices of protest that were being stifled by Chicago's red-faced Irish cops. Receptions, charity balls, club meetings, summer gaiety, and dashing swains like Fred Tuttle ("Everybody's favorite beau!") were the important things for Chicago society in 1885. For the eighties were elegant, and the nineties were gay. Except for the "Roaring" 20s, no adjective has been applied to a decade since that might capture the feeling of a time.

One by one the old robber barons and family patriarchs died off. Their children abandoned the south-side mansions for more opulent surroundings. The old houses stood for a time, finally succumbing to urban blight. High weeds . . . crumbling stone . . . decay. Their houses became tenements. The tenements were leveled, and in their place stood parking lots or housing projects. All that is left behind for us to look at are the impressionist paintings they brought back from Europe, which now hang in quiet repose within the Art Institute. Their enormous marble burial sarcophagi stand side by side in Graceland Cemetery The finest of them all belongs to Mr. and Mrs. Potter Palmer. The tomb stands atop a small ridge, overlooking the grave sites of their friends. Mrs. Palmer would have been pleased.

The social registers listing the days that they accepted visitors for tea (see appendix) collect dust in the library. The Washington Park Racetrack is a ghostly memory now, razed in 1908. Forgotten is Isaac Murphy's run for the money down the sloppy track in June 1885. That Derby Day, the world of Palmers, Ishams, Catons, and all their expensive finery, was doomed to extinction because an idea had reached its time. It was an idea that began many years earlier but really didn't take hold in Chicago until an eloquent young southerner mounted some packing crates to address a torchlight rally on a warm July evening in 1877.

*   *   *

Honesty, sobriety, obedience are the three cardinal virtues of the policeman. With these, if he be a man gifted with a fair share of brains, education, and nerve, he may rise steadily. The present force is one of the best Chicago has ever had. Strict discipline has been maintained for at least six years, and nearly all the rotten timber has been thrown out.

—John Flinn, writing of the police in 1887.

One thousand tired, ragged, but spirited men huddled together in a vacant lot at 12th and Halsted Streets. There was excitement in the air this night. Signs were held aloft, proclaiming "Down With Wage Slavery!" The meeting was called together by a lean twenty-nine-year-old southern man named Albert Parsons. On this evening, Parsons would divorce himself from mainstream politics and a conventional lifestyle that put food on the table for himself and his bride Lucy. Parsons would speak of the labor troubles in the East. He would tell his listeners about the wives of the striking railroad men who were forced to sell their bodies for thirty cents just to put food on the table. Organize, men!

The great Railroad Strike of 1877 began on July 16, at Camden Junction, Maryland. It was a reaction to the Pennsylvania Railroad's decision to cut wages 10 percent, the fourth such reduction in seven years. When members of the blacklisted locomotive, firemen's, and engineer brotherhoods blocked the trains at Martinsburg, West Virginia, a local militia known as the Berkeley Light Guards were ordered to disperse a meeting at a local train station. But they did not wish to fire on their neighbors, so they threw down their weapons and joined the strike. Like wildfire, the strike spread to Pittsburgh, where twenty six were killed, and on to Harrisburg, Scranton, Reading, Columbus, Cincinnati, St. Louis, and Chicago.

Parsons was the son of Samuel Parsons of Maine, a man who traced his lineage back to Narragansett Bay in 1632. Other members of the Parsons family fought alongside of Washington and were prominent in the young republic. It was almost unheard of for members of such old American families to be involved in the radical labor movement. Young Albert was orphaned at age five and was raised by his brother in Johnson County, Texas. He became an indentured apprentice in 1859 at the *Galveston Daily News* and was later a member of the Lone Star Grays during the Civil War.

After the war, Parsons's political connections landed him a job as assistant assessor for the U.S. Internal Revenue Service. The radical transformation for this man of temperate political views began when he relocated to Chicago in 1872. Parsons became politically conscious after he uncovered evidence of graft involving the Chicago Relief and Aid Society, formed by Mayor Roswell Mason to assist victims of the Chicago Fire. The society took charge of food donations, clothing, and raw goods that poured into Chicago from all quarters. But traincar loads of food would often lay idle on the tracks and perish through mismanagement, while people continued to starve.

Parsons joined the Social Democratic Party in 1876, but that group could not agree on principle, so the party splintered into radical and conservative factions. The Workingmen's Party of the United States was organized in Philadelphia in July 1876. The Social Democratic Party, which Parsons joined, later merged with the Workingmen's Party, eventually becoming the Socialist Labor Party of the United States.

To organize a trade union or to overthrow the existing order was the subject that labor leaders debated. The Chicago faction were really "syndicalists," whose members believed in workers' control over business. The radicals favored the idea of "individual anarchism," espoused by Pierre Proudhon, an idea adopted by Parisians during the Paris Commune of 1871 (hence, the word *Communist* or *Communard*).

But it took a German socialist named Johann Most, traveling the American lecture circuit, to bring the idea to the United States. Most was expelled from the Social Democratic Party for his anarchist leanings, but he found a sympathetic following in the German workers who gathered together in the Turner Haus and *Weinstubes* of the large cities.

On July 21, 1877, Parsons had not yet embraced the idea of individual anarchy. He merely urged the men to sign the labor party pledge sheet and to organize trade unions. The crowd was enthusiastic, diverted momentarily by the appearance of a popular stage actor who yelled encouragement to Parsons. The police showed restraint, and soon the meeting disbanded.

The next day Parsons returned to his job at the *Chicago Times*. He was amazed to discover that he had been blacklisted and discharged from his duties as a printer. Later, he was accosted by two plainclothes policemen while visiting the German labor newspaper *Arbeiter-Zeitung*. He was told that Mayor Monroe Heath wanted to see him, but Parsons was actually escorted arm in arm to meet Police Chief Michael Hickey at the city hall.

The room was crowded with police officers and railroad officials demanding some kind of protection from the hostile mobs. Hickey glared at Parsons. "Do you know better than to come up here from Texas to incite the working people to insurrection?" In Hickey's eyes there was nothing worse than a southern rebel. The chief didn't need any problems of this kind, for he was in the last year of a brief, but unspectacular, term as police superintendent. He was a twenty-year veteran of the force, a man whose career was rife with charges of corruption and various intrigues. In 1873, he quit the force in a huff after he was charged with official corruption by the *Chicago Post* and *Mail*. He was reinstated, and his rise in the force was meteoric. Mayor Harvey D. Colvin, an independent elected as a reaction to Mayor Joseph Medill's "Fire Proof," "Liquor Proof" administration, appointed Hickey in 1875.

Honesty was never a saving virtue for Hickey. He invested in some gambling property controlled by Mike McDonald and was later charged with allowing the vice dens in the Lake Street area to operate full blast. Twenty-five patrolmen from the Lake Street Station were brought before a board of inquiry to answer charges, but none agreed to testify.

Hickey replaced Jacob Rehm who resigned the office in 1875 after it was revealed that he had a role in a whiskey ring conspiracy that bilked the government out of thousands of dollars. When the issue of Michael Hickey's retention came to a vote in the city council on July 9, 1878, he was cast out by a vote of 22 to 11.

Parsons tried to reason with Hickey while men in dark suits and derby hats muttered "lynch him." That would never do, someone said. The workers would rise up, and there would be a Chicago Commune. Hickey took Parsons by the arm and escorted him into the hall of the Rookery Building, a symbol of capitalist power to the radicals. "Parsons, your life is in danger. I advise you to leave this city at once," Hickey said. "Why, those Board of Trade men would as soon hang you to a lamppost as not."

Before the Market Street rally, Parsons was an unknown in Chicago. That same night, he visited the composing room of the *Chicago Tribune* to see if he could get in a night's work, but he was slugged from behind by two thugs who dragged him out, threatening to toss him off the fifth-floor stairwell. "Now, go," one of them said. "If you ever put your face in this building again, you'll be arrested and locked up." Parsons then walked the streets of downtown Chicago, populated by Illinois National Guardsmen assigned to keep the peace. Class war had seemingly come to Chicago.

Undaunted by their threats, Parsons appeared the next night at Sacks Hall at Brown and 20th Streets, where the reception was even more enthusiastic. They had read of him in the papers and were anxious to hear him speak. This time the speech took on more militant tones. Parsons called for the nationalization of railroads, adoption of the eight-hour workday, and formation of the People's Labor Party. "And we should be perfectly happy with a bowl of rice and a rat apiece every week," he added.

The great strike reached Chicago on July 23, when the switchmen of the Michigan Central walked off the job. Management had just put through a $10 monthly pay cut. At 9 A.M., the Illinois Central freight men joined their comrades in a march down Randolph Street. The depot at the foot of Lake Street was closed by men carrying sticks and marching two abreast toward the Market Square rally. There Parsons asked the crowd what should be done with the capitalists. "Hang them!" "Throw them in the lake!" Parsons advised them not to attack unless they themselves were attacked. In the background, men carrying the red banner of anarchy began singing the "Marsellaise."

Freight cars were halted the next day, while "committees" of militant workmen visited the depots to advise agents that no trains would be allowed to leave the Chicago yards without the most dire consequences. Trading ceased at the board, and money due Chicago commission men on shipments were unable to reach their destinations. Grain lay idle in box cars, and for a brief time, Chicago commerce was at a halt. The *Tribune* of July 24, 1877, castigated the labor men for their actions.

> In ordering and compelling the cessation of freight trains on all the railroads, the wedge has been entered for overturning the whole commercial and industrial structure, and the houses if pulled down will fall upon those who have started the work of revolution.

Revolution it was not. But the paper was correct in its initial assessment. By the 1870s, the railroad was the master of American interstate commerce. Cities and towns were born, and many more withered away simply because a railroad baron could decide which town would be granted a connecting line and which wouldn't.

In addition to creating massive wealth, social mobility, and progress for the chosen few, the railroads also had a terrible power to corrupt and exploit. The little man who risked life and limb in a rail yard was often the victim of wage cutting, hour reduction, and blacklisting.

The next day the RED WAR! (as the Tribune headline writer described it) began. The opening skirmish has been called by some the "Battle of the Viaduct." It was probably worse than that. One thousand five hundred tradesmen, socialists, and several vagabonds gathered at the Chicago, Burlington, and Quincy viaduct at Halsted and 16th Streets to stir up a little trouble. Historians sympathetic to the labor movement have lost sight of the fact that there were those present who engaged in riot for the sheer sport of it. Of this, there can be no doubt. The men smashed windows in the roundhouses so that they could advance on the idle locomotives. Engines were demolished and track was torn up before a detachment of police from the 12th Street Station arrived on the scene. Lieutenant Callahan and his twenty men surveyed the mob that had grown to 3,000, thought the better of it, and returned to the station for reinforcements.

John Hickey of the Madison Street station commanded forty armed reserves, who fired warning shots over the mob. This whipped the rioters into a greater frenzy. They began throwing stones and railroad spikes at the cops, who fired directly into the crowd. Nine of the sixteen rounds the police had were discharged. Fourteen were killed, dozens more were wounded. But the sheer size of the mob drove the police back to the station. Meanwhile several men took charge of the mob, leading them down Halsted Street toward a gun and hardware store. From a second floor window a man poked his head out.

"Give us some knives and powder!" someone called.

"You'll have to talk to the boss on that score," the man said.

They didn't want the boss. The door was broken down, and the store was looted. A streetcar was overturned at the viaduct before Lieutenant Vesey of the Hinman district appeared. As one paper so glibly put it, the "cheerful sound of cracking heads could be heard."

Six companies of the 22nd Infantry had just arrived from the Sioux territory but were pressed into duty by President Hayes to restore order to panic-stricken Chicago. With some stern help from the Chicago police, incidents of riot were scattered by July 26 and ended completely the following day.

"Perhaps the most credible performance of the police was the almost total annihilation of the notorious Hassett family. They were the ring leaders in the mob and are a good riddance to the community," the *Tribune* said the day after the riot. The strike in Chicago cost the city $2.3 million. One by one other cities witnessed the cessation of violence, but a scorched earth of dead and bleeding men was one direct result. Concessions were made by the railroads, and the trains moved once again. Activity resumed in the grain pits, and society matrons peeked out at the streets from behind lace curtains to see that life had returned to its leisurely pace. But had it really?

The Workingmen's Party ran aldermanic candidates in Chicago, but Parsons himself was defeated in the fifteenth ward because of some ballot-box manipulations. Better results were achieved in 1879, when Parsons and August Spies held rallies in the Exhibition Hall on Michigan Avenue to raise money to purchase the German-language newspaper, *Arbeiter-Zeitung*. Parsons later edited the English-language newspaper, *Alarm*. Spies, a former furniture dealer and native of Landeck Castle in Germany, was installed as editor of *Arbeiter-Zeitung*. Through his efforts, the paper became the most widely circulated German weekly in the city.

Of a more serious concern to the city was the organization of secret paramilitaristic societies in the German community. The *Lehr-und-Wehr-Verein* (Study and Resistance Group) was an armed elite of German socialists who practiced sharpshooting and close-order drill at their headquarters at 58 Clybourn Street and 636 Milwaukee Avenue. A group of foreign-speaking men parading about the city streets with Springfield rifles scared the legislature into outlawing the possession of guns. The demonstrations of marksmanship was not done without a purpose. The fears of the government were probably justified, for there is little doubt that the bombs and rifles would have been used by certain members of the socialist movement.

Carter Harrison ascended to the mayoralty in 1879. No other mayor of that time had the worker's interests at heart more than "Our Carter." Harrison's administration was the first of several Chicago "machines"—one based on patronage and the ethnic vote. In return for their votes, Harrison gave them the wide-open town, a political advantage the blue bloods like Joseph Medill failed to seize. The mayor allowed Mike McDonald to have a free hand in running his Randolph Street gambling dens for six years. The chip charmers and shoestrings up and down Gambler's Row were a necessary diversion for the workers. Harrison realized this, but when Boss Mike showed signs of relinquishing some of his power, the mayor ordered the first gambling crackdown on June 3, 1885. McDonald then fled to Europe for an extended vacation.

Through the early and mid-1880s, the labor movement struggled to establish its course of action. These were generally quiet times because Carter Harrison allowed the socialists the right of assembly and free speech. The movement got going again on November 27, 1884, after the president and governor signed into law the first national Thanksgiving Day. On that day, a thousand less-than-thankful men gathered in the drizzle to hear Parsons, Spies, the Methodist minister Samuel Fielden, and editorial writer Michael Schwab address the gathering. "Our capitalistic robbers may well thank their lord that we, their victims, have not yet strangled them!" Parsons said.

Parsons quoted passages from St. James and St. John while addressing the crowd from atop some chicken crates. After the speeches were concluded, the crowd fell in line behind two men carrying the red flag of revolution and the black flag of hunger. What a sight it must have been to see the ragged mob appear first on Rush Street, and later

Chicago's Labor Pains

on Prairie Avenue, ringing the door bells of Swift, Armour, McCormick, and Palmer. The *Tribune* reported that most of the marchers were "slick and fatted," but that seems unlikely.

Labor unrest flared again in 1885, first with the March on the Board of Trade (which was of relatively minor consequence) and later that summer, the Streetcar Strike. The Board of Trade march received little attention from the press, partly due to the effective measures taken by the police (it was probably the last time that the police of this era *did* use common sense).

For several years, the board of trade utilized Chamber of Commerce facilities to transact business. But on April 28, 1885, William W. Boyington's magnificent monument to American commerce was to be officially dedicated. The building was constructed at the foot of LaSalle Street at a cost of $1,730,000. The stairs were made of imported granite; frescoes depicting the stages of man's evolution from the primate onward adorned the walls. The spacious interior was finished in rich mahogany, and in the "big room," light poured in through huge windows overlooking the famous "pit." The second part of Frank Norris's masterful trilogy of grain (*The Pit*) described the room as best as any. Dreams, deals, and the crushing failures to corner a market came to symbolize the Chicago pit.

For three years, workmen labored on the building. It came to symbolize something different from a big wheat deal to the socialists. Just as the doors opened to several thousand financiers, visiting foreign dignitaries, and society swells, the socialists began their own rally. Albert Parsons organized the meeting in front of *Arbeiter-Zeitung* offices on Wells Street, posing the question: "How many of my hearers could give $20 for a supper tonight?" The supper was being served later that night at the Grand Pacific Hotel to 457 members.

The march began on Fifth Avenue with Lucy Parsons and Oscar Neebe at the front. At Jackson Street, they were turned away by forty cops under the command of Sergeant Bartram. The building had been cordoned off so that people alighting from their landaus would not have to see the communists.

Inside, Fredrick Austin's band played Meyerbeer's "Prophet," but echoes could be heard in the vast chambers. People spoke in hushed tones, for the building was cathedral-like and somber. It was built to last a hundred years. It didn't. The Board of Trade Building was razed in 1928 for a functional skyscraper that lacked the original charm and palatial elegance. Only one incident was reported that night. Restaurant man R.D. Kadish's carriage was stoned by someone in the march, hitting his wife in the face.

Calm relations between the police department and the labor movement ended for good on June 30, when the car conductors and drivers of the West Division Streetcar Company walked out in sympathy with fifteen members of the Conductors Benevolent and Protective Association, who were fired for labor agitation. Three weeks earlier, they succeeded in winning a raise and shortening the sixty-day probation period from company president J. Russell Jones.

The company hired scabs to replace the striking drivers, and right away there were problems along the Madison Street Line. Stones were hurled at the drivers who stood in the exposed portion of the cars. Carter Harrison even got involved. While riding his steed down Halsted Street, the mayor noticed a man tearing up some railroad track with a pickax. He dismounted the horse and disarmed the man before a throng of curious spectators.

At the Western Avenue car barns, angry strikers jeered the scabs as they appeared for work. Answering the distress call was Captain John Bonfield of the 22nd Street detail, one of Chicago history's real villains. Bonfield was a man of modest talents who was thrust into a position of responsibility due to his influential family connections. His brother Joseph was a corporation council during Mayor Monroe Heath's term. His younger brother James began as a bailiff in the criminal court before earning a promotion to the detective force in 1881. When Heath added men to the force, John Bonfield began his police career at the advanced age of forty-one. Previously he had failed as a grocer and fertilizing company owner.

During the streetcar strike, Bonfield got his name in the papers for his treatment of strikers. While Carter Harrison offered to arbitrate the dispute, Bonfield settled matters with the free use of his club. The cars ran on Friday, July 3, thanks to Bonfield's curfew. Anyone on the street for any suspicious purpose would be clubbed. "So-called innocent men were hurt, but warnings had been given," John Flinn reported in his history of the department.

There were those standing on the corner of Madison and Western who did not understand this order. They were waiting for an express wagon to take them to their downtown jobs, when the police appeared with upraised clubs. John Schulkens sued Bonfield for $2,000, while a group of workmen vowed to lynch the captain from the highest lamppost.

Those who were subdued by the club were taken to the Des Plaines Street station, where 150 men were confined in the basement. They sang "John Brown's Body" and another popular song of the day, "Stick to Your Mother." But the mothers and wives were not allowed to visit the prisoners. Anyone heard uttering the word "scab" or "rat" was arrested on the spot and was also sent to the hole.

On July 6, the transit company hired 150 new men. The strikers responded by throwing a bomb at a streetcar pulling up to the intersection of Robey and VanBuren. The driver, Thomas Caruth, was taken from the car and beaten. The next day President Jones of the company backed down and agreed to review the cases of the sixteen men who had been fired. The brutal streetcar strikes ended, but many people complained to Police Chief Austin Doyle about Bonfield's abusive tactics, compelling the mayor to interview him. "Mr. Mayor, I am doing it in mercy of the people. A club today to make them scatter may save use of a pistol tomorrow."

The Chicago Police

Before the Civil War, Chicago was protected by a constable's force that proved to be inadequate for the burgeoning city. Policemen were identified by a leather badge worn on their hats but were poorly trained and ill equipped for their jobs. The Metropolitan Police Force was created in 1855, and for five years was under the jurisdiction of a city marshal, but real power was in the mayor's office.

In 1860, the state legislature created the Board of Police Commissioners, which effectively checked the mayor's authority over the hiring and deployment of officers. This did not meet with the approval of Mayor "Long" John Wentworth, who called the force together for a 2 A.M. meeting on March 21, 1861. He told them that they were all fired, and if Chicago didn't need a mayor to oversee the police, then Chicago didn't need the police either. For twenty-four hours Chicago was at the mercy of thieves and second-story men.

The Two O'Clock Purge resulted in a new and superior force, hired by the board the next day. Jacob Rehm was appointed deputy superintendent at a salary of $1,500, but fell victim to Chicago politics.

Rehm resigned twice, retired once, but was called back each time. He was forced to resign in 1875 after the Whiskey Scandal broke.

Chicago's police department has always been plagued by men who acceded to the top position who had no business being there. During one of Rehm's absences, Mayor Joseph Medill appointed Elmer Washburne, former warden of the Illinois Penitentiary and a man who agreed with the Sunday dry law. Washburne meant well, but was verbose, pompous, and the perfect bureaucrat for a job that required political savvy and tact. The Committee of Fifteen wanted a man who took a tough stance on the temperance issue. Charges of neglect of duty were brought against Washburne by the secretary of police, but the chief was cleared of charges on April 28, 1872. Medill then took political revenge on two of his accusers, E.F. Klokke and Charles Reno, who were fired from the police board.

The large immigrant population wanted beer on Sunday, so Medill was swept out of office in 1873 in favor of Harvey D. Colvin, one-time agent for the U.S. Express Company and a political stooge of Mike McDonald. Colvin had run as a liberal independent, easily defeating the Fireproof Ticket headed up by L.L. Bond. It was Colvin who promoted Michael Hickey to police superintendent, whose three-year term established the pattern of police overreaction to the anarchist issue.

When Hickey failed to secure his reappointment, Mayor Heath appointed Valdous Seavey, hero of the 1877 riot, to superintendent. Seavey lasted one year. It was on October 15, 1878, that Seavey, Mayor Heath, and policeman Henry O'Neil were arrested for assault and battery after O'Neil prevented employees of the Metropolitan Railway Company from laying track along Lake Street. A detachment of cops freely used their clubs, driving the workmen off. A $200 bond freed the mayor, his chief, and O'Neil from the lockup while the case was quietly settled out of court. Seavey took ill and died on September 8, 1879.

Next came Simon O'Donnell, the most forthright of the group, but forthrightness was not a good quality to have at this time. O'Donnell joined the force in 1862, working the intersection at Clark and Lake, which were the only paved streets in the business district at the time. He became known to the ladies as the "dandy cop" for his exceptional charm and good manners. But he cleaned out the bribe takers and crooked bondsmen at the Armory Station and arrested Paddy Guerin after he knocked off the Galesburg Bank of $12,000. O'Donnell also helped form the auxiliary court to handle the overflow of cases from the criminal court.

O'Donnell replaced Seavey on December 15, 1879. The department was woefully mismanaged and needed 800 more men to function properly. But O'Donnell wouldn't cooperate with the aldermen, who sought political appointments for friends. He had actually staged unauthorized raids on Mike McDonald's gambling dens. This earned him a demotion back to the 12th Street district on November 28, 1880, though the official accounts of the move describe O'Donnell's unhappiness as police chief and his wish to return to an area smaller in size.

Carter Harrison appointed William McGarigle, former secretary to Elmer Washburne, as the next superintendent in 1880. McGarigle, (whose infamous exploits are detailed elsewhere in this book) is credited with starting the patrol box system, which was the most important police innovation of the 1880s. The telephone and signal system began in 1880. Three-hundred-seventy-five hexagonal pine boxes that supported a lamppost were installed in each of the police districts. Inside the box (which resembled a wooden phone booth) was an alarm box dial, which the caller could use to notify the local station. By placing the pointer on one of eleven "categories" (that included thievery, forgery, riot, drunkards, murder, accident, fighting, violation of city ordinance, and fire), a person could summon instantly a five-man patrol wagon that included a stretcher, cuffs, blankets, and clubs. Each of the boxes could be opened with a specially numbered key that was given to 2,144 citizens of the districts. A trap lock secured the key in place, and only the officer of the patrol wagon could release it after the call had been answered. In this way, false alarms were minimized. Each box cost the city $25, and by 1884, McGarigle's innovation resulted in 857,084 distress calls placed to the station.

Diminutive Austin J. Doyle replaced McGarigle on November 22, 1882. During Doyle's term, 418 more men were added to the force because of a growing concern over foreign anarchists. The Citizen's Association purchased a gatling gun and 296 Springfield rifles in anticipation of future labor unrest. Doyle's career paralleled those of other Irish policemen who had risen through the ranks of patronage—first as a clerk in the recorder's court and later as clerk of the criminal court in 1873. Doyle was a hand-picked favorite of Carter Harrison, but his term of office was characterized by the free use of clubs and blackmail. Under some pressure, Doyle "retired" on October 15, 1885, following the negative fallout resulting from the streetcar strike. Doyle accepted a job as general superintendent of the Chicago Passenger Railway through the intervention of Carter Harrison. Harvey Weeks was the president of the line, a major contributor to the Harrison reelection campaign and Democratic leader.

In selecting Doyle's replacement, Harrison faced a real dilemma. The trade unions were up in arms at the prospect of John Bonfield becoming superintendent, but this was Harrison's first choice. He had been pleased with the captain's work in implementing the placement of the signal boxes and his suppression of streetcar rioters. But the Irish already commanded a majority of the city offices, and with the election a year away, it would be politically expedient to appoint someone of German descent. On October 16, a former Bavarian war hero who fought alongside of Sherman at the battle of Shiloh was named. Harrison said this of Fredrick Ebersold: "Men of Irish descent now fill a large share of the offices at my command. It seems to me that the 160,000 Germans in Chicago should be recognized."

Bonfield, who wanted to be police chief very badly, was relegated to the lesser position of inspector. "Captain Bonfield will be made inspector, and I know that he will be an inspector who inspects and a splendid drill master," Harrison told the press. Bonfield smarted over his lost opportunity, but he embarked on an ambitious campaign to drill his men in riot control. A serious power struggle in the police hierarchy was about to begin, a conflict that ran along German-Irish ethnic lines and personal jealousy. It was then that the Haymarket bomb was thrown.

What Happened at the Haymarket

The festering problems between labor and capital flared again at the McCormick Reaper Works (now International Harvester) on the southwest side during the winter of 1885 and 1886. Young Cyrus Hall McCormick succeeded his more liberal father as head of the concern but attempted to regain some lost profits by imposing an unpopular pay cut and attempting to break the union.

In April 1885, the McCormick employees won an agreement that union organizing would not be grounds for dismissal. There were other issues at stake. Many of the foreign-born Catholics objected to the huge endowments given to the Chicago Presbyterian Theological Seminary in the face of severe pay cuts. The struggle to win the eight-hour workday began in earnest in 1884, when Samuel Gompers of the Federation of Organized Trades and Labor Unions set May 1, 1886, as the date of a general strike if the shorter workday had not been adopted. Despite the support of President Grover Cleveland and others, the eight-hour day was not received with enthusiasm by capital. Employers were free to regulate their work schedules as they pleased following an 1868 Supreme Court decision that declared that the government was entitled to make separate agreements with their employees (certain federal employees already had the eight-hour day).

There were numerous labor clashes that winter, culminating in the lockout of 1,482 employees, many of whom belonged to the Molder's Union #23, on February 16, 1886. McCormick had incurred the men's wrath by hiring Pinkerton agents to infiltrate the shops to weed out the organizers.

Chief Ebersold placed 350 policemen at McCormick's disposal along the "Black Road," so named because of the charcoal and cinders that gave this stretch of road from Blue Island Avenue to the Reaper Works a black, sooty appearance. Scabs were escorted safely into the Reaper Works on March 1, but on March 2, there were more reports of police harassment of strikers.

To understand the Haymarket Affair is to understand the "war of words" that transpired between the socialist newspapers and the daily press. Parsons and Spies resorted to dangerous rhetoric (that was probably *just* rhetoric) but scared the people and alienated the police who took them at their word. The English-speaking *Alarm* ran this little item on June 27, 1885: For those who will sooner or later be forced to employ its destructive qualities in defense of their rights as man [sic], and from a sense of preservation, a few hints may not be out of place. [The article goes on to describe the construction of a gas pipe bomb.]

The explosive nature of the *Alarm* did not fit the generally passive nature of Albert Parsons. It can be assumed that many of the editorials were written by his wife Lucy, a Negress with a trace of Spanish blood. She was an uncompromising radical who later worked closely with Emma Goldman and others till her death in 1942. The notorious *To Tramps* article that she wrote on October 4, 1884, did much to seal her husband's doom: "But each of you hungry tramps who read these lines avail yourselves to those little methods of warfare which science has placed in the hands of the poor man, and you will become a power in this or any other land. Learn the use of explosives!"

She was responding out of emotion to Joseph Medill's equally incendiary comment that "the simplest plan is to put a little strychnine in the meat or other supplies given tramps." The Chicago daily papers spared no adjectives in describing the men. The *Times* called Samuel Fielden a "villainous looking fellow," and the *Tribune* called Parsons a "blood preaching anarchist fiend."

May 1 dawned, and 30,000 tradesmen marched peacefully down Michigan Avenue, led by Albert Parsons. This was the first May Day, a holiday that would later be celebrated worldwide. May 2nd, a Sunday, passed quietly. The next day trouble broke out again at the McCormick factory. Two members of the Lumber Shover's Union had gone to Grief's Hall at Clinton and Lake to ask Spies if he would go to the factory to address the striking men. The editor agreed, appearing that Monday afternoon before an estimated crowd of 6,000. Spies delivered a mild-mannered speech from atop a railroad car outside the plant.

Spies was heckled by a number of the men present, but he seemed to maintain control over the crowd. At 3:30, the scabs that McCormick had hired began exiting the plant. They were given the afternoon off, perhaps as a symbolic gesture toward the strikers. Just as Spies concluded his talk, portions of the mob drifted toward the gate to harass the scabs. Spies cautioned the men to restrain themselves, but many were of Polish and Bohemian descent and could not understand.

The scabs were driven back into the factory under a hail of stones and bottles. Two patrolmen on duty, J.M. Hanes and J.J. Egan, alerted the Hinman station for assistance. Estimates of just how many cops appeared vary greatly. Haymarket historian Henry David suggests that 200 were on hand, but that seems unlikely since each station employed less than 75.

In the volley of shots that were exchanged, one striker was killed and six were wounded. Simon O'Donnell, considered by historians to be sympathetic to the labor movement, drove to the scene in a buggy from the 12th Street station. When pushing and shoving men surrounded his carriage, O'Donnell lashed them freely with his whip, while he fired into the crowd.

Spies watched the carnage only briefly. Unnerved, he flagged down a Blue Island streetcar and rushed back to the newspaper offices on Wells Street to pen the famous "revenge circular." Had Spies remained to gauge the lesser significance of the event, circumstances might have been different. He imagined that he had witnessed the massacre of a dozen men, when in fact only one had been killed. (Perhaps he read the afternoon *Daily News*, which reported six deaths.)

Chicago's Labor Pains

The circular, which became exhibit no. 1, read: "Workingmen! To Arms! Your masters sent out their bloodhounds—the police—they killed six of your brothers at McCormick's this afternoon." The notice was concluded with an urging to "destroy the hideous monster." However, a compositor inserted the word "Revenge!" without Spies's knowledge. Another circular read "Workingmen! Arm Yourselves and Appear in Full Force!" Spies ordered the word *revenge* deleted, but several hundred escaped the printer's office. The call-to-arms flyer was an announcement of a mass meeting to be held at the Haymarket on Tuesday, May 4. The Haymarket was an open area on the western fringe of downtown where wholesale meat, produce, and dry goods could be purchased directly from the farmers and manufacturers. It was bounded by Randolph, Des Plaines, and Halsted Streets.

But Spies did not organize the meeting. It had been planned earlier in the day at Grief's Hall. Inside this plain four-story meeting hall, the "Monday Night Conspiracy" (as the state later called it) was hatched. George Engel, a toy store owner, and Gottfried Waller, member of the International Working Peoples Association (IWPA) and one of the state's key witnesses, organized the Haymarket meeting from the basement of Grief's. Forty men gathered together to decide on a plan of action. Engel proposed that the word *Ruhe* be inserted in *Arbeiter-Zeitung* to signal the men to gather at Wicker Park, but only if a revolution broke out. The state contended that Engel had been in constant communication with bomb-maker Louis Lingg, and that the devices would be brought to the Haymarket from Neff's Hall on Clybourn Street.

The state contended that the Monday Night Conspiracy meeting hatched a revolution that began at Haymarket, but that does not seem to be the case. Very little was said about the meeting, but once again their timing was bad. The word *Ruhe* appeared against Spies's wishes and was another in a series of unfortunate coincidences.

Mayor Harrison issued a permit for the gathering because he believed that nothing would come of it. Captain Bonfield assured the press that while there might be a few "sanguinary conflicts," there would be no repetition of the 1877 riot. The next day Bonfield contradicted himself. He declared that there would be "bad work" at the Haymarket. Six hundred police reserves were transferred to the West Chicago, Harrison, and Central stations downtown in anticipation of the bad work that Bonfield described. Yet there is no record of any large concentration of police at the Hinman station, which served the sensitive Black Road. This potentially explosive area was left in the control of O'Donnell and the seventy-five regulars.

Early in the morning on that fateful May 4, an angry crowd assembled on the corner of 18th and Center Streets. The incident is a footnote to the Haymarket Riot, but the actions of the police raise some more questions about a general conspiracy whipped up by Bonfield to keep tensions high.

In less than a half-hour, the mob swelled to 3,000 persons. Sam Rosenfield's corner drugstore was the target. Insults and accusations that Rosenfield was a hired police agent were leveled at the druggist, who removed his family upstairs. A wagonload of O'Donnell's men appeared, and in a few minutes the disturbance was quelled. But for some reason known only to himself, O'Donnell did not leave a guard on duty.

Some time later, the mob reassembled, this time succeeding in its original intention to loot and pillage the store. The mob advanced on Weiskoph's Saloon, a short distance from the drug store. The building was sacked, and the liquor barrels were cracked open. Only then did the police arrive. The saloon was reputed to be a favored spot for the socialists.

Had Bonfield seen to it that the police response would be deliberately casual so that the labor tensions would be fanned and a strong case could be built against the movement? The defense charged the police with forming a secret plan to crush the labor leaders by hiring an *agent provocateur* paid for by the Chicago industrialists. Gottfried Waller turned state's evidence and testified freely against George Engel. It was alleged that Waller was the mysterious agent, but evidence shows that Captain Schaak promised him immunity while paying his rent and salary while he testified. This was certainly preferable to the gallows.

When the Spies revenge circular was shown to Chief Ebersold, he dismissed it as unimportant, but police reserves were still added to the Des Plaines Street station that served the Haymarket district. The Des Plaines district covered just one mile of the third precinct, an area normally patrolled by seventy-three men. On this night, a detachment of 100 officers under the direction of Captain William Ward were added.

The Haymarket meeting was scheduled for 7:15 P.M., but did not begin until 8:30. A crowd estimated to be 2,500 milled about the square, certainly not the size that Spies had hoped for. Fearing that the police would cite the blockage of streetcar traffic as a reason for dispersing the gathering, Spies directed everyone toward Des Plaines Street,

Chicago's Labor Pains

adjacent to the alley next to the Crane Brothers Factory. Parsons and his wife had arrived at 8 P.M., but were told that they were not scheduled to speak, so they took a streetcar downtown to address a group of sewing girls attempting to form a trade union.

August Spies arrived late, for it was the custom for the German speakers to appear last on the billing. He mounted a truck wagon in front of the factory and called the meeting together in English. Spies looked about him to see if Parsons was present. Rudolph Schnaubelt, the prime suspect in the bomb throwing, was sent to get Parsons and Fielden.

Spies told the crowd that the day would come when McCormick and his kind would be hanged. He warned against making idle threats but to use the time to act. This was the tone of the speech that lasted twenty-five minutes. Parsons arrived. He put his wife and children in a wagon twenty feet away and delivered a speech that was heard by Mayor Harrison. The mayor decided that all was well, so he went to the Des Plaines station to inform Bonfield to send the extra men home.

At 10 P.M. a drizzle began to fall, accompanied by a stiff wind. Parsons proposed an adjournment to Zepf's Hall at Lake and Des Plaines, but someone in the crowd said the building was in use. Fielden replied that he only needed a few more minutes to speak. Parsons returned to Zepf's Hall to have a drink with Adolph Fischer, the man who printed the handbills to announce the meeting. At 10:20, Fielden began his conclusion. It was at that very moment that a detachment of 176 policemen that had formed in the alley next to the Des Plaines station, marched on the meeting.

They marched in columns covering the span of the street. The crowd, which had been standing south of Crane's alley retreated northward. The size of the meeting had dwindled to less than 300 at this point. The police halted three paces from the speaker's wagon, just as Captain Ward uttered the famous words to Fielden, who alighted from the wagon. "In the name of the people of the State of Illinois, I command this meeting to disperse." Ward repeated the directive once more. Fielden replied: "We are peaceable."

Suddenly a luminous object thrown from a vestibule at the northeast corner of Randolph and Des Plaines sailed through the air. Sixteen witnesses saw the bomb in flight, but none were able to identify the thrower. The dynamite bomb exploded with fearful intensity, landing at the feet of the first detail of police.

Contemporary illustrators portrayed the anarchists circling the police and drawing on them. However, the opposite was true. A hail of gunshots were fired blindly at the crowd, several of which landed in the door at Zepf's Hall (where Parsons and Fischer were) a block away.

A volley of shots directed at themselves finally forced Bonfield into ordering ceasefire. The following chart lists the police wounded.

Policemen Suffering Injury as a Result of Bullet Wounds**

Officer	Location of Wound
John Reid	Both legs below knees
Lawrence Murphy	Two in right leg, one in left side of neck
John Doyle	Two in right leg below knee
Arthur Connolly	Right Arm
Nicholas Shannon	In back
Adam Barber	Right heel
Patrick Hartford	Right heel, three left toes shot off
August Keller	Left side grazed
John King	Two in right leg
Lieu. James Stanton	Right arm
Alexander Jameson	Left thigh
Timothy O'Sullivan	Right thigh
Jacob Hansen	Left hip
Michael Horan	Right thigh
Peter Butterly	Right forearm
Charles Fink	Each thigh
*Henry Smith	Right shoulder
*Daniel Cramer	Neck grazed
Frank Tyrrell	Bomb fragments in head and back

*It is interesting to note that only two officers from the final two detachments (which brought up the rear of the police line) were injured by gunfire. If gunfire had come from both the east and west sides of Des Plaines Street (as the prosecution later testified), then it stands to reason that more of Lieutenant Beard's rear detail would have suffered injury. Twelve of the nineteen wounds were inflicted below the belt. The force of the blast had knocked much of the detail to the ground. In their haste to respond, it is feasible that the rear detail fired into their own ranks blindly, thus absolving the crowd of guilt.

***Source: Police Report for 1886.*

The Chicago press does not tell us how many bystanders were killed or maimed, just a characteristic headline that said, "Now It Is Blood!" An ex-convict named Frank Louis was the first to be arrested in the dragnet that began immediately. It was his misfortune to be struck in the right side of the back while returning home from a shopping errand. The extracted bullet was fired from a standard police .38.

Patrolman Mathias Degan of the Lake Street station was the first victim of Haymarket. He was a two-year veteran appointed during the recruitment period of 1884. Of the six officers who died from their wounds, only Thomas Redden of Lake Street had more than two years on the force. Interestingly, none were in supervisory positions. Degan had attempted to walk away from the blast but collapsed as a result of a severed artery. In the next twelve days, George Miller, John Barrett, Timothy Flavian, Nels Hansen, and Nicholas Sheehan died from their wounds.

The Actions of the Police

Earlier in the day Bonfield predicted "bad work" at the Haymarket, and for those reasons he insisted upon personally commanding the Des Plaines reserves. Through most of the evening, Bonfield sent detective Louis Haas and two other men to observe the progress of the meeting and report back to him. But other officers at Des Plaines were chiding Bonfield about his timidity in breaking up the gathering. And when Carter Harrison called on Bonfield, the captain said that he knew of a plan to blow up the Milwaukee and St. Paul freight houses, and therefore the men must be retained for security purposes.

Then without warning, Bonfield ordered the detail to fall in on the double quick. The three divisions were commanded by five lieutenants and a sergeant. The rear detail barely had time to fall into position when Bonfield moved them out. The captain was in a hurry to disperse a meeting that was about to end—so much so that the detail was almost trotting. At the trial, a traveling salesman named Barton Simonson testified that he visited Bonfield and Ward at the station earlier in the evening. "The trouble there is that these anarchists get their women and children mixed up with them, and we can't get at them," Bonfield said. "I would like to get 3,000 of them in a crowd without their women and children. I would make short work of them." It is unlikely that Bonfield would hire a bomb thrower to kill policemen in a column that he himself stood at the front of. It seems more reasonable to believe that his motives were simply to undermine Ebersold. In a letter to the chief dated June 1, 1886, Bonfield recounted his actions that night.

> At different times between 8:00 and 9:30, officers in plain clothes reported the progress of the meeting and stated that nothing of a very inflammatory nature was said until a man named Fielden or Fielding took the stand. He advised his hearers to "throttle the law." It would be as well for them to die fighting as to starve to death. He further advised them to exterminate the capitalists and to do it that night. Wanting to be clearly within the law, and wishing to leave no room for doubt as to the propriety of our actions, I did not act on his first reports, but sent the officers back to make further observations.
>
> A few minutes after 10:00 the officers reported that the crowd was getting excited and the speaker growing more incendiary in his language. I then felt to hestitate any longer would be criminal on my part, and then gave the order to fall in, and our force formed on Waldo Place.

Bonfield's attitude concerning the anarchist question was at odds with the chief, who naturally wanted to play it down. The whole issue put the mayor and himself into a tight position with the city election only months away. Ebersold pursued radicals with enthusiasm during the 1877 railroad strike, so his stance does not show a concern over the anarchist's civil rights, but a desire to save his political hide.

Sharing this desire to purge Ebersold was Michael John Schaak, second only to Thomas Byrnes of New York as the nineteenth century's most famous policeman. He was the prototype of the intense, brooding cop with extra girth and a handlebar mustache. He was driven and dedicated to his twenty-eight-year career—one that never included a vacation.

Born in the Grand Duchy of Luxembourg in 1843, Schaak joined the department as a patrolman in 1869. Within three years, he advanced to sergeant. In five years he had made over 865 arrests and was said to be familiar with every back alley, gaming house, and sporting domain north of the Chicago River.

In 1879 he was transferred from the Armory Station to Chicago Avenue, where he was promoted to lieutenant. On two occasions Schaak was shot by levee hoodlums but avoided serious injury. It was his good fortune to have a part in solving three of the most prominent

Posturing, defiant, self-assured, Michael Schaak strikes a pose for his entertaining, absurd book *Anarchy & Anarchists*. Schaak purported to be an expert on the socialist movements of the world.

police cases of the late nineteenth century: the Kledzic murder case, Haymarket, and the Leutgart "sausage vat" murder of the 1890s.

Two days after Schaak was promoted to captain, a Polish woman named Anna Kledzic was found clubbed to death in her house. After pronouncing the detective bureau incompetent (and reorganizing it),

Schaak unraveled the mystery himself. He found some burned letters in the stove from a man named Mulkowsky who had just escaped a Polish jail on a murder charge. Using the name Brunofsky, the man got to know Anna Kledzic, who stored some valuables in her home. While she bent over a wash tub, Mulkowsky clubbed her, stole a wedding ring and some jewelry and vouchers. Schaak dressed up Mulkowsky's sister in men's clothing and had a photograph taken. The picture was circulated in the Polish ghetto, and he was soon apprehended. It took a jury just twenty minutes to convict.

Schaak joined forces with Bonfield, which split the department into two feuding cliques at the time of Haymarket. The captain later wrote a lavish, but far-fetched book entitled *Anarchy and Anarchists* that painted Ebersold into a compromising corner.

> The department was rent and paralyzed with the feuds and jealousies between the chiefs and subordinates. This too was at a time when the people of Chicago were in a condition of mind bordering on panic. It is charity to say no more. He [Ebersold] had neither a proper conception of his duties nor the ability to perform them.

Ebersold reluctantly agreed to let Schaak handle the investigation when the captain stated that he had access to informers and was privy to secret evidence. "I am going to work this case day and night until it is cleared up," he promised the chief on May 7.

Captain Schaak gathered together his favorite detectives, each of whom went on to achieve degrees of dubious notoriety. They included Charles Rehm (a relative of Jacob Rehm, showing once again the influence of Chicago patronage), Michael Whalen (suspended for complicity in the Dr. Cronin murder case of 1889), Jacob Loewenstein (suspended with Schaak in 1889 for fencing stolen goods), Michael Hoffman, John Stift, and Herman Schuettler. Of Schuettler, a historian later wrote: "Clubs, bricks, and stones were common weapons of offense, and Schuettler was as adept with them as he was with his knuckles. He was arrested for fighting with a truck teamster at age seventeen." His rapid climb in the department began in 1883 when he helped secure the first poisoning conviction in Cook County. Wealth, power, influence . . . and a term as police chief awaited Schuettler in the next thirty years.

Minutes after the bomb landed, the dead and wounded were taken back to the Des Plaines station while the block was cordoned off. Chief Ebersold pacified the public fear by informing the governor that the state militia would not be required.

The Des Plaines Street station as it looked at the time of the Haymarket Riot. The police formed up in a column on Waldo Place, adjacent to the building. Today it is a parking lot.

Inspector Bonfield sent the first detachment out at 11 P.M. to *Arbeiter-Zeitung* offices at 41 N. Wells, but the building was deserted. Parsons borrowed a five-dollar gold piece from a man named Brown (who was arrested for this crime) so that he could flee to Elgin. Later, Parsons went to Waukesha, Wisconsin, to work as a painter at a summer resort. Safe but torn by a guilty conscience, Parsons returned to Chicago on June 20, to stand trial with his comrades. Accompanied by attorney William Perkins Black, Parsons made a dramatic courtroom appearance on June 21.

The first socialist was arrested on May 4. The unnamed man was in possession of four revolvers when he attempted to escape. He was booked for murder. Bonfield theorized that the Haymarket bomb was a result of an armed conspiracy engineered by the *Lehr-und-Wehr-Verein*.

The discovery that each member of the elite was assigned a number to correspond to his gun number was made when Chris Komens of 231 20th Street was arrested while in possession of dynamite and rifles. He belonged to the No. 3 armed group and owned rifle 400. The police did find some storerooms of bombs and rifles, thanks to heavy infiltration.

Spies, Fielden, and Michael Schwab were arrested quietly on May 5. Spies and his brother Christian were working at the newspaper office when James Bonfield presented them with their arrest warrants. Arrests came quickly after that, and often illegally. If there was any official negligence on Chief Ebersold's part during the investigation, it occurred in relation to Schwab's brother-in-law, Rudolph Schnaubelt. Two of Bonfield's men, Palmer and Cosgrove, arrested Schnaubelt on May 5. When he was taken to the central station for booking, Ebersold ordered him released for lack of evidence. Schaak claimed that Schnaubelt lingered at the station after he was told to leave. One week later, Schnaubelt was arrested again by Stift and Whalen. Palmer and Cosgrove told the men to "lay off," so he was released again.

Judge Joseph Gary and State's Attorney Julius Grinnell believed Schnaubelt was the bomb thrower, and defense attorney Sigismund Zeisler said that Schnaubelt told him he was leaving town on May 7. Schnaubelt was active in the movement but was considered an unstable personality. He stood six foot four and was more than capable of throwing a heavy bomb the required fifteen feet. Sensing the dangerous feelings against him, Schnaubelt fled to London, Argentina, Bavaria, and other unknown ports-of-call. Only two letters of dubious origin (published in the German papers) gave any clue to his whereabouts in the next fifty years. Was Schnaubelt the perpetrator of the deed? It is believed today that the bomb was thrown by someone in the movement. It was a dynamite pipe bomb, the kind manufactured by Louis Lingg and William Seliger.

It seems odd at this late date that Schnaubelt was released twice when others were held for more flimsy reasons. Examples of police overreaction in other arrests are public record.

Robert Blumenburg was arrested by officer Jerry Donahue of the North Avenue station on May 9. The man's only crime was that he was preparing a manuscript with the heading "socialist" in it. He was locked up without the formality of a booking. That same day, George Bartels and Frank Schmidt were arrested at 71 Lake Street by George Hubbard for possession of socialistic literature. When their friend Charles Franks came to visit them at the Central station, he too was arrested. An officer asked him if he would participate in a socialist parade. He said yes and was booked.

Ebersold tried to force a confession out of Gustave Stange, who was arrested for possessing several Remingtons, labor pamphlets, and a bayonet. He told the press that he *knew* Stange threw the bomb and there were witnesses to prove it. But nobody has heard of Gustave Stange since. Seen in this context, Ebersold's actions were strange.

Schaak enhanced his legend after Herman Schuettler brought in twenty-two-year-old Louis Lingg on May 14, following a fierce struggle. Lingg was the youngest and most radical of the Haymarket men. He was a drifter and draft evader from Mannheim, Germany, when he emigrated to the United States in 1885. He was given a job and a small house by carpenter William Seliger at 442 Sedgwick Street. The two of them manufactured the bombs in their spare time, but Seliger turned state's evidence against his young associate. He told the court that he talked Lingg out of a scheme to throw a bomb through the window of the Larrabee police station. In return for his cooperation, Seliger and his wife avoided prosecution and were given one-way fares back to Germany, where they remained until they died. Shortly after penning his autobiography in jail, Lingg committed suicide on November 10, 1887. He exploded a bomb in his face, in what has become another of the great unsolved Haymarket mysteries. How did he receive the material to construct a bomb?

Meanwhile, Schaak planted detectives in labor meetings and met mysterious women in the middle of the night (or so he claimed). In the meantime, someone set his house on fire.

"Are you the chief or am I?" Ebersold asked him on May 11. Schaak accused Ebersold of keeping company with Clark Street drunks and allowing the reporters to become cozy with the incarcerated anarchists. Ebersold then took a vacation to California, which earned him Grinnell's wrath. "What do you want me to do? Throw my train tickets in the lake?" Ebersold asked. When Schaak's book appeared in May of 1889, Ebersold answered his accusers by saying that "Schaak wanted to keep the pot boiling, keep himself prominent before the public. Well, I sat down on that . . . and of course Schaak didn't like it." He went on to say that he began to think that there wasn't much to all the anarchist business, but in his report to the city council of 1886, Ebersold described the "extensive preparations which these people had made and planned for the destruction of life and property."

By May 27, thirty-one indictments were presented. The investiga-

tion was over, and the trial was about to begin. Two-hundred arrests were made; ten labor meeting halls and seventeen saloons were raided by the police. Forty-five families were being directly supported by the police in exchange for their testimony. Several others were coerced into presenting false evidence.

Nine men stood trial for conspiracy to riot and commit murder. The prosecution tried to establish a direct link between the men in their attempt to prove a general conspiracy. George Engel was home with his wife when the bomb was thrown but had attended the Monday night meeting. Adolph Fischer was also at the meeting, but his crime was of a more serious nature. As compositor for *Arbeiter-Zeitung*, the usually mild-mannered Fischer inserted the line "Workingmen! Arm Yourselves and Appear in Full Force!"

Michael Schwab left the Haymarket meeting at 8 P.M., but he had helped Spies edit the flyers earlier in the day. The cases against Parsons, Spies, and Fielden are well known, but consider the crime of Oscar Neebe, brewmaster. The state based their case against him on the fact that he owned two dollar's worth of stock in *Arbeiter-Zeitung* and that he was in the newspaper office the first time it was raided.

Presentation of evidence began on June 21 in the courtroom of Judge Joseph Gary, who was anxious for a speedy conviction. The Haymarket men were defended by four attorneys—Captain William Perkins Black, Sigismund Zeisler, Moses Solomon, and William A. Foster.

The case against the anarchists became a general indictment of the movement. The march on the board of trade was irrelevant but was introduced as evidence of a general plan to overthrow the existing order. Unreliable witnesses were paraded to the stand, and despite discrediting cross-examination, their testimony was accepted as the truth. Lieutenant Martin Quinn of the Chicago Avenue station testified that he heard Samuel Fielden tell the crowd to "do your duty, and I'll do mine," just before pulling a revolver and firing at the police from atop the wagon. Quinn said that he heard Fielden make this statement from fifty feet away, while Louis Haas heard it from fifteen feet. Both of their statements were contradicted by William Ward who said

(Left) "A Fierce Struggle." This romanticized version of the arrest of bombmaker Louis Lingg originally appeared in *Anarchy & Anarchists*. On the left, Herman Schuettler struggles with Lingg at the point of a gun, while a police officer prepares to cane the anarchist. During the fight, Schuettler bit Lingg's finger, almost severing it.

that he was close enough to Fielden to touch him and that he didn't remember him making any comments of that nature.

Julius Grinnell's most important witness was Harry Gilmer, a former deputy marshal and employee of the West Park commissioner. Gilmer testified that he had stopped at the Haymarket meeting while returning home from a meeting with the governor of Iowa at the Palmer House. While standing near the lamppost by Crane's Alley, Gilmer claimed to have watched Spies light the match to the bomb, before handing the infernal device to Schnaubelt. Sixteen other witnesses swore that the bomb was thrown at a location *south* of the alley. Gilmer said that he noticed Fischer at the meeting, but it was conclusively proven that he was at Zepf's Hall the whole time.

Gilmer's integrity was discredited by several who knew him. Ex-Deputy Sheriff John Garrick told how he once had Gilmer as a tenant but evicted him because of "bad character." John Brixey knew Gilmer since 1880 but said he could not believe him under oath.

Carter Harrison appeared for the defense, recounting his movements that night. He told the court that he believed that there was no threat to the public safety and had called for the police reserves to be sent home. His testimony cost him the 1886 election.

Judge Joseph Gary bent the scales of justice through his broad instructions to the jury, which implied that if suitable evidence could not be found, then the past record of the men would be sufficient:

> The bomb might have been thrown by someone unfamiliar with and unprompted by the teachings of the defendants or any of them. Before defendants can be held liable therefore, the evidence must satisfy you beyond all reasonable doubt that the person throwing said bomb was acting as the result of the teachings or encouragement of the defendants or some of them.

There could be little doubt of the verdict when the jury retired on August 20, 1886. The public, the press, and indeed many in the labor movement screamed for a hasty conviction. They were not disappointed. Only Oscar Neebe was spared the hangman's noose. Gary sentenced him to fifteen years at hard labor for his ownership of *Arbeiter-Zeitung* stock and suspected involvement with the *Lehr-und-Wehr-Verein*. In a stirring speech to the court, Neebe asked for the death penalty, saying it is better to be executed than to die by inches.

An appeal to the Illinois Supreme Court was made by Perkins and a friend of Abraham Lincoln named Leonard Swett. When a petition to the federal Supreme Court was also denied, attention centered on Governor Richard Oglesby, the only man alive who could issue a pardon.

It was at this time that the intellectuals and parlor socialists rallied to the men's cause. William Dean Howells, George Bernard Shaw, and Henry George all contacted Oglesby, who began to hedge. Judge Gary even asked for clemency for Fielden and Schwab, in what ranks as one of history's amazing turnarounds.

A number of Chicago industrialists concluded that the men had been railroaded, but Marshall Field silenced them. Oglesby reduced the sentences of Fielden and Schwab to life imprisonment. Spies, Parsons, Engel, and Fischer refused to consider asking for clemency. There was some noticeable softening in the media attitudes as the fateful day drew near. The *Tribune* even reserved its criticism when Oglesby issued his reprieve.

> It must be remembered that Governor Oglesby is a humane and sympathetic man, and averse to the shedding of blood and that more than once he has shown himself the warm friend of the working class [November 11, 1887].

Of course the governor was a Republican, and Altgeld was not, which probably saved him a bitter denunciation.

Public sympathy for the men grew, as they spent their final days in the old county jail located at Dearborn and Illinois Streets. Each day, a beautiful twenty-four year old socialite named Rosnina Clarke Van Zandt visited Spies in his cell, accompanied by her father and mother. The girl was the only daughter of a wealthy chemist who lived at Huron and Rush Streets. Her story is one of the more pathetic aspects associated with Haymarket. A world of ease and grace awaited Nina if she hadn't fallen in love with Spies. It began sometime during the trial.

The press commented favorably about her many charms during her visits to the courtroom. In the morning she wore one elegant outfit, and in the afternoon she changed to another. Somehow they began to communicate with each other, and for a while, she assisted Spies in preparing his autobiography. When the attraction took on serious overtones, Sheriff Canute Matson informed her that he would not permit a jail marriage if that is what she was considering. Van Zandt found out that a proxy marriage would be legally recognized in Illinois. Christian

Spies took his brother's place. Van Zandt became a social outcast because of it, but went through with the ceremony in suburban Jefferson on January 29, 1887. Captain Schaak called it the "product of a deranged mind."

Spies hung a photo of Nina in his cell, while she kept a medallion engraved by an Italian artist on top of her fireplace. Still, Matson refused to allow the couple to meet with each other in the jail, ignoring two letters written by Spies and the girl's concerned father.

February 17, 1887

Dear Mr. Matson:

It is very painful to be so importuning—but when I see the distress and anguish of my child there is nothing for me to do but plead with you to turn the key. Looking at the matter, I am satisfied if we cannot do something very soon, my sorrow will only have begun. May I beg for you to let her in today or tomorrow?

Very truly yours,
Jas. K. Van Zandt

February 23, 1887

Dear Sir:

My wife is ill. Will you kindly give her permission to visit me, and if you fear another newspaper sensation, she might vail herself so that nobody would know her. By granting the above request you will greatly oblige.

Your most respectful,
A. Spies

(Right) *Frank Leslie's Illustrated Newspaper* was the *Life, Time,* and *Newsweek* of the 1880s. It was a delightful package of news and woodcut drawings known for their clarity and detail. Here we see the Haymarket men incarcerated in the old county jail, formerly located at Dearborn and Illinois Streets. Nina Van Zandt and August Spies are shown in the upper corners. (Courtesy of the Chicago Historical Society.)

FRANK LESLIE'S ILLUSTRATED NEWSPAPER

No. 1,672.—Vol. LXV.] NEW YORK—FOR THE WEEK ENDING OCTOBER 1, 1887. [PRICE, 10 CENTS.

Nina threatened suicide and locked herself in the house for days following the execution. She placed a photograph of Spies in her front window; in time, she became a radical herself. An aunt in Pittsburgh disinherited her. She joined the IWW, but was out of place among the labor leaders. In 1891, she temporarily abandoned the movement to begin a forelorn marriage to Stephen Malato, an Italian lawyer suspected of belonging to the Black Hand. In May of 1907, Malato divorced her, charging infidelity and moral degeneracy. Among other things, Nina was a dog-and-cat woman. Malato said that she preferred their company in bed to his own. Fed up with being chased around the room by Nina and her washboard, Malato moved out. He claimed at the time that he was unaware of her marriage to Spies. He found out about it after Van Zandt sold the medallion of her former husband to a dime museum. Indeed, Nina was a rudderless ship cast adrift in the world. With her fortune gone, she spent her final days running a small rooming house in the crowded tenement district along Halsted Street. When she passed away on April 9, 1936, those in the movement were angry that she chose to leave her remaining $3,000 to an animal welfare station known as Orphans of the Storm. They wanted her money, but neither the labor leaders nor animal shelter saw fit to build her a grave at Waldheim Cemetery.

The Chicago Police Department feared a red revolution on November 11, 1887. Three hundred cops, armed with bayonets and revolvers were deployed around the county jail. Chief Ebersold, with Captains Buckley and Schaak, commanded the details from Harrison Street and East Chicago. Reserves were pressed into duty in the outlying neighborhoods to quell any disturbances. The streets around the jail were cordoned off with heavy rope, preventing any street traffic (or bomb throwers) to get near the building.

When Nina Van Zandt and her mother arrived in their carriage, they were turned away by the police. Lucy Parsons tried to force her way past the police line but was arrested and taken to the Chicago Avenue station. She and her children were detained there until the execution had been performed. So sure that the workers would riot, Ebersold dispatched two detectives to infiltrate the crowds that stood outside the jail. Two companies of sharpshooters were positioned on the roof, while the police who circled the building were deployed in open order. In that way, should a bomb be thrown, there would be minimal loss of life. The police could reform quickly and return the fire. Things never reached that point. The mood was somber. Most of the people who gathered outside the jail were just curious sightseers. Two arrests were made that day. A man described as a "genius crank" because he wore glasses was taken in for concealing a pistol.

Inside the prison, two hundred men assembled to witness the execution. A representative of the German government was on hand to file a report. Spies, Parsons, Fischer, and Engel were executed in the courtyard between the jail and the courthouse. "Will I be allowed to speak? Let the voice of the people be heard!" Parsons said before the trap was sprung. Spies issued a prophetic warning to his accusers: "There will come a time when our silence will be more powerful than the voices you strangle today!"

The room was filled with silence. When it was over, Schaak turned to Ebersold. "The law is vindicated." Ebersold nodded. "The anarchists will understand they cannot do as they please in this country."

Inspector Bonfield wept openly. The *Tribune* said, "It had taken nearly two years to see the disciples of anarchy get their desserts, but he saw it at last, and felt that the brave men who went down that night had been avenged."

Reporters found Sheriff Matson in his office several hours after the execution. He had put in an honest day's work, but there was nothing to be jubilant about. In his view, he had upheld the law. "Do you take any significant meaning from the last words of the dead men?" someone asked.

"No, I do not. With the strained public sentiment, I did not deem it expedient to have the men make long speeches at that time."

And so it was. The plight of the surviving Haymarket men—Fielden, Schwab, Neebe—rested with the governor. No one was willing to commit political suicide, so the men continued to languish in the penitentiary. In 1892, a stoop-shouldered, sour-looking man, beset by various physical ailments, was elected governor. His name was John Peter Altgeld, and his parents were poor German immigrants. Altgeld's career was nurtured by the big-city Democratic bosses. He counted among his supporters the gambler Joseph Martin and the gambler's boss, Mike McDonald. As a jurist, he was unremarkable. In fact, he resigned his judgeship so that he could devote more time to his downtown real-estate holdings. He explained his action at the time by saying that men in public office were a "cowardly hanging-on class, always careful to see how the wind blows before daring either to have or express an opinion."

Altgeld never shirked from expressing his opinions. As governor, he struggled with his conscience concerning the Haymarket men. He studied the issue but reserved judgment. Finally he concluded that the charges were true—Judge Gary had been prejudiced, the evidence of guilt was flimsy, and the jury may have been packed. On June 26, 1893, Altgeld's message of pardon was given to the press. There was an immediate uproar, as the press labeled him the "viper" Altgeld, friend to anarchists. Even those who supported clemency found fault with the governor's stern criticisms of Judge Gary. He accused Gary of conducting the trial with "malicious ferocity."

Deeply disturbed by the hue and cry of the press, Altgeld turned the cheek to an imprisoned, dying young man, whose mother had requested a pardon. The day the boy expired in his cell, Altgeld signed the release papers. He did not know the young man died in the morning.

Altgeld went to his grave with the courage of his convictions. He had done the right thing. Later, his actions would be justified to historians, but they did not see it that way in 1893.

Schaak and Bonfield basked in their publicity, and, for a time, they were called heroes. The Chicago industrialists expressed their gratitude by contributing $31,371.50 to the Policeman's Benevolent Association and another $31,371.93 to the heirs of the slain policemen. The railroads, which had felt the brunt of labor agitation, donated a combined $10,759. But the man most responsible for the troubles along the Black Road, Cyrus Hall McCormick, chipped in a meager $250.

Aftermath

The cause and the deed would not slip from memory. The very issues that the Haymarket men fought for would be adopted by the coming generations. When the last of them were dropped to eternity, it insured their place in history as martyrs, while setting into motion the wheels of change that ended the laissez-faire lifestyles of the Chicago rich. The old ways do not change overnight, and for many other summers after 1886, Derby Day, cotillions, and afternoon tea would be observed on the south side. But it would pass from view.

Would these men of average means become martyrs if the state had responded in a sane, rational manner? Probably not. Haymarket would have become a nonevent in Chicago history, if not for Bonfield, Schaak, Judge Gary, and Grinnell. What happened in the weeks following May 4, 1886, deeply influenced a new and more radical generation that included Emma Goldman, William Z. Foster, and Elizabeth Flynn. On June 25, 1893, a monument designed by Albert Weinert was dedicated at Waldheim Cemetery in Forest Park to the Haymarket men who were buried there. William Haywood and the legendary Joe Hill requested that their ashes be scattered over the grave sights following their deaths. Haymarket became a worldwide symbol to the laboring classes, but Bonfield and company could not see that.

One thousand thirty-six policemen were on the city payroll in 1886. That represented a 100 percent increase in manpower since 1881. Seventeen thousand more arrests were made in 1886 than in 1878. Most of the crimes were petty offenses: lounging on street corners, vagrancy, thievery, and failing to hitch a horse. These are numbers that indicate that the suspected socialists and street-corner loungers were pursued doggedly while society's ills, represented by Mike McDonald, were ignored. After Haymarket, the stench of scandal filtered into the press once again.

A former Lake Street machinery merchant named John Roche replaced Carter Harrison as mayor in 1886. Roche allowed Bonfield and Schaak to continue their red-baiting tactics. Meetings were infiltrated, while Lucy Parsons complained of having her mail tampered with by the post office. To Schaak's delight, Ebersold was replaced on February 14, 1888. "Ebersold is charged with being partial in giving soft snaps to certain favorites, and extending advantages to his own nationality, German,"the *Daily News* reported. But Schaak was passed over for promotion in favor of George Hubbard of the Central Station. The new chief allowed Bonfield to chase the socialists, so Lucy Parsons was arrested for selling her husband's book that year.

But finally, the *Chicago Times* exposed the red-scare tactics of the police department in a series of bold exposés during January 1889. The paper accused Bonfield of allowing gambling along Halsted, State, and West Madison streets. A raid would be engineered now and then, but the only ones brought in were "suckers and irresponsible darkies" (respect toward blacks in the press was years away).

Bonfield used his position to play politics. When former Captain William Buckley of the first precinct ran for a seat in the Illinois General Assembly, Bonfield threatened saloon keepers into supporting his opponent "Ike" Abrahams. Ike was known as a bondsman and attorney whose clients were well-known low life. The elderly Buckley had trained Bonfield years before, but the inspector held a grudge. He tried to deny Buckley his pension. The paper went on to explain how Bonfield accepted a gold police star from the madam of a notorious Clinton Street house in return for protection. For several days, Bonfield strutted about the station displaying his new star before the *Times* city editor got wind of it. Bonfield allegedly visited the editor to plead for mercy, explaining that his sick father could not bear the public scandal.

The Louisiana Lottery opened an office directly across the street from the Central Station in open defiance of the law, while Bonfield and William Ward ran a secret protection racket in which the gamblers and call-house madams were forced to contribute or be raided.

There was more. A former Chicago policeman and noted pool hustler named John Brennan opened up a saloon next to the Des Plaines station, which was frequented by uniformed men. Brennan was allowed to shake down the call girls in the lockup in return for a piece of the profits. Several cops were made silent partners.

But the whole story was not killed. (Carter Harrison later bought this paper for use as his political organ, so it can be assumed that *his* motives were not entirely civic.) Bonfield reacted to these charges in his usual cavalier fashion. On the morning of January 5, editors James West and Joseph Dunlop were arrested for criminal libel. Bonfield timed the arrest so that Dunlop would not be able to meet the bondsman at the Harrison Street lockup. Since the bondsmen were out of the building, the editor was installed in a basement cell that was a cesspool, even by 1889 standards. Mayor Roche condemned the actions, so Dunlop finally got to meet his bondsman. Upon leaving the jail, Schaak tried to arrest him again, but was shown the necessary bond.

While the details of open gambling shocked the public and helped sink Bonfield, Schaak had some problems of his own. At the time, his Haymarket partner Jake Loewenstein was recovering from a gunshot wound put there by his wife. Mabel Loewenstein told her lawyers that she was tired of seeing her house turned into a warehouse for stolen merchandise. She told of how Schaak and her husband confiscated the personal property of their prisoners, using her home as a drop off. Prisoners would be routinely taken to the house to be "sweated" into confessions, while witnesses were coerced into presenting testimony that was the opposite of what was known to be true. Louis Lingg willed a gold watch, brooch, shawl, and a vase to his fiancé. However, Schaak never returned the goods to the rightful owner. The stories were remarkable in the sense that it was a departure from the usual coverage of police affairs at that time. Witness this *Chicago Times* quote of January 6, 1889:

> If an inoffensive citizen was arrested without cause and the outrage was denounced, Bonfield's cry of anarchist would be heard. Again the *Times* does not, and will not shut its eyes to official attempts to hoodwink the public. If a judge on the bench or a police officer at his desk lays the plans for an alleged dynamite plot, engages the men to work it, takes measures that will insure notoriety and on the strength of exposure, jeopardize the liberty and perhaps the lives of the innocent for his own glorification, the *Times* will expose the diabolical work.

Schaak, Loewenstein, and Bonfield were suspended from the force on February 7, 1889. Lawsuits were introduced against the newspaper, but nothing came of it. Schaak was eventually reinstated, but Bonfield never wore a police uniform again.

Anarchist raids to Grief's Hall continued into 1892. The *Chicago-Herald* charged the police that year with engineering raids to con the Citizen's Association into keeping the anarchist funds alive. But the business community had already cut the fund, while the first red scare faded into history.

Bonfield and Schaak died the same year. The inspector started his own detective agency following his 1889 suspension. There was a business failure, so Bonfield drifted into permanent obscurity. He died from the effects of Bright's Disease on October 19, 1898. Michael Schaak remained flamboyant to the bitter end. A few weeks before contracting pneumonia, Schaak predicted his own death. He turned over all of his evidence in a poisoning case to an assistant, saying he knew it was time for him to die. Schaak survived bullets, arson attempts, police scandals, and shakeups, but died on May 18, 1898.

Fredrick Ebersold was collecting the largest pension given to a retired policeman up to the time of his death on January 21, 1900. The spectre of Schnaubelt's release haunted him to his death. He secluded himself in his Chicago home, receiving no callers and eating no food. The cause of death was listed as starvation.

Outside the doorway between Jackson and Taylor stands the police memorial to the Haymarket Affair. The statue was designed by Frank Batchelder of St. Paul, Minnesota, and was dedicated on May 4, 1889. Construction funding was raised by Richard T. Crane and the *Chicago Tribune*.

Policeman Thomas Birmingham was selected to pose for the statue created by John Gelert. Birmingham was one of many cops selected from the central detail to serve at the Des Plaines station the night of the tragedy. He was later suspended for neglect of duty, but made money during the 1893 World's Fair by conducting guided tours to the Haymarket site. He died destitute at the county hospital on September 26, 1912, after spending his last six years in the county infirmary at Oak Forest.

The statue is the only known monument dedicated to the police. It features the upraised hand of William Ward. After the statue was blown up during the "Days of Rage" in 1969 and 1970, the city moved it to the police headquarters. Today, only the base remains. It stands like a broken sphinx east of the Kennedy Expressway on Randolph Street.

Very little of the original Haymarket area is left. Zepf's Hall at Lake and Des Plaines still stands, but the original store front has been boarded up. It is a gray, withered building that houses the Grand Stage Lighting Company. On another May night, bullets whizzed into the door, sending Parsons and his family sprawling to the floor.

The site of the Des Plaines station is now a parking lot. The ancient, cobblestone alley still exists, but the building containing the vestibule where the bomb was thrown is gone. If you let your imagination wander, you can visualize columns of blue-coated men advancing down the street. It is an old area. The feeling of history is here. It is unmistakable. Tucked into a grimy, industrial area, the event that helped change the Western world remains anonymous to the casual visitor. There is no plaque or museum because old feelings have refused to die.

2
Close-up on the 1880s: The Boodler's Bathroom Escape

boo dle, böd' al, n. 1. a bribe or other illicit payment. 2. loot or booty.

IT WAS TO BECOME AN OLD CHICAGO TRADITION USUALLY IDENTIFIED with John Coughlin and Michael Kenna. But the Bath and the Dink were political novices when William McGarigle pulled a scam on the county that helped put the word *boodle* in the dictionary.

They remembered McGarigle's boodle for years. He set a new standard for corruption in Cook County and then was forgotten about. It seemed so incredible at the time. How could this rising young man of Democratic politics and a Freemason involve himself in such an odious political scandal?

He was born to a middle-class Milwaukee family on September 9, 1850, and was educated in one of the better German institutes in the city. His father was a postal clerk and general contractor, but young McGarigle had designs on the bigger things in life, when he moved to Chicago in 1868. He joined the police force in 1871 as a patrolman at Webster Street. With a quick wit and a fine mind, McGarigle ingratiated himself with Jake Rehm and Elmer Washburne. Rehm promoted him to the detective bureau in 1873, and Washburne made him his private secretary.

Carter Harrison promoted him to general superintendent in 1879 when he was only twenty nine. As police chief, McGarigle systemized the reports of arresting officers, created a workable bookkeeping system, and even made the grand tour of Europe in May of 1881. In what was supposed to be a fact-finding mission, McGarigle took time out to visit County Cork and to kiss the blarney stone.

McGarigle's integrity was questioned by those who sought an end to organized gambling. The charge was made that police secrets were being given to the gamblers and that Mike McDonald's operations were being shielded by McGarigle. "So far as anyone giving away the secrets of the department to any gambler is concerned, no matter who the man might be, he would not remain a minute on the police force after I found out," McGarigle said. But there was little doubt that

William McGarigle sketched from an official portrait. Here we see him as chief of detectives, circa 1879, and as commissioner, 1886.

McDonald's influence with Carter Harrison helped McGarigle land the job of police superintendent.

In 1882, the Republican Party of Cook County mounted a serious prohibition campaign. Mike McDonald perceived this to be the first step toward a general suppression of his enterprises. To check this latest Republican move, McDonald talked McGarigle into running for Cook County sheriff. The press attacked the cozy relationship between the police chief and the gambler before the state convention even took place. The outcry against McGarigle was so strong that Harrison warned him about the consequences of running for office. He couldn't win, and he would not be given back his position as police chief after the election should he lose. The advice was ignored, and McGarigle was the unanimous choice of the Democratic State Convention. Harrison was out of town at the time.

McDonald spent $50,000 trying to elect McGarigle. At the beginning of the campaign, he coached McGarigle on what to tell the press.

Close-up on the 1880s

It was important, McDonald said, to criticize the gambler alliance openly and to disavow any personal association with him.

But then, McDonald began showing up at McGarigle's campaign rallies. In the sixteenth ward, McDonald marched into the hall with his candidate trailing right behind. The marching band played "See the Conquering Hero Come," while McDonald took his place at the rostrum. "Gentlemen, I didn't get up here to make a speech, but to treat you to some beer," he said. McGarigle helped pass out the beer while McDonald distributed victory cigars. The meeting was well attended because McDonald had mailed out form letters bearing the signatures of the party brokers—Harvey Weeks, John Mattocks, and John McAvoy—to stimulate monetary contributions.

Meanwhile, the mayor stumped the German and Irish wards, reminding them that the Republicans would take away their drinking privileges. "I think the best plan is, since you are going to let men drink, to let them have the good stuff," Harrison said. "Kentucky, where I was raised, is a great state for making whiskey. Up to the time I was twenty-five years old, I never saw a man who had the delirium tremens. I knew a good many men who drank too much and a good many of them were not often sober. But they were not poisoning themselves, for good old bourbon didn't give them the delirium tremens [as beer would]. A fellow would drink, go to bed, sweat it off, get up in the morning, do his work, and yet he was a tolerable good sort of fellow after all." On the subject of Mike McDonald, Harrison told the Germans, "He is a pretty good man. If Mike ran the city government the people of Chicago were to be congratulated that he was born and lived among them."

The German weekly, *Staats-Zeitung*, endorsed the mayor but expressed reservations about his comments pertaining to McDonald. The *Tribune* just bristled.

> If the Bourbons get control of the county as well as the city offices, McDonald's bread will be buttered on both sides. The safer the business of buying and selling justice is, the more largely will he go into it. If he can get his creatures in the County Board, and so direct the drawing of juries, he will be able to not only furnish bail-bonds on "short notice and easy terms," but to guarantee an acquittal on any charges at "greatly reduced rates."

On the subject of the gambling dens and the mayor's speech, the *Tribune* of October 28, 1882, editorialized that:

How Mike McDonald runs this city is shown in the gambling houses of Clark Street and the horrible dens on State Street and Third Avenue and Canal Street, where every special vice is openly practiced and defies interference from the police or the law authorities. Well may honest, moral, temperate citizens look on with astonishment that even Carter Harrison ventures to go so far at Mike McDonald's bidding as to stand up in his place, the mayor of a great city, and openly advise people to drink whiskey, with the horrible effects of it all around him, cursing the city and injuring its good name. How long will it be before law abiding Americans and the temperate Germans will indignantly rise and crush out this McDonald and his man Carter Harrison, and rescue the city from the thugs and harridans that infest its principal streets?

That November, McGarigle won the city by 1,500 votes but suffered defeat in the outlying areas. McGarigle lost to Seth Hanchett by 4,900 votes in an election he was expected to win. The prohibition ticket was weak, and even the *Tribune* conceded that Democratic prospects were excellent. At least until the media exposed the liaison between city hall, the gambler, and the candidate.

On September 1, 1883, McGarigle was appointed warden of the Cook County Hospital, following a brief business venture with his friend E.J. Lehmann. the new position required the careful administration of county tax money. In his role as commissioner, McGarigle worked closely with other members of the county board.

The board was bloated and corrupt. The capable businessmen of Chicago wanted no part of the committee meetings that somehow always adjourned to the saloon across the street. The fourteen positions on the board could have been easily attended to by three or four commissioners. Instead, the county taxpayers had to pay five dollars a day in salary to the commissioners of printing, finance, education, roads, bridges, town accounts, juries, taxes, jail and criminal court, public buildings, charities, hospitals, licenses, courthouse and records, and outdoor relief.

Under the pretense of attending to county business, the commissioners convened unnecessary board meetings and ran up expense accounts making useless sidetrips to the outlying institutions. A commissioner's job was a political plum if used wisely. And McGarigle was the latest addition to the Mike McDonald-infested board.

Close-up on the 1880s

On his first day in office, he toured the spacious grounds with outgoing warden Joe Dixon. He told McGarigle of unfulfilled plans—walls in need of paint, broken sidewalks, and faulty plumbing. There was no mention of Dixon's scandalous practices. Reports had leaked out that patients were given heavy doses of morphine each night, so they would not bother the night nurse, and that the inmates were forced to eat their food without silverware.

McGarigle listened carefully to everything that was said. There was much repair work to be done . . . and he knew the right people who could do it.

Boodle for the Gang

Just six days after the Haymarket bomb fell, a resolution was entered in the county record: "A communication from Warden McGarigle submitting a proposal from the American Stone and Brick Company for necessary repairs and work on the hospital buildings was read and referred to the committee on buildings and hospitals."

McGarigle told fellow board members about a wonderful new method of restoring crumbling masonry that he found. It was called the "Lundberg Process."

The proposition to apply the Lundberg Process to 4,090 square feet of the county hospital at a cost of thirty-five cents a foot was approved by the board. But then a second, revised report was filed just two weeks later. Could the first estimate have been wrong? An additional 7,991 more feet of front stonework had been "found," bringing the initial cost (with other various expenses) of $1,400 up to $8,044 total.

The "boys on the board" (and there were thirteen of them) made a tidy little profit from the hospital paint job. Nobody noticed . . . or cared. There was money to be spread all around—commissions for the contractor, commissions for the county board members, and a fat profit to Michael Cassius McDonald, the gambler king whose career deserves closer examination.

King Mike arrived in Chicago in 1855. He was a snappy, roguish gambler, fond of the drink. He learned his trade from Colonel Jack Haverly, the first to make gambling a full-time occupation in the days following the Civil War. During the war, McDonald did his part for the Union. He worked as a recruiter, collecting commissions from the government for every man he signed up. When they deserted their regiments and enlisted *again*, McDonald split the second commission with them. But this was strictly small-time stuff. After the war, McDonald drifted into the Democratic circles, after he first established his reputation among the sportsmen in the Loop poolrooms. McDonald organized the campaign of Harvey *Doolittle* Colvin, Chicago's postfire mayor, who gave the gamblers an open town.

One night, he met a young clerk from the Chicago Dock Company. The clerk gambled away some of his employer's money at a parlor that Mike was "roping" for. After he lost all his money, Mike pulled him aside and told him to return the next night with some more. Mike had a great plan to make them both a fortune and to cover his losses.

The next day, McDonald and his new friend left Chicago to start a traveling faro bank. But with the money in his hands, there was no need to continue the game. McDonald told him that due to some unforseen luck, the bank was broke. The clerk went to the police, and both of them were arrested. However, Mike was released to his Democratic pals, who posted the bond. With his ill-gotten $30,000, Mike opened the "Store" at 176 Clark Street. It was a four-story building with Mike's wholesale liquor business occupying the first floor, his private residence on the third, with faro, roulette, hazard, and card games conducted night and day on the second floor. Harry Lawrence and Morris Martin were two investors that Mike eventually bought out. During the gambling inquest, he swore that his connection with the games ended in 1874, when he decided to devote all his time to his wholesale liquor business.

Up and down Randolph Street, the boys called him "Sure Thing Mike." Professional out-of-town gamblers were barred from the Store. Mike never needed ropers to steer in the traffic because they cost too much, and he hired the right people to make sure that only suckers were allowed in. The dealers were Billy Tyler, George Noyes, Charley Winters, Cliff Donaghue, and Frank Gallin—bad boys all. By the time of Carter Harrison's first election in 1879, McDonald was receiving tribute from other gamblers operating in the Loop. He regularly took 25 percent of Jeff Hankins's profit at 134 Clark for "protection." It was understood that there was to be a divvy for Mike, or there would be raids.

As a professional bondsman, McDonald supplied sixty-six offenders in the lower court and twenty-one cases under appeal with their tickets out of jail. Political favors in the ethnic wards translate into votes on election day. Buying and selling justice was just one way McDonald became the silent partner to the Democratic machine of Chicago. With his friend McGarigle installed as sheriff, McDonald could have had his own man see to it that forfeitures on bonds would not be pressed against him. The sheriff could also assist the bondsman by driving the crook out of town, after he already deposited his money with him. The scheme was foiled by the Republicans in 1882, a bad year all around for Mike.

On March 7 of that year, McDonald was indicted for keeping a gaming house. He was among illustrious company. In addition to "Mockingbird" Whalen, "Kid" Leonard, Johnny Dowling, Jeff Hankins, and Jim Conlisk, James C. Gore, proprietor of Chapin & Gore's Restaurant, and Potter Palmer himself were also indicted. Palmer was charged with maintaining a gambling den next to the Lawler & Smith establishment at 178 State Street. Indeed, it was a strange gathering that faced Judge Joseph Gary.

Several of the small-fry gamblers were convicted, but Mike walked out of court a free man on April 17. There was no evidence to prosecute. McDonald disclaimed any knowledge of a game on his premises, but he did admit to "loaning" money to gamblers from time to time. Carter Harrison was called as a witness. He told of meeting with McDonald several times and had even visited the Store to advise him against harboring large groups of drinking men in the "upper quarters." When asked about a southern boy who lost some money to Mike's game, Harrison replied that if a Kentuckian wasn't sharp enough to save himself from gamblers, then he wasn't going to interfere. Earlier, McDonald was arrested by Captain Buckley of Harrison Street after a sailor named Joe McDowell of Cleveland swore out an arrest warrant. He claimed to have lost all his money in a rigged faro game at the Store. When the trial convened at the Armory Police Court, the man said he couldn't remember the dealer or who started the game. Mike walked out of that one laughing.

Keeping a gaming house was a serious charge, and it took considerable money and influence to win an acquittal. The police officers who had battered down the door leading to the upstairs parlor could not recall ever seeing Mike on the second floor. The charge couldn't stick. Once again McDonald proved to be above the law, despite the testimony of a Chicago detective who saw thirty people playing roulette or faro.

By 1887, Mike not only had the Store but the city and the Democratic Party as well. The American Stone and Brick Preserving Company was just one of his many enterprises. The company was administered by Henry L. Holland, McDonald's bookkeeper. When a reporter asked Holland about the special Lundberg Formula, he smiled and said nothing.

Inside the county board room, Holland won his contract by using a time-honored Chicago ruse, the old "brick trick." A very old and crumbling brick would be pulled out of a bag for the commissioners to inspect. In just one day, they would treat the brick with the formula to remove all incrustations and foreign matter. The pores of the stone were closed with a water-proofing compound that was a part of the process. The next day Holland returned with a new brick that he said was the old one transformed. Somehow the commissioners believed him.

The county courthouse was another public building in need of this special service, so Holland was first in line with a contract offer. Work on the courthouse was twofold. The firm of E.R. Brainerd was hired to remove porticoes and granite stairs from the Washington Street side and to replace them with a cheaper grade of Bedford Stone. The firm's bid was significantly higher than that of the Hallowell Granite Company but was accepted anyway. Brainerd was a noted first-ward resident whose partner was "Oyster" Joe Mackin, resident of the Joliet Penitentiary. Mackin was secretary of the Democratic Central Committee. During the Cleveland-Blaine election, he was caught in an elaborate ballot-box fraud and later convicted of perjury. But he was still one of the bosses.

If all this wasn't bad enough, the board changed its mind and had to pay Brainerd $52,000 *not* to tear out the porticoes. In October of 1886, the county agreed to allow Holland to supply the magic formula to 600,000 square feet of the courthouse. At thirty-cents a foot, the total cost of the paint job came out to more than $180,000. Months later an accurate measurement was taken. The total surface to be painted measured only 329,373 feet. By this time Holland and McDonald had collected $98,812. As for the magic Lundberg Formula? Well, it's charitable to say that they did it big in the old days.

Two separate paint samples were sent to Professor Walter S. Haines of the Rush Medical College for chemical analysis. Sample #1 turned out to be linseed oil (this sample had been used only on bricks that had been encrusted or rough following a sanding by workmen). Sample #2 was a cheap grade of paint consisting of linseed oil, turpentine, white lead, zinc white, carbonite of lime, oxide of iron, silica, and

Close-up on the 1880s

alumina. Conclusion: Any commonly used white lead paint would have done a better job than the formula.

The Tabernacle Building stood directly across the street from the courthouse. It too was coated with the Lundberg Process. In eight months time, it had to be repainted. This was boodle, performed Chicago style, and the courthouse job was only the beginning.

The *Chicago Tribune* zeroed in on the affairs of the county commissioners in a series of probes that began in mid-January of 1887. McGarigle's ties with Mike and Ed McDonald (who was the engineer at the hospital) and various other shady contractors helped draw the entire board into a public scandal.

There were three ways the commissioners turned taxpayer money into boodle. Private contractors, who were anxious to land choice county jobs, eagerly paid a lump sum to the board. A second way was taking "commissions" collected on the bills paid by the city, and a third method of boodle was the payments received from the haul-away services. Food wastes and offal were not just discarded by the hospital. McGarigle saw a way to make a profit by selling garbage to farmers, who in turn fed it to their pigs.

There were no checks and balances on the commissioner's authority to push through illegal bids. They were simply approved and sent on to the county clerk, who prepared a warrant to the county treasurer, who paid the money.

The revelations of open corruption by those trusted with the county money was swift and startling. On February 10, 1887, the *Tribune* reported that $16,222.67 had been paid to lumber supplier J.G. Lobstein for a ten-month period ending on November 29, 1886. As far as anyone could tell, the only thing done with the lumber was in conjunction with a new sidewalk for the hospital and a small barn built next to the insane asylum.

The contractors that the board preferred to deal with were the small independents. One of them was Theodore Clemenz, who ran a beer saloon from the basement of his home. He supplied McGarigle and Commissioner Harry Varnell of the asylum with eleven cases of Rhine Wine costing $1,650. Normal retail prices for a case of wine at that time was only $6.

Everything from pipe fittings, to clothing, to bread became boodle targets. The company of Heissler and Junge provided the county institutions with bread at a cost of $2.70 for one hundred pounds. The firm routinely picked up stale, unsold loaves from its retail customers every day. Before landing the fat county contract, Heissler donated the unsold bread to the farmers who used it for hogfeed. Later, he sold it to the county facilities, which used it to feed patients.

Fred W. Bipper of 375 State Street was a merchant who sold the county pig's heads at the rate of nine cents a pound. The original contract called for salt pork at that price, but they received pig's heads instead. Pig's heads normally retailed for two cents a pound. Bipper's profit was estimated to be $50,000.

While the county treasury was being bled dry and McGarigle and his cohorts grew rich, conditions at the county hospital had not improved. The Knights of Labor sent a delegation on a fact-finding mission and to interview McGarigle. The warden ushered them into his private office where they were served sherry and fine cigars. Mac pointed with pride to the improvements made while he was in office. A new stable had been built. Imported vases, fine damask draperies, and china cuspidors were now displayed in the hallway, and the death rate had dropped 7 percent.

All these things were true, of course, but what McGarigle neglected to show them was the infamous Ward Eighteen, located on the second floor of the county morgue away from the main building. Ward Eighteen was above the morgue for good reason. It was the contagious-disease ward, where there were just six available beds to serve the entire city. In a cramped, fetid, 18' x 40' room, men and women were mixed together, often lying side by side on the floor waiting to die and to take the short trip downstairs. Smells of rotting corpses filtered upstairs, and it was said that strong men turned away sick after being led through the morgue and upstairs.

Drunken nurses, poor sanitation, and rotting foods were the services provided by the master boodler. A workman who suffered burns on three-quarters of his body was brought to the hospital, where he was left to himself in a room for three days without a change of linen. After being discharged, the bed sheet was found to be black and reeking from open wounds on the man's body.

When these facts were revealed, State's Attorney Julius Grinnell began an investigation. The fate of the Haymarket men was still in the hands of the Supreme Court, so Grinnell hired a team of detectives to track down evidence of boodle. They had to find the weak link in the chain . . . someone who could be pressured into giving evidence. Such a man was Nicholas Schneider, a rotund, obsequious type, who was a steamfitter by trade and a close partner of Edward McDonald.

Schneider had completed $94,000 worth of work for the county but had little to show for it. Nick was in debt to McGarigle, who had loaned him $5,000 so that he could purchase material. The trouble was, the five thousand was money owed to the hospital employees. Believing that Schneider would confess under pressure, Grinnell assigned the Mooney and Boland Detective Agency to follow him around town. Then one night he disappeared. Grinnell would not reveal whether he was taken into custody or whether Schneider had fled town. Schneider's panic stricken wife appeared at the courthouse door pleading for some news but was turned away.

The detectives raided his office at 234 Honore Street to impound his ledgers. Falsified bills of every county job going back three years were seized and held as future evidence. The legality of the raid remains questionable but at last Grinnell had material to take to the grand jury. The other boodlers were edgy. McGarigle blasted the state's attorney. "Now Grinnell knows the county commissioners have done no wrong. He knows that they are honest men, but simply because they have been a little careless in some of their methods, he wants to blacken their characters before the community."

John VanPelt, former chairman of the Democratic Central Committee and a retired commissioner who was also under a cloud of suspicion, offered another view: "I'll give you a pointer. If they take me, I'll not be alone."

Joe Dixon could laugh about the whole episode. He told a grisly story about the time he served as warden of the hospital. To pick up a few extra dollars, he sold corpses lying in the morgue to local undertakers for $25 a stiff. We can only guess what happened to the bodies afterward.

"Grinnell will sweat blood before he's through," McGarigle vowed. But that would not be the case. A special grand jury was summoned on March 8 by Judge Elliot Anthony. The boodlers rejoiced when they learned that several members of the jury were former business associates. John A. King had sold wholesale drugs to the county, while juror Michael Keeley was a brewer who knew Commissioner Richard Oliver well. "He's a whiskey man," Oliver exclaimed. "Whiskey men stick together."

Jury-packing charges were leveled against the boodlers throughout the following months. When the bailiff went to select a prospective juror, he carried with him a secret list provided by McGarigle.

McGarigle, Varnell, Driscoll, and McDonald were arrested on March 16. Nine days later the first indictments were returned against Commissioners Dan Wren, Adam Ochs, John VanPelt, and grocer Elisha Robinson. Robinson testified that he made payments to VanPelt

ILLUSTRATED GRAPHIC NEWS

VOL. VII, No. 9. CHICAGO, SATURDAY, FEBRUARY 26, 1887. TERMS: { TEN CENTS PER COPY. $4.00 per Year, in Advance

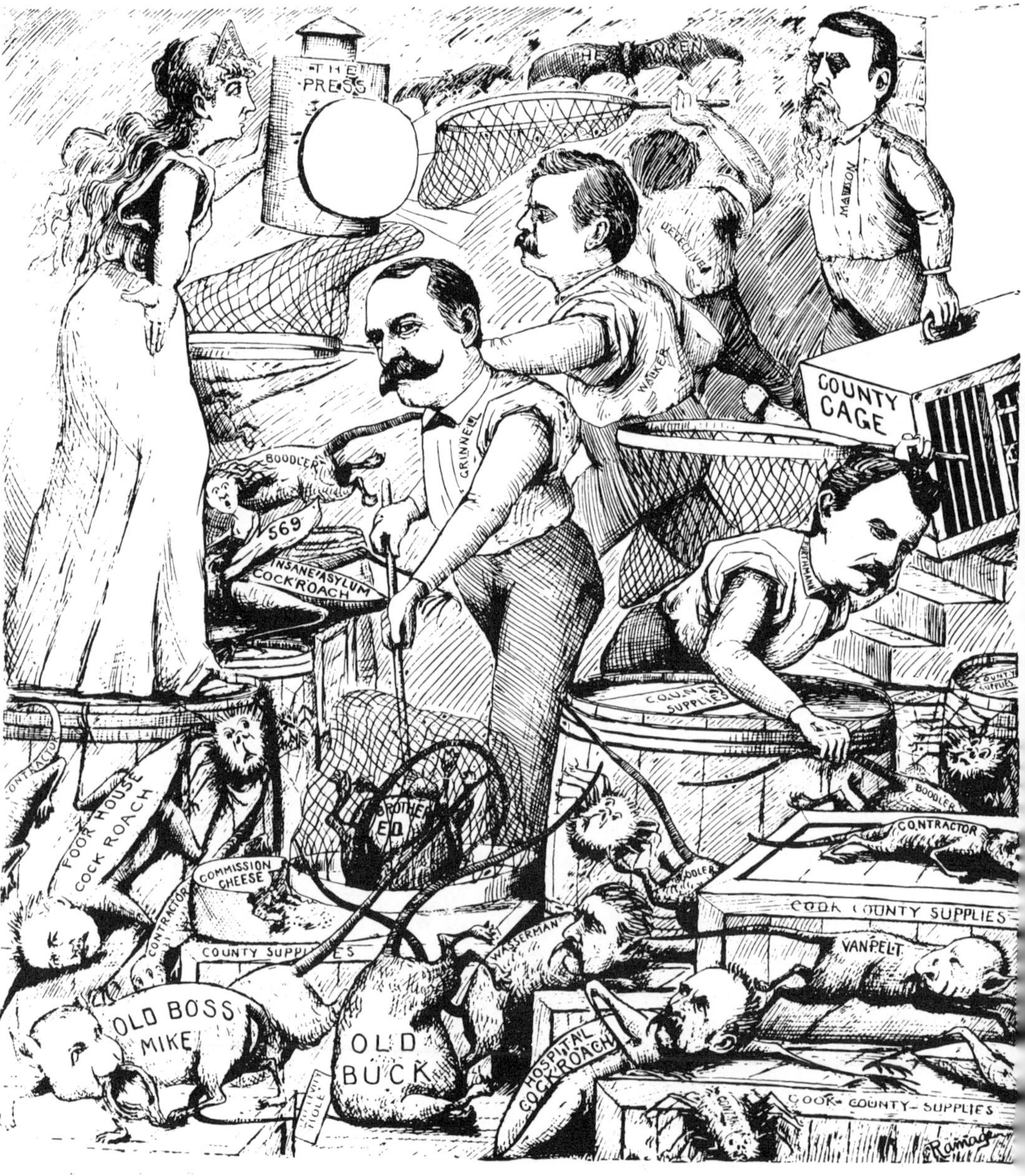

THE RAID ON THE VERMIN.

Close-up on the 1880s

totaling $1,300 over a six-month period. Payments would be slipped into an envelope and taken to the cigar stand at the Sherman House by a bookkeeper. Not only did Robinson have to stand trial, he was also out the $42,000 he claimed the county owed him.

Mike McDonald was not among those who would stand trial. The king of Chicago politics and gambling was just another interested observer to lend his opinions: "Well, according to the newspapers I'm into everything nowadays. But I notice after it's all over that I generally show 'em a pretty clean pair of heels and I'll do it this time or I'm very much mistaken. Most everybody's a boodler nowadays, you know."

The trial commenced in the courtroom of Judge Henry Shepard of the superior court on May 25, 1887. Though Mike had arranged with the First National Bank to cash Nick Schneider's illegal vouchers and had funneled him money through his saloon trade, he would not spend a minute on the witness stand. Younger brother Ed would take the fall instead.

During a cross-examination of Ed, Mike got bored and left the room to pay a social call on his friend, Judge John Peter Altgeld, who was in his chambers down the hall. "How you doin', Judge?" Mike said. "I have been listenin' to that little brother of mine. I had a little experience with a jury in the courtroom once myself. They had me charged with gambling. I let my lawyer pick out eleven of the jurymen until they came to Miner T. Ames [who also served on the boodler jury]. My counsel objected to him, but I said no. Well, he stayed on the jury and was the only one who held out for conviction. The other eleven wanted to acquit. If I ever have any more experience with juries, I'm going to leave it to the lawyers." McDonald turned and walked away. Altgeld remarked to a clerk; "Smart man, smart man, one of the smartest in the country."

(Left) The *Graphic* was a newspaper published in Chicago to serve the greater Midwest. Through the mid-1880s and 1890s, it presented a digest of the news in timely, interesting manner. The illustrator of this issue portrays the rats nest of corruption being "cleaned out" by Julius Grinnell, Sheriff Matson (holding the cage), and prosecutors Walker and Furthmann. (Left to right on the bottom, Mike McDonald, Buck McCarthy, Michael Wasserman, McGarigle, and John Van Pelt are fleeing from the commission cheese, which was sampled by the vermin. Interestingly, Matson holds the cage. His stupidity allowed McGarigle to open it up. (Courtesy of the Chicago Historical Society.)

General Israel Newton Stiles, hero of the Battle of Franklin, Tennessee, opened for the state at 11:45 A.M. on May 25, 1887. Stiles was known for his easy, persuasive way with a jury. He spent much of his time courting their favor before getting down to the specific charge: an attempt by Edward McDonald, William McGarigle, Nicholas Schneider, and architect Fredrick Faber to conspire to defraud the people of Cook County.

The Cook County Normal School at 15 Illinois Street was the first boodle case to be presented to the jury. When the school officials alerted the county board that they were in critical need of a new heating apparatus, Ed McDonald and Mike Leyden went out. Leyden brought along McGarigle because he had done such a "wonderful" job putting the hospital in order. It didn't matter that the hospital was twenty miles away from the school and that McDonald had no business being there.

So Schneider, McDonald, and McGarigle entered into a conspiracy to do the job at a 30 percent commission rate for each of them. There was no contract drawn up, nor formal bids accepted, and no estimates prepared for board debate. When the thirty-year-old architect Faber told his story, McGarigle bowed his head in repose. As the chief architect, it was Faber's responsibility to review the work and okay the estimates. But Faber was signing bills he knew nothing of. McGarigle had directed the bills to Commissioner James "Buck" McCarthy, a roly-poly, sarcastic little man from the stockyards district. "What are you employed for, if not to sign these bills?" he told Faber. "I don't know anything about them." "Well, what are you paid for then?" he told Faber again. Faber protested that the bills seemed too high, but McGarigle dipped his pen in the inkwell, telling him that quantity was none of his business.

Nick Schneider, resplendent in a scotch-tweed suit, was kept on the stand for three days. He told of his arrest and incarceration by the Mooney detectives in Hyde Park and how he attempted to flee from the city. Nick set out for the East Coast but was trailed by Grinnell's detectives. After three months on the road, Schneider returned to Chicago to turn state's evidence to escape imprisonment. On the stand, Schneider was grilled at length by General Stiles. His Normal School bills clearly showed the waste and the steal.

	Used	*Charged*	*Steal*
1½" pipe	$1,730	$3,500	$1,770
1" pipe	$ 710	$2,300	$1,590

1½" ells	$193	$500	$307
1" ells	$461	$800	$339
1¼" pipe	$ 19	$250	$231

The trial proved that no county contract could be given out without McGarigle's tacit approval and that he controlled the commission pool within the board. It was Ed McDonald's job to see that no bill went through the committee unless the 20 percent commission first went into the pool.

McGarigle sat through the proceedings in a comatose state. He stared at the floor for long periods of time; the only emotion shown was utter disgust. Thoughts of suicide raced through his mind, for he was trapped by irrefutable evidence. His whole life was shattered, his promising career in politics gone. There had to be ways out.

Charles R. Abbott of the Columbus and Hocking Coal Company told of an $11,000 payoff to McGarigle at the hospital. The company's bid for a contract was instantly approved.

One by one, the contractors testified against the gang. Thomas Middleton, State Street carpet man, agreed to pay the boodlers 15¢ for every yard of carpeting furnished the county. But the carpeting that was supposed to go into the courthouse ended up in Commissioner Charles Lynn's home instead. Middleton only received a few of the promised vouchers and was lucky to break even on the deal.

Through the proceedings, Ed McDonald and McGarigle shared a berth in cell 79 of the county jail. While Mac sat on his bed refusing to eat, McDonald welcomed everyone who came to visit him and remained confident even after the two men were convicted on June 18 and sentenced to three years apiece by Judge Shepard. But their situation was hopeless after the Republican Mayor John A. Roche timed a gambling crackdown to coincide with the boodle case. With the gambler's income dried up, any funds that were to be channeled toward the defense also ended.

Judge Shepard and McGarigle were both Democrats, and the temptation was strong to grant Mac bail before sentencing. But Shepard was a noted jurist, who later championed the eight-hour workday. He put partisan politics aside in refusing to grant bail. "I have known and liked McGarigle and would have been glad to see him out on bail if it were right." But Mac didn't need the bail anyway. Cook County deputies who also knew and liked McGarigle escorted him about Chicago whenever he pleased. On one occasion, a deputy got so drunk that McGarigle had to drive the buggy back to the jail with the man passed out in his seat.

Ed McDonald's only son was killed in a freak accident June 20, while playing on a fire escape at the county hospital. The sympathetic courts allowed the two prisoners some time to clear up their affairs and to attend the funeral.

This time away from the jail allowed McGarigle to formulate his plans. For Mac, there was no worse fate than to go to prison. He would do anything to avoid it, and for this reason an escape plan had to be formulated.

The second stage of the trial was known as the "omnibus" phase. Indictments were returned against Commissioners Adam Ochs, Michael Leyden, Chris Giels, Richard McLaughery, Christian Casselman, Dan Wren, Michael Wasserman, Varnell, VanPelt, Oliver, McCarthy, Lynn, and the chairman of the county board, George Klehm. The commissioners were average men, thrust into political jobs they were incapable of administering squarely. McLaughery was a farmer from the town of Palos, Wasserman owned a restaurant, and Leyden was a butcher from the old Irish neighborhood. Giels spoke with a heavy German accent, and his answers to General Stiles questions were confused and irrational. McLaughery was the oldest at age 65. VanPelt was short and wiry. To a man, the commissioners were corpulent, sarcastic, and confident that the system would take care of them.

This phase of the trial was held in the courtroom of Judge Egbert Jamieson. Grinnell quickly went to work to show that a larger conspiracy existed among the board members. He showed that McGarigle had been appointed "collector" of the commissions in a secret meeting held in the janitor's room at the courthouse. The days passed. The contractors were called to the stand to explain how they did their business with the county. And in the end, the only penalty they would pay would be one of disgrace. None would go to jail because their testimony assured them immunity. Through their statements, it was learned that boodling had existed in the county for at least six years.

For example, James W. Kee, milk distributor, told of charging the county 12½ cents a gallon. He did not pay the yearly tribute (which had spiraled from $1,000 in 1881 to $2,500 in 1886) to any of the commissioners but directly to Fred Bipper, the meat man, who called the shots for the contractors.

Close-up on the 1880s

The Great Escape

Meanwhile, McGarigle languished in cell 79 while he awaited a motion for a new trial. When his prospects seemed remote, Mac asked his friend and business associate Edward S. Dreyer (whose bank had cashed a number of the suspicious vouchers) to contact Grinnell about a tradeoff.

McGarigle promised to tell what he knew about boodle in return for a penitentiary reprieve. Grinnell hedged. His case was almost complete; conviction was certain. The only loose end was Mike McDonald, whom Grinnell wanted very badly. Henry Holland had been indicted for conspiracy but not fraud. Holland proved to be an evasive witness. He covered for McDonald, and he covered for "Oyster" Joe Mackin, the man whom he owed his political allegiance to. When he failed to crack Holland, Grinnell made it known to Mike McDonald that he might release brother Ed if McDonald would give testimony about boodling aldermen.

The deal, of course, could not be made. So Grinnell let McGarigle have his say. McDonald was McGarigle's bondsman, political mentor, and a close friend. There would be no agreement, just two unproductive meetings at the Union League Club and at the residence of Sheriff Canute Matson. But McGarigle was looking for a way out. He asked for a third conference with Grinnell, this time for Friday, July 22. The state's attorney agreed but changed his mind late in the day because he was tired. He agreed to meet with McGarigle the following morning at 10 A.M. On each occasion, McGarigle was in the custody of Sheriff Matson, who continued to take extreme measures to insure his prisoner's comfort. Meals were catered in each afternoon from the luxurious Revere House at Hubbard and Clark directly to cell 79.

But Grinnell canceled out again, and Matson felt sorry for him. The sheriff felt obligated to honor a request by McGarigle to visit his home in Lakeview later on in the day. (This is the same Sheriff Matson who refused to allow Nina Van Zandt to visit Spies, even after the proxy marriage had taken place outside the city limits in Jefferson.)

That afternoon Henry Varnell and Buck McCarthy visited McGarigle in his cell. They were joined by the defense attorneys Alexander Sullivan, William Forrest, and Luther Laflin Mills in a conference that lasted nearly two hours. When they left, physician Leonard St. John of 539 W. Monroe Street appeared. If the witless

Matson did not suspect anything odd at this point, perhaps he should have.

The mysterious St. John was a thirty-three-year-old Canadian who was a member of the county hospital staff. He was a man of independent means and co-owner with his brother Fred of the Canadian schooner *Edward Blake*. The doctor was popular and outgoing with his patients but was viewed with distrust by his colleagues in the medical field. McGarigle earned his loyalty after saving him from an embarrassing malpractice suit.

An hour passed. McGarigle asked the jailer whether he could telephone Sheriff Matson to find out what time he was coming to pick him up at the jail. The whole plan hinged on Matson returning to the jail, but McGarigle worked out a second plan of escape with the jail clerk, B.P. Price, if things didn't work out. At 5:30 P.M., they received the happy news that Matson would appear for McGarigle at 8:30.

While all this was going on, the *Edward Blake* was loading grain at the Pacific Elevator at Archer and Ashland Avenues. She was a twenty-year-old schooner that just arrived from Michigan with a load of salt for the Philip Armour Company, before continuing on to Kingston, Ontario. At 3 that afternoon, St. John showed up at the dock before meeting McGarigle at the jail. Captain John Irving chatted with him for several minutes before he took out a small slip of paper. The captain reminded the first mate to make sure the *Edward Blake* would be moored at the north pier near Rush Street at eleven sharp and to arrange for a tugboat to be there. Irving left with St. John in his buggy.

Sheriff Matson kept his word. He showed up at the jail promptly at 8:30 P.M. McGarigle maintained his composure, acting like this was just another weekend visit home. Matson stopped to purchase a basket of fruit before driving on to McGarigle's residence at 832 Grace Street, near the corner of Evanston Avenue (now Broadway) in Lakeview. Mac had worked with law-enforcement people all his life. He knew that Matson could easily be duped. Two weeks later, the sheriff would sadly recall one of Mac's statements which should have told him something: "If I had a ten minute start, I could get away from the Chicago Police and every detective in the county. It would be much easier to hide here in Chicago than endeavor to get to Canada by the ordinary routes."

McGarigle and Matson arrived at the house a few minutes after 9 P.M. Mac summoned his coachman Jacob Spiegel to remain with the sheriff's rig while the men went inside. The house was spacious two-story brick building purchased for McGarigle by E.J. Lehmann the same time the first boodle indictments were returned. There was a library, a bedroom, two parlors, and, of course, a bathroom on the first floor. Exquisite oil paintings and an upright piano were in the front parlor. A portrait of McGarigle as chief of detectives hung near the front hallway.

A druggist named Edward Doepp and a hospital electrician named Oakley were waiting for him on the front porch. They were called to the house by a mysterious voice who told them to put aside their card game and get out to Lakeview as soon as possible. The druggist asked who was calling and why.

"You know. The people who moved out there a little while ago." The phone line went dead, but the message was understood. The call had been placed by Levi Dell from a drugstore at the corner of Indiana and Paulina. Dell was the hospital janitor, but on this evening, he was accompanying Dr. St. John on a professional call to a family living near Wells and Wisconsin Avenue.

Edward Doepp was asked to bring the hospital clerk Edward Dougherty along because McGarigle had some accounts to settle. But the accounts had been disposed of long ago, and Dougherty was not available to meet with the warden. When they arrived at the house, Mrs. Anna McGarigle expressed surprise. She knew her husband was coming home to take his usual Saturday-night bath, but he did not tell her that company was expected.

When Doepp and Oakley said they had better return to work, she asked them to remain just a bit longer. She barely finished her words, when the sheriff's buggy pulled up to the house. Greetings were exchanged, and the fruit was spread out for everyone to sample. After several minutes, McGarigle went upstairs to say goodnight to his younger children. The oldest son, George, called to his father from the yard. Matson remained in the parlor while the boy and his father examined one of the family horses that had been scratched by a nail. (The coachman Spiegel was later arrested as an accomplice for following McGarigle to the barn to attend to the horse.)

After determining that the horse was all right, McGarigle went inside to take his bath. Anna laid out a set of clean underwear in the adjoining room while Matson continued his chat with Doepp in the front parlor. Another half-hour passed.

"This is certainly getting monotonous," Matson finally said. The sheriff sent McGarigle's eleven-year-old daughter Bessie to the rear of the house to see what the delay was. She went into the bedroom (which was connected with the bathroom) but did not return. Matson stood up, unsure of what to do next. Good manners dictated that he wait politely in the living room, but finally he went to the bedroom and knocked on the door.

Anna McGarigle emerged from the bedroom. She had taken a nap. "Your husband does not answer. Have you seen him?" She opened the door and stepped inside. With a look of surprise, she told Matson that he had gone. McGarigle had used his time wisely. Matson stuck his head through the open bathroom window and saw that it was only an eight-foot drop to the ground. A sick feeling of panic swept over him.

Oakley, Doepp, and the children searched the house and stable. A buggy, carriage, and a phaeton remained undisturbed in the coach house. Matson ran to the Webster Avenue police station (which was coincidentally McGarigle's first assignment as a young policeman) to report the disappearance. Within an hour, a score of policemen and

The house at 832 Grace Street was purchased for William McGarigle by his business partner, bondsman, and friend E. J. Lehmann. In the 1880s, the McGarigle home in Lakeview was considered to be an ideal "suburban" dwelling for a man of position.

detectives from the Mooney-Boland Agency were combing the north side, but it was too late. Anna McGarigle thought that he might have dropped in on his bondsman and friend E.J. Lehmann, who lived several doors away. Lehmann was out of town.

A German named Frederick Miller told the police that he saw a buggy and rider parked by Rockeby Street (now Fremont), shortly before 9 P.M. At 9, Dr. St. John completed his medical call. He excused himself, telling his patient that he had another call to attend to. McGarigle waited in his bathroom until a signal was given from a red lantern inside the carriage. He jumped through the window, retrieved his suitcase from the coach house, and was on his way to freedom in exile. A Clark Street barkeep told the police that he watched a covered carriage being driven by a lathered bay horse. The driver lashed the animal freely to make his appointed rounds. Captain Irving waited for his passenger inside a cigar store at Illinois and Rush Streets. McGarigle was dropped off a block before the bridge, walking the remaining distance to meet Irving. The two men shook hands and proceeded to the boat.

The *Edward Blake* arrived at the north pier at 8. A Swedish sailor named Paul Swanson remembered that the man introduced as "Mr. Williams" cautiously avoided the light, making a hasty retreat to the lower berths. The *Flossie Thielcke*, a tugboat belonging to the Dunham Line, steered the *Edward Blake* into Lake Michigan to begin its journey.

McGarigle presented Irving with a pass signed by St. John, allowing him on board the *Edward Blake*. Irving later told officials that he never did find out who his passenger really was. St. John owned two-fifths of the boat, and it was his privilege to select the passengers.

Mac appeared on deck the following afternoon wearing a beige Prince Albert suit and a plug hat. McGarigle looked sallow and depressed, but he puffed his cigar with high hopes for his new life.

Inspector Bonfield, who had once felt McGarigle's squeeze, organized the forces at 3 A.M. for a house-to-saloon dragnet. (Bonfield received his first assignment from McGarigle, but there had been a falling out. In Canada, he passed McGarigle on the street but could not recognize him.)

A $2,500 reward was offered by the police the next day. Crowds of onlookers gathered outside the McGarigle residence on Grace Street. The wife fought her way past annoying reporters from the *Record-Herald* and *Inter-Ocean* to her awaiting carriage and a ride with her children. They badgered her with questions, but she handled them with cool abandon. There was no question the escape was premeditated and that she had full knowledge. But proving that was quite another matter.

"Do you know where he is?"

"I told you, I do not."

"He will probably come back in a few days, won't he?"

"You bet he won't!" piped up nine-year-old Eddie McGarigle.

The mother smiled, and the carriage whisked away, but the questions still remained. Was he in Canada? Was he in Mexico? Was he still in Chicago? Someone suggested he might have been kidnapped.

The *Edward Blake* continued northward toward Mackinaw without incident. A revenue cutter off the Milwaukee shoreline refused to intervene on behalf of the Chicago authorities, who wanted the boat stopped and searched. Such was McGarigle's luck. Remember, he once kissed the blarney stone.

Outside Mackinaw City, his run of luck continued. While the *Edward Blake* passed through the Straits of Mackinaw, an American schooner named the *George Marsh* finished loading cedar at Point LeBarbe. The seas were made choppy by a fierce northern gale. The *Edward Blake* passed by St. Ignace and went out into Lake Huron. At 4 A.M. on July 31, a tugboat named the *Merrick* hauled three schooners toward the *Edward Blake*. Meanwhile, another tugboat named the *Orient* was steaming furiously toward the rendezvous. A *Herald* reporter chartered the boat with the intention of apprehending McGarigle. He didn't want to take him back to Matson. He just wanted an interview.

The *George Marsh* came alongside of the *Edward Blake*, but the storm tossed the two boats like pieces of cork. The *Edward Blake* crashed into the starboard quarter of the *George Marsh* and in the confusion that followed, McGarigle leaped on board the damaged schooner. Mac was shaking with fear because he thought the *George Marsh* was a police boat that had been sent for him. According to official accounts, McGarigle begged Captain John Freer to put him ashore. The captain was moved by his plight. He agreed.

A yawl was dropped from the side of the *George Marsh* just as soon as the *Edward Blake* had been cast adrift. What happens next is almost comic. The *Orient* raced toward the shore, only a few hundred feet in back of the yawl that was rowed by one seaman. McGarigle jumped out of the boat at Green Island Shoals, just as the *Orient* abandoned the chase because of the shallow water.

McGarigle ran up the beach, dodged between some railroad cars, and headed for the nearest town. A dozen people on the shore cheered

Mac, for it was not uncommon for escaped American fugitives to land here. For some reason, McGarigle decided he needed a disguise. His first known movement in Canada was to go into a store in Sarnia to buy a hat. The clerk asked him whether he was McGarigle, since he was a stranger in the town. Mac turned and walked out.

He slept in a livery stable that night but was finally cornered by the *Herald* reporter. McGarigle granted him an hour interview in exchange for one night's room and board at the Western Hotel. "If I stay in that jail, I would have a spell of typhoid fever. My system could not stand it, and it became imperative for me to get out," he told the reporter who waited one day to file his story.

The *Edward Blake* continued on to Port Colborne, Ontario, where it was met by Fred St. John and later by Captain Freer of the *George Marsh*, who told of dropping McGarigle off at a desolate beach near Point Edward. When McGarigle's trunk was unloaded, Captain Irving denied any knowledge of the affair. "Where did that come from?" Charles Chapin of the *Tribune* was there to file his story. He wanted to see whether it was true that McGarigle absconded with $30,000 in county money. There was no truth, just a lot of news-hungry reporters who chased every rumor.

In Chicago, there was gloom from the Republican camp and jubilation among McGarigle's many friends. Jokes were told at Matson's expense in the bar at the Sherman House. Leonard St. John laughed; young Georgie McGarigle said he knew his father could do it, and there wasn't a thing anyone could do. The United States was bound to the Ashburton Treaty, which had been signed with Canada in 1842. Forgery and fraud were not extraditable offenses. Cook County officials asked Secretary of State Thomas F. Bayard to pursue the matter with the Canadian government, since their citizens had knowingly assisted a fugitive. But the Cleveland administration was not prepared to break any existing treaties for the sake of apprehending a minor Democratic official.

Before he gave up, Julius Grinnell would try desperate measures. The authorities tried to have McGarigle arrested on an old libel charge, stemming from an attempt by McGarigle, Allan Pinkerton, and Michael Hickey to damage the reputation of James Baxter of Cook County. When McGarigle was police chief, he circulated the photograph of Baxter in the Rogues' gallery of wanted felons. At the time, Baxter was involved in litigation before the Queen's Bench in Montreal. McGarigle and Pinkerton were trying to influence the jury to a speedy conviction. Baxter was offered a $5,000 bribe by McGarigle's friends if he would drop the case. When he didn't, the Queen's Bench signed a warrant for his arrest.

The detectives assigned to the case had difficulty tracking McGarigle, who drifted from St. Catherine's to Toronto, to Niagara Falls, Sarnia, and finally to Banff in the British Northwest Territory. Convinced that the big cities were too dangerous, McGarigle journeyed where the law-enforcement people were reluctant to follow. While Mac moved westward, a railroad conductor from the Detroit & Milwaukee Road found a bottle washed ashore at Grand Haven, Michigan. It was wrapped securely in oil cloth and contained the following hand-written dispatch:

> To my friends in Chicago: A few more hours and I will be safe through the straits and in Canada. Sheriff Matson, please accept my thanks for the bath, but I have concluded it in British waters. Oh, Ed, I wish you were here with me. Goodbye till we meet.
>
> W.J. McGarigle

Under the shadows of Sulphur Mountain, in the cold, clear air of Banff, citizen McGarigle took up residence at the Sanitarium Hotel. He soon involved himself in the affairs of the community, forming a livery business and investing in the local hotel. His roommate was the Reverend Charles Williams of the Banff Methodist Church. Being the pious soul that he was, McGarigle joined the church choir and directed a number of their theatrical productions. When he wasn't shooting bear or fishing for speckled trout, McGarigle took time out to canvass the political district on behalf of a friend running for the legislature. Some old-fashioned, underhanded Chicago electioneering got the man his office. In Banff, the grateful townsmen elected McGarigle the chief of the village fire department. But when he declined, they threw him a banquet instead. In January of 1889, a *Tribune* reporter got a first-hand exclusive interview with McGarigle at his new home. Mac took him on a midnight sleighing party through the forest, a swim in a sulphur pool in zero weather, followed by a sumptuous dinner of venison. When the dishes had been cleared, each of the guests stood up and sang a song. When it was McGarigle's turn, he stood up and sang "My Country, 'Tis of Thee." After which, he cried.

In time, the Canadian detectives abandoned the search after the money funneled to them by Grinnell dried up. Leonard St. John and

Captain Irving were indicted in Cook County, but since both men were Canadian subjects, their cases were dismissed.

In Chicago, the "omnibus" case continued without McGarigle. Judge Jamieson reviewed the cases of the thirteen commissioners whose misdeeds were front-page news for weeks. George Klehm, chairman of the county board, entered into a secret agreement with Grinnell to tell what he knew in exchange for a reprieve. He said that he never wanted to go about boodling but had been forced to it. The two men agreed to meet secretly in Lakefront Park each night, and the story Klehm told was one of political influence, intrigue, and corruption.

He revealed the secret details of the jury-packing scheme and how juror George C. Tait had been picked by the boodlers. During the proceedings, Klehm communicated with Grinnell by a series of prearranged hand signals that told the state's attorney when a particular statement was true or a lie. While he never looked at Grinnell directly, he would tug at an earlobe or curl his index finger. For his cooperation, Klehm received the minimum $1,000 fine and avoided the penitentiary. In Joliet, Joe Mackin said that a real man of honor would rather go to the pen than squeal on his pals. This view of life was a noble one, and "Oyster" Joe (nicknamed for inventing the free lunch with a glass of beer; in this case, oysters) later earned a pardon from Governor Fifer for his sins. The *Tribune* just referred to Klehm as the "meanest pecksniff of them all."

Seven of the commissioners resigned their offices on August 8, 1887, but the other six refused. Since their convictions constituted a violation of their oaths of office, formal resignations were not required. "This thing of administering the affairs of a great county from the jail cannot be tolerated," Judge Jamieson said. "Prisoners in the county jail cannot and will not legislate for the county." The boodlers were not interested in doing any work from the jail anyway. Each morning they ordered expensive breakfasts from the Revere House that included nutmeg melon, cigars, and their morning newspaper. This was followed by mutton chops, porterhouse steak, wines, cheese, and cheesecake.

At 8:50 P.M., on August 5, 1887, the great boodle trial came to an end with an eleven-to-one vote for conviction by the jury. Leyden, Van Pelt, Varnell, Wasserman, Ochs, and McLaughery received two-year sentences, while Lynn, Oliver, Casselman, Klehm, Giels, and McCarthy each received $1,000 fines. Buck snapped at a reporter who asked whether he was satisfied. "What in hell do you mean? I shouldn't have been fined a goll-darned cent. I say it's an outrage."

Buck's crimes would be excused. He paid his fine and was later elected alderman. In 1896, he was a delegate to the Republican convention. During a caucus, another delegate punched him in the eye.

Chris Giels went with Grinnell to the clerk's office to find out what the total fine with court costs would be. "I had to borrow the money once before to settle up, but I paid that amount and I can pay this." Giels said. "When was that?" the clerk asked. "That was the time I was drafted into the army and had to pay a substitute."

There were handshakes all around and back slaps for the jurors. Little VanPelt, who once served a term as mayor of Jersey City, turned to a spectator and said: "I can live through two years, and when I get back here I will live long enough to get even with the sons-of-bitches who worked so hard to put me in the hole." He died in 1902, without any reports of violence against the jurors.

Ed McDonald was denied a motion for a new trial by the lower courts of Illinois, but he did win his appeal in the Supreme Court. After eighteen months in jail, Ed was back on the streets.

After nearly two years of exile in Banff, McGarigle struck a deal with the new state's attorney, Joel Longnecker (Julius Grinnell had since become a judge). He would agree to return to Chicago and enter a plea of guilty on the condition that his sentence be reduced to a fine. The maximum penalty under Illinois law for McGarigle's fraud was $1,000. It seemed a reasonable thing to do rather than allow him to remain a fugitive from justice. McGarigle met Longnecker at London, Ontario, returning to Chicago the morning of May 30, 1889. They drove straight to Judge Shepard's courtroom from the Grand Trunk depot, interrupting a case in session.

Dressed in a dark gray tweed suit and graying noticeably around the temples, McGarigle approached the bench with his head held high. One of the jurymen bolted from his seat to shake Mac's hand but was restrained by a bailiff. With Longnecker, E.J. Lehmann, and attorney Francis Adams in back of him, Mac stood before the judge while his lawyer read a statement.

"The state's attorney," said Adams, "is placed in about this position. McGarigle was in Canada, and there was no law by which he could be extradited. And he could have stayed away as long as he pleased. He wanted to come back, and if a new trial is granted upon the conditions that we have talked about, he will plead guilty and submit to a fine."

Close-up on the 1880s

Judge Shepard said he was inclined to follow the state's attorney's recommendations. Longnecker withdrew the motion for a new trial. Mac stepped into the judge's chambers to sign the order which set aside the forfeitures of bonds and the remaining cases against the boodlers.

McGarigle stepped into the light of Clark Street a free man. He climbed into a carriage and was driven back to his Lakeview home. After a private reunion, the reporters besieged the house. "I have always loved Chicago," he said in slow patient tones. "I could not live long away from it. Chicago is the only place on earth—the only city in which life is worth living. Can you wonder then that I have suffered so much for being compelled to leave it?"

Would McGarigle get back into the political field again? "I have friends in Chicago and good friends, some who would not be afraid to trust me with all the property they possess."

McGarigle never got back into public life. Like other politicos before and after him, he bought a Clark Street saloon, which he called the Round Bar. He died in Chicago on April 29, 1917, forgotten but content. The other commissioners served their three years at Joliet, some retiring to private life, others staying in politics.

Mike McDonald was too smart and too powerful to be caught in the boodle trap. It was his love life that messed him up. His first wife Mary ran off with an actor named Billy Arlington. At the point of Mike's gun, she returned to Chicago for a time. But she took off with a Catholic priest named Father Joseph Moissant, who had been attending to her religious needs in her own private chapel that Mike had built.

In 1898, Mike renounced his faith and converted to Judaism for the benefit of Flora Feldman, a thirty-year-old chorus girl who danced at the Chicago Opera House. He was taken by her, even though she was still married to Sam Barkley, a former second baseman for the St. Louis Browns and Pittsburgh Pirates. Barkley could not compete with Mike McDonald, so he reluctantly accepted a $30,000 divorce settlement. It was said at the time that Barkley was hopelessly depressed and had considered suicide. But when the going gets tough . . . well . . . what was there to do but open a Clark Street bar? The Old Rag Shop opened up a few doors away from McGarigle's Round Bar.

Flora and Mike married in Milwaukee and returned to Chicago to settle into the Ashland Avenue mansion. But there were immediate problems. Mike's son Guy hated Flora, and the two of them were caught one day kicking and punching on the front lawn. McDonald ordered his son from the house.

It was at this time that Flora met a young high school boy named Webster Guerin, who lived at 655 Harrison Street. She was thirty, and he was fifteen. This peculiar liaison began and continued for nearly *ten years* underneath Mike's nose. Flora was a generous lover. She indulged her protégé with expensive finery and wrote him love poetry. But she was also insanely jealous. When Guerin tried to break it off, she followed him to California and induced him to come back. When the boy's aunt, Nellie Fitzgibbons, asked Flora to leave him alone, she pulled a gun on her and told her to mind her own business.

Guerin invested his savings in a haberdashery business, but that failed when he spent more time riding around Chicago in hansom cabs with Flora than attending to the business. Guerin believed his true calling in life was that of commercial artist. With Flora's help, he went into business in Suite 703 of the Omaha Building at Van Buren and LaSalle. The business wasn't very profitable, and Guerin was accused from time to time of swindling potential customers.

But Flora visited him each day, becoming more pronounced in her jealous accusations. When she brought him the morning newspaper, it was filled with holes. She had carefully cut out all the pictures of lovely women.

On the morning of February 21, 1907, she sat down to breakfast with Mike and told him that she "was tired of being blackmailed and was going to put a stop to it." McDonald laughed and told her that he had better attend to it because he had some experience in that field himself. Nothing further was said, as Flora slipped out of the house shortly before noon to pay one more call on Guerin.

She arrived at the Omaha Building in a nervous frenzy. When Guerin heard her coming, he sent a junior clerk away. Nobody witnessed what happened next, but the argument was heard one floor down. She pulled a pistol from her bag and fired a shot that landed in Guerin's neck, just below the ear. Flora then began pounding at the glass door, breaking it into shards. When they found her, she was covered with blood and wailing frantically. The poor woman had gone off the deep end.

In her purse, they found several stained and torn love poems. One of them said: "What became of those pearls of mine? Oh nothing, I just threw my pearls to the swine."

Close-up on the 1880s

She was taken to the lockup and was given bromides and a hypodermic needle to quiet her. Old Mike appeared, and she seemed to recognize him. "Papa! Papa!" she cried, "I will mind you." The devoted husband remained at her side the next three days, holding her hand and soothing her. When a policeman asked her whether she knew Guerin, she cried; "Web! Oh my God, bring him to me. I want my dear Web!"

Her mind was gone, but Mike was a forgiving husband, even after the police uncovered a cache of photographs in Guerin's office. Some of them featured Flora in daring poses taken in hotel rooms. Leonard St. John was summoned to administer to Flora, while Mike "bottled things up." A second scandal was just too much to bear for the ex-king.

He died on August 9, 1907, some say of a broken heart. His death scene at St. Anthony's Hospital was attended by Mary, who was seeking a second act of forgiveness. Younger brother Ed was there also, but Flora was confined to the insane asylum. Mike saw to it that her defense fund was paid for, and that she received one-third of his $2-million estate. Mary the faithless one was left nothing. The church and hospital received the balance of the fortune.

On that last sad note, we take leave of the county boodlers and their legacy. Their crimes have not been duplicated since, though many in high places have tried. McGarigle, with the drooping mustache, balding head, and rich baritone voice that brought tears to everyone's eyes when he sang "My Country, 'Tis of Thee," had style. We must give him that. "I have taken a bath every day since I went to Canada," he told Longnecker minutes before arriving at the courthouse. "They were always good for my health."

3
A Summer of Gold: Chicago in 1896

"Tell me, what wonders have you built in Chicago?" Reporters with notepads and bothersome agents stumbled over themselves trying to oblige with an answer. "Tell me, cheri, are any of the World's Fair buildings left?" They shuffled. There wasn't much left from the great fair since the Divine Sarah Bernhardt passed through Chicago, but there was the new Masonic Temple, the spacious Public Library, and the Art Institute—all constructed in her absence. *"C'est un merveille!* What men to dare so much! Why, the city is quite changed!" Sarah at fifty-two was just as pleasing to behold as she was twenty years earlier when she first visited Chicago.

She was the world's consummate actress, a fair-skinned enchantress whose golden voice captivated European theatregoers for a quarter of a century. Men fought duels to protect her honor, and several fans attempted suicide when they were denied entrance to her performance. She played tragedy, and she played comedy. And finally on May 3, 1896, Sarah Bernhardt played Chicago.

Her traveling company filled three coaches and three baggage cars, but Divine Sarah had one car for herself and a collie named Game. In the company of her valet Emile, Sarah was taken to a private suite at the Auditorium Hotel, while the rest of the cast spent their first day looking for cheap lodging because tour promoters refused to pay for their keep.

Madame Bernhardt opened the 1896 summer season in *Izeyl* at the Columbia. It was a four-act drama written by Armand Sylvester and

A Summer of Gold 75

Eugene Morand, based on the life of Mary Magdalene and set in ancient Hindustan. Bernhardt played the role in verse and rhyme. "Beautiful youth and all the fires of passion" was how one critic summed up her performance. For four splendid days, Bernhardt recreated her greatest roles— *Gismonda, Phédre,* and *Camille.* She answered their curtain calls, even though the theatre was packed and an annoying blue haze made it difficult to see her from the back row.

Intensity characterized her every move. Despite illness, she went on stage to play Gismonda, a role that paralleled her own life. The pope would not allow Gismonda to marry the father of her illegitimate child, the same way she herself, was prevented from marrying Prince Henri de Ligne who sired her son.

When Bernhardt left Chicago, so too did Chicago society. It was the summer resort season and a time for the wealthy to flee the city to cavort with nature. The favored gathering places for midwesterners included Green Lake, Wisconsin; Hot Springs, Arkansas; Colorado Springs; and the opulent Grand Hotel at Mackinac Island, Michigan. Chicago yachts filled the harbor, while inside the casino, southern minstrel singer Polk Miller told stories of the antebellum South to an audience that included Vice-President Adlai Stevenson. What did Chicago's out-of-town innocents do while on vacation? They attended religious lectures, outdoor theatre, yacht regattas, and, in the case of Charles Tyson Yerkes, imperial wizard of Chicago traction, oversaw the construction of his observatory at Lake Geneva. All this wasn't nearly as extravagant as the arrival of the New York Yacht Club at Newport, Rhode Island, but Chicago society still enjoyed roughing it in the frontier. Others played golf and bicycled, two new sports on the American scene that came into their own during the 1890s. When the city passed a law forbidding betting at Washington Park, society discovered golf. Within six months, a course was constructed where the pacers and trotters once ran. The first tee overlooked the track, and it proved to be a tricky shot over and across the rails. The jockey quarters were converted into locker rooms for the duffers, and a Scotch golf pro named Richard Leslie was brought in from St. Andrews to teach the game to club members. Leslie hand-made the niblicks, lofters, and spoons (words that were creeping into the boardrooms of LaSalle Street). The course required constant maintenance. Secretary James Howard retained a horse-driven mowing machine and 100 grazing sheep to take care of the problem. Golf was an elite sport, not readily available to the masses. To many, it was a confusing, infuriating game, associated with the crusty British. (The United States nearly went to war with England in 1887 over Venezuela. Among the lower classes, there was a decided Anglo prejudice.)

Bicycling was accepted for everybody else. It was not so much a sport as it was a *craze*. During the 1870s, a few courageous souls guided their six-foot-high "front-wheelers" down the rough Chicago streets, where the slightest rut would cause a serious overturn. In 1884, Englishman John Kemp Starley corrected all that by inventing the safety bicycle with two wheels of equal size attached to a frame. In 1894, the invention was modified to include a coaster brake. It was around this time that the sport captured the public fancy.

Bicycles were costly, but everybody in Chicago had to own one. Retail installment credit may have begun with the bike. A typical cycle cost $100 in 1896, but most retailers allowed their clients to purchase one with just twenty dollars down. The purchaser had to provide three references and make a one-dollar payment each week thereafter. A blacklist of bad debts was maintained by the Cycle Board of Trade and by the numerous clubs that flourished in the city at this time.

The best cycles were built by the Pope Manufacturing Company and by A.G. Spaulding. But in 1895, a German immigrant named Ignaz Schwinn and meat packer Adolph Arnold set up shop at Lake and Peoria Streets. The rest, as they say, was history.

If there was any doubt about Chicago being the capital of cycling, consider the numbers. By 1896, 6,000 workers were employed in bicycle factories. There were 600 dealers, 200,000 riders, and over $500,000 spent annually on riding paraphernalia. There were forty-eight cycling clubs, with 10,000 members. Each club flew its own colors, organized century runs, and lobbied for political causes favorable to cyclists. Better roads, new signs, and the construction of bike paths were the issues the clubs fought for, and who but Bathhouse John could speak for them so eloquently? In May, the Bath won their votes by introducing a resolution in the council for the construction of three-foot-wide asphalt bike paths to be built adjacent to downtown streets. Coughlin proposed a $1 licensing fee to pay for construction costs. That meant $200,000 to the city treasury and a new source of boodle. "I am in this thing heart and soul," the Bath said. "If there is any legal way of having it done, I will fight hard for it." Despite the support of the clubs, the bill was buried in the judiciary committee.

The Lincoln Cycling Club, Lakeview, Aeolus, Thistle, and Smalley clubs were just a few of the organizations that began the summer season with group rides through the neighborhoods. Five hundred members of the South Side Cycling Club filled Grand Boulevard each Thursday night for three months. The front column of bicyclists sported two Chinese lanterns on the front handle bars. The police routinely sent plainclothes "spies" in their ranks to look for "scorchers." (Where have all the brave young scorchers gone?) They were a menace to the police and a hero to the young. We see them now with their baseball caps worn at a jaunty angle and their coattails flapping in the breeze behind them, as they gathered speed. They pedaled all over Chicago, and their exploits were reported faithfully in the papers.

Bicycles were used by real-estate agents, butchers, messengers, and mothers who built hammocks for their infants, so they could ride on the handlebars. The *Tribune* of May 17, applauded the noble machine as a modern-day wonder.

> The vehicle of the future, say those who ought to know, are the horseless carriage and the bicycle. For luxury, speed, and scenic effects, the motorcycle driven by electricity and built in any of the magnificent forms of which it is capable will be the proper thing, but as a poor man's vehicle, both of pleasure and business, the bike is going to have no rival.

With every new enterprise comes crime. In 1896, bikes were pilfered from outside stores, factories, and taken to shops where they were dismantled for shipment to St. Louis, Cincinnati, and Indianapolis. The chop shop is not such a new idea after all. The first bicycle bank robbery was reported on May 14, at Buffalo, Illinois, a small town ten miles outside of Springfield. Two men wheeled up to what once was the hitching post. They walked in and demanded $10,000 from the astonished tellers. They got back on their bikes and rode away, never to be seen again.

The bicycle liberated women and brought them out from their Victorian shells. It was a participation sport that they could share equally with men. Overgaiters, leggins, and a Knox sailor hat were some of the new fashions designed for her comfort. One journal posed the question: Which makes the better wife, the Bloomer Girl or the clinging vine? Charlotte Holt of the Chicago Society for the Protection of Women and Children answered the moralists who saw a decay in society when a girl's figure was outlined while riding a bike. "Of course, wheels have made greater freedom possible among our young women," she said. "It is nothing uncommon for a girl to be away all day with her wheel, but what of it? One reason I like the wheel so thoroughly is that it has done away with the chaperone who was beginning to be foisted on us."

Emancipation from the home meant more family outings. On Sundays from 2 o'clock till 5 o'clock, Jackson Park was a whirl of cyclists. Picnics were held in a grassy knoll that was ringed by a cinder bike path. When the 1893 exposition dismantled, the Jackson Park grounds were designed by Frederick Law Olmstead. The result was a pleasing array of public park, bike paths (one for women, and one for men), and even a designated area for infant nannies.

The era of the cyclist was a brief, exciting epoch of Chicago history. For a time, the great Arthur Zimmerman, Willie Windle, and Harry Tyler were as well known as Cap Anson. The bicycle fad never officially died, but if there was one date in city history when the wheelman surrendered his reign, it was July 15, 1903. On that day, Chicago dentist Ernest Pfennig bought the first Ford in the city. He paid $850.

Incident on a City Street

The woman held her brother's arm as they crossed Van Buren Street for their rendezvous. She wore a brown muslin dress; he looked like any other Loop businessman out for a walk. Nellie English was a dark-haired twenty-year-old. She had arrived in Chicago just several months earlier from Galesburg, Illinois, and she was doing the typical thing that thousands of other rural farm girls had done, since the railroad linked together the prairie towns of Illinois. Nellie was taken in by her sister on Portland Avenue, while she tried to save her money by working as an operator at the Chicago Telephone Company. Brother Joseph was a bartender at Houlihan's on Root Street, and on July 30, 1896, a small-town score was settled.

Walking toward them was William Hawkins, her one-time boyfriend. "English, is it true that you have threatened to kill me?" Hawkins demanded. The couple paused in front of George Baker's Drug Store at Clark and Van Buren. It was 2:45 P.M. Joseph English narrowed his gaze. "Yes, and I will do it if you don't quit talking about my sister." Hawkins cast an aspersion about Nellie's moral character. "So that's the way you want to talk about my sister, is it?" Joe English drew his .32-calibre pistol from his vest pocket. Hawkins turned away, but two shots struck him in the hip and face. Hawkins collapsed, while English handed the gun to his sister. He nodded solemnly, for this was a mission of honor, after all. Nellie closed her eyes and fired two more shots into him. A bystander finally wrested the gun away from her. The sister and brother surrendered quietly to officers McKenna and Riley, who escorted them to the Harrison lockup.

Three other officers carried the stricken man into Baker's Drug Store. (One of them was Frank Tyrrell, who was a Haymarket veteran. In later life, he was president of the Haymarket Riot Veterans Association. He conducted tours for out-of-state visitors, pointing out the exact spot where the bomb fell. Tyrrell was the last surviving Haymarket participant at the time of his death in February 1947; he was eighty-eight years old.) "Boys, publish just what I am going to say," Hawkins told the gathering crowd. "For I am a dying man, and God knows I am telling the truth." He told of Nellie's various affairs with men, including a Chicago policeman. He said that her parents once asked him to find her a responsible position in the city. Hawkins, a tailor by trade, found her a job as a seamstress. To work in a sewing room was not for her.

"The Tuesday after Easter, I went to Galesburg to see about some patterns I had cut, and I met her at the depot," Hawkins said. "She showed me a piece cut from the paper telling about eloping. I arranged it so that it would appear that I had eloped with her. Her sister then came to me and asked me if I would correct the statement. I said I would if her sister would tell the priest the truth. On Thursday I heard that her brother had threatened to shoot me, and I at once wrote her the letter which was received by her this morning."

At the lockup, Nellie and Joseph talked freely about Hawkins. They seemed to enjoy the limelight that is often associated with sex-related shootings. "He even told my dearest and most intimate friends what he knew of me and drove me from my home. I asked him this afternoon if he wouldn't as a man please take back what he said about me and he answered no and called me a name you would not call the lowest woman in Chicago."

Hawkins and English were engaged in Galesburg, but he claimed to have heard some disturbing rumors about her moral character, so the engagement was broken off. When the story of their elopement hit the Galesburg papers, Hawkins tried to clear his name after English refused to issue a retraction. Hawkins was admitted to St. Luke's

Hospital, where bandages were liberally applied to his wounds. He resembled a mummy but continued his cheerful banter with reporters. "Tell me, boys, do I have long to live?" Frank Hawkins, his older

It was just another busy afternoon at the corner of Clark and Van Buren, when Joseph and Nellie English pumped four shots into William Hawkins. The lady's honor was saved. The cad was taught a lesson he would not soon forget.

brother, stood by his side when suddenly two policemen brought English and her brother to the bedside. It was a peculiar thing to do, but apparently a bedside statement had to be made in the presence of a notary public. Frank tried to slug English but was subdued. "Oh, leave him be. He's a blow just like his brother." Several white-aproned nurses guarded the patient. "Oh, that wretched woman!" "That man and that woman both shot me! And I'm dying!" Joseph English wrapped a comforting arm around his sister's shoulders. They were led back to their cell at Harrison Street, where their needs were attended to by old Alex Beaubien. (Beaubien, the lockup keeper, was the first white child born in Chicago. That was in 1822, and at age 74, he was still on the payroll.)

Hawkins vowed not to die, and he didn't . . . or so the public record has it. He remained on the critical list for some time and probably suffered a small relapse when he found out that Nellie and Joseph were released on a $10,000 bail on August 3. "My, but won't this affair be a surprise to the folks down there!" Nellie beamed. In Chicago everyone had their day. There is no moral to this story. Better to be presumed an innocent than proven guilty, at least when it came to the state of marriage in the 1890s.

Hawkins probably loved English very much. When he could no longer have her for his own, he took revenge on her, hoping that no one else would want her either. A couple of slugs in the belly was his reward. "I know now that Holmes was a better man than Hawkins," Nellie said.

The Real Bluebeard

Well, that's not quite true. Herman Webster Mudgett, a.k.a., H.H. Holmes (and many other assumed names) swung from the scaffold on May 7, 1896, at the Moyamensing Prison in Philadelphia. Two priests, a lawyer, and Assistant Superintendent Alexander Richardson accompanied Holmes to the platform. The black cap was placed over his head by Richardson. In jest, Holmes remarked, "Don't be in a hurry, Alec." For there was something the killer had to say. "Gentlemen, I have a few words to say. In fact I would make no remarks at this time, but for my feeling that in not speaking I would appear to acquiese in my execution."

He denied his guilt, choosing to die as he lived—in a lie. The noose

Herman Webster Mudgett, a.k.a. H.H. Holmes, a.k.a. Henry Howard, a.k.a. O.C. Pratt. We shall never know the *real* story.

dropped him at 10:12 A.M., and for a full half-hour the officials did not dare cut him down. Holmes was cunning and dangerous. They feared he might survive the hanging. He didn't.

The "serial killer" was an anomaly in 1894. People were unaware of the kind of man who would roam the streets of the twentieth century, randomly killing innocent people. Arguably, Holmes was the worst. He was part Machiavelli, mad scientist, cad, and bluebeard. On the day of his execution, he told his jailer that he was "born with the

Devil" in him, but would he please test the rope? Holmes wanted the rope to be firm and strong, so that his neck would break cleanly (it did not). Holmes feared a death by slow strangulation, a consideration he did not extend to any of his victims. The rope was a half-inch hemp variety, manufactured by the E.H. Fitler Company. It proved to be the perfect fit.

H.H. Holmes's execution ended a ten-year crime spree that saw the disappearance of scores of women and children. He showed no tendency toward butchery during his early years. Herman Mudgett was born to Christian parents at Gilmanton, New Hampshire, on May 16, 1860. His father Levi was the local postmaster.

One of his uncles was insane, but Holmes showed no signs of an early psychosis. Stoop-shouldered, deliberate in speech, but always polite to the ladies, Holmes married Clara Lovering of London, New Hampshire, on July 4, 1878. She was the wealthy farmer's daughter, and Holmes took advantage of his position to gain an education, first in Burlington, Vermont, and then at the University of Michigan at Ann Arbor. Holmes entered the medical program in September of 1882, after working as a sales clerk in East Concord, New Hampshire. His wife worked as a dressmaker to support their only child and to help put him through medical school. He told university officials that his tuition was guaranteed by Nathan Wright. Wright was actually a lonely widow who trailed Holmes to Ann Arbor. She helped pay some of the tuition costs with the understanding that he would marry her later (bigamy was second nature to Holmes). She later sued him for breach of promise but mysteriously dropped the case. Holmes earned money on the side by insuring corpses that he removed from local graveyards. Classmates later remembered Holmes as a listless student whose sole interest was *Gray's Anatomy*.

When Holmes tired of his marital arrangements, he sent his wife and child back to Gilmanton, while he went to Clinton County, New York, to teach school. He left a series of unpaid debts and a trail of broken hearts before fleeing to St. Paul, Minnesota (perhaps at the point of a gun). This time he invested in a restaurant but absconded with the profits, leaving the business in the hands of a bondsman. He drifted to Terre Haute, Indiana, where he began his long association with a watery-eyed sot named Benjamin Pitezel. Ben was the ideal accomplice, the kind of man who would do anything for a pint of gin. Pitezel took the rap for an insurance forgery, while the boss skipped town again. Holmes next turned up in Moore's Fork, Pennsylvania, where he practiced medicine at a local insane asylum. A story was circulated that a wealthy inmate bribed Holmes $5,000 if he would look the other way during an escape. He escaped all right—to another world. They found him face down in a reflecting pool with his pockets picked. Holmes was not implicated in the affair, but he moved to Chicago under a cloud of suspicion.

He tried to secure a divorce from Clara on the grounds of adultery, but the claim was denied. This setback did not prevent him from marrying Myrtle Z. Belknap of Wilmette, on January 28, 1887. She was the daughter of a prosperous merchant named John Belknap and due to inherit some property. Holmes tried to wrest the land away from the Belknaps in 1893, by forging his father-in-law's signature to a trust deed for $2,500 and securing the money through David Fiske of 150 LaSalle Street. Afterwards, Holmes attempted to poison the father and kill the uncle by means of asphyxiation.

Jonathan Belknap went to visit Holmes at the "castle" on 63rd and Wallace to confront him with hard evidence concerning the forgery. Holmes reassured the man that everything was all right. There had been a misunderstanding, but wouldn't Belknap join him for dinner and spend the night? It was a long way back to Wilmette. Belknap softened. Holmes led him through what seemed to be a maze of passages and twisting corridors to his room. "Goodnight, Mr. Belknap." Holmes closed the door behind him, leaving his guest in a small airless bedroom without a window. Belknap was apprehensive; he remembered an earlier conversation with Horace Drury of the Wilmette Village Board, who warned about some of the rumored goings-on at the castle. So he kept the gas jet on all night, unable to fall asleep.

After a while the light went out, but the gas remained on. Fortunately, Belknap was awake and had the presence of mind to relight the jet. An hour later he heard shuffling in the hall. He opened the door and found Patrick Quinlan, the janitor, standing in the hall. He mumbled something and walked away. Belknap discovered that the gas jet in his room was controlled from a pipe at the end of the hall. Holmes or Quinlan opened the jet sometime in the night. By blowing air into it, the flame extinguished in Belknap's room. Then, assuming he was unconscious or dead, Quinlan was sent to carry him away. (Holmes was already out of Myrtle's life. She went into seclusion in Wilmette, but later stated that she knew her husband was a fraud but certainly not a murderer. Children seemed to take to him and surely a child knew best.)

A Summer of Gold

By the time Belknap confronted Holmes with the evidence of fraud, the fiend was operating on the south side. Already in 1887, he had secured a job in the drugstore of Mrs. E.S. Holden, across the street from where Holmes was to erect his castle. He maintained the books, impressing the widow with his alacrity. Holmes proposed a buy out, and the woman seemed willing. But he never paid for things he bought. When she grew tired of waiting for the funds, she introduced a lawsuit. Shortly after this, she disappeared. The city directory for 1887 does not list a Mrs. Holden. Gone to California, Holmes explained.

Holmes took control of the drugstore, but he decided to mortgage it in 1892 so that he could build his famous castle on a vacant lot 701 63rd Street, directly across the street.

Much has been written about the Englewood Castle. The *Chicago Tribune* described it as best as any on November 25, 1894.

> In America's wide domain there is not a house like unto that one, and there probably will never be. Its chimney sticks out where chimneys never stuck out before. Its staircases do not end anywhere in particular. It has winding passages that bring the rash intruder back to where he started from, and altogether it's a very mysterious building.

They called it a castle because it hovered over everything else on the block. It was constructed of brick, with wooden bay windows and a stone basement. The castle stood three stories high and measured 162 feet long by 50 feet wide. The second floor contained thirty-five rooms, with fifty-one doors cut into walls in every imaginable place. Holmes intended to rent these rooms to World's Fair visitors. Various construction crews were hired and fired at his whim. That way, nobody was really sure of what was going on. A mortgage was held by a loan agent named Chandler, and an insurance policy was secured through the Gerard Company. When a rooftop fire broke out on August 13, 1893, Holmes collected an $800 payment through Minnie Williams, whose name the policy was in.

Businessmen who should have known better rented his first floor storefronts. C.H. Gove and Delos Matteson agreed to pay Holmes $300 a month for a small space fronting 63rd Street. After serving notice on the current tenant, Holmes concluded his agreement with Gove. They didn't have the necessary funds, but Holmes accepted a first mortgage on their furniture. They paid him $200 toward the first

The most evil building in Chicago during the not-so-gay nineties was the Holmes Castle. Before his crimes were discovered, the building at 63rd and Wallace disguised unspeakable perversion and horror.

month's rent, and $100 out of their own pocket went into general repairs. Gove and Matteson also agreed to give promissory notes for a half-month's rent for the rest of the year. The notes that Gove signed turned out to be *judgment* notes. Holmes served a five-day notice on them, keeping their money and furniture and, thanking them for their repairs, sending them on their way.

What is a castle without furniture? Holmes stocked his building with the finest sofas, chairs, and tables from the Tobey Company and the French-Potter Crockery firm. Both of these firms accepted the written guarantee of H.S. Campbell, the man Holmes identified as his backer. His lawyer, Wharton Plummer, forged the name of Campbell (who in reality did not exist) on the guarantee. The scheme worked to a charm. When the company sent agents to repossess the goods, they found the place empty. Holmes moved all the furniture into a spare room, bricked it up, and applied wallpaper. Later, a black man who lived in the neighborhood tipped off the furniture company about what really happened. They burst in and recovered their merchandise. They did not press charges.

At this time, Holmes involved himself in numerous business frauds. The Silver Ash Institute was a noble scheme to cure Englewood residents of alcoholism. He bottled a patent medicine and sold the cure for $50 from the castle. In fact, there wasn't any manner of larceny that escaped his eye. On one occasion, he represented himself as a bicycle agent. He went from dealer to dealer, purchasing parts in return for worthless securities. By the time the retailers discovered they had been swindled, Holmes sold the parts for full value and was able to buy *two* fully assembled bicycles.

Holmes bought and sold patents for all kinds of things. Even the gas company was fooled when he claimed to have invented a process that would convert ordinary water into gas. A company expert was sent to the castle to inspect the contraption. It resembled a wash tub that had pulleys, pipes, and wires protruding from it. The funny thing was, it seemed to work. Water churned through the machine, and the smell of gas was distinct.

The excited gas-company inspector rushed back to the office to convince the company that this man Holmes was a genius. They offered $25,000 for rights to the invention, and of course, Holmes agreed. When they came to haul the thing away, workmen discovered that Holmes had somehow tapped into the gas line below the house. Not to be discouraged by this setback, Holmes made good use of the gaping hole in the cellar floor. He did a little more digging and found a trickle of water. This he declared, was an artesian well gushing pure, natural mineral water. He bottled the stuff as a miracle cure, selling it to Englewood residents for five cents a glass at the soda fountain. A chemist had to tell them that it was just ordinary Lake Michigan water.

In May of 1890, an inventor named Frederick Nind came to Chicago to start a copy-machine business. He formed the ABC Copying Company in the Monon Block, on Dearborn Street, but his business partner sold his shares to Holmes. When Nind was away on business, Holmes schemed to steal the business from under him. Wharton Plummer informed Nind that the business was in a serious peril, but there was an interested party in Pittsburgh who would buy him out. The Pittsburgh group was really Holmes, but Nind did not know this, of course. After securing his new business, Holmes set out to lure out-of-state clients interested in duplicating their blueprints at

ABC. When they came to inspect the facility, they found an office staffed by young men rushing to and fro, pretending to be order fillers. These important clients signed bogus contracts with Holmes. What had started as a legitimate business enterprise ended in fraud, but Holmes had their money.

A glass-bending process made him a few dollars, but Holmes murdered Mr. Warner, the founder of the company. Warner helped Holmes install a firebrick kiln in the cellar. The immediate benefit of the oven was realized when Holmes induced him to step inside. He slammed the door on him, incinerating the man to a pile of dust.

Murder, not larceny, was Holmes's true calling in life. Estimates of how many girls entered the castle to board there or work as stenographers vary. By his own account, Holmes killed twenty-eight people. Others will swear this figure is closer to a hundred.

Typical of the girls who became enchanted with Holmes's easy style was seventeen-year-old Emily Van Tassel of 641 Robey Street. She worked at a small candy store on Milwaukee Avenue that Holmes had a financial interest in. The girl's mother even accompanied her daughter during their carriage rides through the streets of Chicago. What a fine catch for a poor girl without an education! Several weeks later, she was murdered in the candy store after Holmes ruined her. The body was later cut up. If Holmes did not dissect his victims, they were sold as cadavers for twenty-five to forty dollars apiece.

The third floor of the castle contained the guest rooms. There were sliding walls and, in the south front room, a murder vault. It was large enough for one person to stand in. A noxious acid (usually benzine and oil) would be spread on the floor or placed in a bowl inside. When the doors were closed around the intended victim, the oxygen would be absorbed by the acid. The person would die slowly, choking in his own spit. Police found a single female footprint on the door, indicating that the person had tried to batter down the door with no avail. Afterward, the bodies were carried to the bathroom and through a secret passage way leading to the basement. In this infernal room, they were dissected, placed in the vat of quicklime, or burned in the kiln. A policeman later found a ball of woman's hair wrapped in a cloth under the stairwell.

How did Holmes get away with it? Clara Lovering recalled that it must have been his eyes. That he was a skilled hypnotist, there can be no doubt. He used his talent in 1890, when he took on another lover.

A Summer of Gold

Her name was Julia Connor, of Davenport, Iowa. When she met Holmes, she was unhappily married to a meek little jeweler named Icilius "Ned" Connor and was the mother of a twelve-year-old girl named Pearl.

Ned Connor answered Holmes's newspaper ad asking for a watchmaker and jeweler. Arrangements were made, and soon Connor moved his wife and child into an apartment directly above the Holmes drugstore. He was paid twelve dollars a week. Julia was an ambitious, jealous woman. She threw tantrums if her husband showed extra attention to female customers. Perhaps sensing a possibility here, Holmes discharged his bookkeeper to hire Julia. Meanwhile the title of the drugstore was transferred to Connor to fool the creditors. Julia moved into her new position with ease. She was impressed with Holmes, and during her nightly tirades against her husband, she reminded him about his ambition. "Why can't you be more like Dr. Holmes? What kind of man did I marry?" It's unclear whether Connor suspected his wife's affair, or whether he was just tired of the harangues. Whatever the case, he left his wife and child behind to work for a downtown jeweler. Connor eventually remarried and was able to restore a degree of dignity to his life.

Julia and her daughter moved into one of Holmes's buildings at 7403 Honore Street. An insurance policy was taken out on their lives, something Ned Connor refused to allow Holmes to do. More than once, Julia threatened suicide, so Connor was naturally reluctant to provide her with encouragement. Business dealings brought Connor together with his wife one more time. She sat in Holmes's office staring vacantly at the floor. She pretended not to see her husband, while Holmes brazenly asked Connor whether he could borrow $5. Afterwards, the police brought Connor back to the castle for purposes of identification. As the police led him through the dank basement, the poor man stopped in his tracks. Hanging from a hook was an oil-stained garment that was apparently used by one of the domestics. Connor identified it as a dress his wife had made.

There is no question that Julia knowingly assisted Holmes in his shady dealings with insurance companies and private speculators. When Holmes incorporated his jewelry business on August 15, 1890, Julia was listed as a director along with her friend Kate Durkee and his insurance agent C.W. Arnold. Then the mother and daughter disappeared. "They have gone to Michigan," Holmes told Ned when he came looking for them. Holmes revised this story to say that her death resulted from a bungled abortion that he performed on her. Pearl was poisoned, and their furniture was shipped to St. Louis.

Julia was expendable at this time because there was a new woman in Holmes's life. Her replacement was a plump twenty-one-year-old blonde named Minnie Williams, who was born in Mississippi and educated at the Whitworth College in Boston. She came to Chicago in 1893, after meeting Holmes at a private gathering following one of her recitals. Her ambition was to become an elocutionist. Holmes intro-

Minnie Williams was considered to be a plump, somewhat unattractive woman. But she was an accomplished elocutionist when such things symbolized breeding and refinement in a young woman. Why then could she have been so completely cowed by Holmes?

duced himself as Harry Gordon, wealthy Chicago patent man. The girl was lured to the mansion after Holmes found out that she was scheduled to inherit some prime downtown Fort Worth real estate valued at $60,000 and a farm worth $15,000. The property was owned by her uncle, C.W. Black of Jackson, who raised Minnie and her sister Nannie after their father was killed in a train accident.

Holmes persuaded Nannie to abandon her teaching position at the Midlothian Academy in Texas to come to Chicago to witness the "wedding" of her sister to Holmes. The story takes on bizarre dimensions at this point. Julia Connor was still alive at this time, and there were reports of hair pulling and cat fights between the two women. After Holmes grew tired of the jealous escapades, he eliminated the Connor woman in favor of the *real* money. We'll never know whether Julia was pregnant with Holmes's child or whether he even performed an abortion. We do know that her last day was spent inside the murder castle.

Nannie came—and went. She was murdered by Holmes in June of 1893. The killer later said that Minnie clouted her sister over the head with a chair because she was jealous of her attention to Holmes. There were those in Englewood who believed Holmes when he said that he helped cover Minnie's crime by dropping the body into Lake Michigan in the dead of the night. Letters sent back to Texas described Holmes as a "wonderful man" who was going to send her to Europe for a vacation. This was his favorite tactic. Before their execution, Holmes's victims would be forced to write a letter to a loved one telling of some plan to leave town. What thoughts go through a person's mind when she knows she is about to die but must perform a humiliating act first?

In April of 1893, the Fort Worth property was deeded over to Benton T. Lyman, who was really Ben Pitezel, the drunk. The deed was filed in the Fort Worth county clerk's office and was personally notarized by Holmes. Minnie was the personal love slave. She willingly turned over her property and assets. But for what? In October of 1893, her brother Baldwin was killed in a mining accident that Holmes arranged in Leadville, Colorado. Minnie assigned the $1,050 life-insurance benefit to Holmes at 701 63rd Street, but the company hesitated. So Holmes, Minnie, and another romantic interest named Georgianna Yoke of Franklin, Indiana, headed west to settle the estate.

Georgie Yoke was the daughter of a high school principal. She was a blonde, considered to be beautiful in all respects, except for her very large eyes, which were set apart. Miss Yoke escaped a tarnished reputation in Franklin, for the excitement of the World's Fair midway. Like other small-town girls, she came to Chicago to work in a department store (Siegel-Cooper). She later applied at the castle for a job. This time Holmes identified himself as Henry Howard, nephew of Henry Mansfield Howard of Denver, Colorado. Minnie Williams posed as his cousin during the entire trip. It's unclear why Holmes went to these lengths to deceive. Georgie Yoke's inheritance was a modest $3,000, not the kind of estate that Holmes was used to plucking. Maybe he was in love. Miss Yoke was the one woman he cared for the most. When the police closed in on Holmes, he sent her back to her family when he could have easily ended her life. Charitable fellow, that Holmes.

He registered at the Vendome Hotel in Denver, remaining long enough to marry Miss Yoke, with Minnie Williams serving as *witness*. This was on January 17, 1894, and we can only guess at her real motives. It seems unlikely that Minnie was after a share of Georgie's estate, since she had already given Holmes her own. The honeymoon entourage traveled to Fort Worth, where Holmes claimed Minnie's property. Holmes negotiated a $10,000 mortgage on a building he constructed on the grounds, *after* it was finished. While in Texas, he engineered a horse swindle on the good citizens. He bought carloads of horses with bogus notes signed by O.C. Pratt (Holmes) that were delivered to St. Louis, where they were sold.

Minnie was taken to Momence, Illinois, where she was poisoned. Holmes covered his latest murder by sending his janitor Pat Quinlan to Fort Worth to work on the construction site. This seems to absolve Quinlan of any direct involvement in murder. When he reached Texas, he found the construction men sitting idle at the site.

While all this was going on, Holmes hired and murdered *another* stenographer. Her name was Emmeline Cigrand, of Anderson, Indiana. She was considered to be the prettiest of the Holmes women; Pitezel told him of her charms while he was an inmate at the Keeley Institute. Miss Cigrand was hired because of her experience working with inebriates at the Keeley Institute, a rehab facility at Dwight, Illinois. She had the perfect references for Holmes's very own Silver Ash Institute. Miss Cigrand was an efficient clerk and the one girl that Holmes felt remorse over killing. On summer nights, they cycled through Englewood with the bikes that he secured through the parts swindle. Then, for some reason, Emmeline lost interest in her boss, expressing a desire to return to Indiana. Holmes murdered her in the castle, explaining in a detailed letter to her parents that she had left his employ to marry Robert Phelps. He even went to the trouble to print engagement cards with their names but no forwarding address. (Phelps was just one of several aliases used by Ben Pitezel at this time.)

We next find Holmes traveling to St. Louis, but this time his ambition was his downfall. In July of 1894, he was arrested for selling mortgaged properties, the complaint having been filed by the Merrill Drug Company. Before Georgie Yoke came to bail him out, Holmes struck up a friendship with train robber Marion Hedgepath (leader of the fearsome Hedgepath Four), who was doing a twenty-five-year stretch. He told Hedgepath that he was an expert at insurance fraud, having done this kind of thing since he was in college. The plan was simple. The Fidelity Mutual Company of Philadelphia would be relieved of $10,000. A policy would be taken out on Ben Pitezel, who would then fake an accident. All Holmes needed from Hedgepath was the name of a lawyer who could be trusted. Hedgepath was promised a $500 commission. Agreed. Holmes was told to see Colonel Jeptha Howe, brother of the public defender assigned to Hedgepath's case (as Mark Twain once observed, there are more "colonels" in the world than whale shit). Howe decided that the scheme was not only foolproof but brilliant.

Pitezel rented a storefront at 1316 Callowhill Street in Philadelphia. The policy was taken out, and Holmes (alias H.M. Howard) hung his shingle outside the building—"Patents Bought and Sold, B.F. Perry." The plan was very simple and was common knowledge to everyone, including Mrs. Carrie Pitezel. Her husband's face would be doctored by Holmes so that it would appear to an examiner to be nothing more than a severe burn. Pitezel would drink a potion that would render him unconscious while the physician examined him. After the doctor left to summon an ambulance, a cadaver would be substituted, and a claim filed. What they didn't know was that Holmes had no intention of substituting a corpse when the real thing would serve the purpose.

The arranged "accident" took place the evening of September 4, when an explosion was heard in the neighborhood. The next morning, a carpenter named Eugene Smith went to visit Holmes about a patent. The door was locked, and Smith was suspicious. He summoned a policeman, and together, they discovered a corpse laying face down with the face and arms severely burned. A broken bottle of benzine, a pipe, and several matches were found next to the body. By all appearances, it looked like an industrial accident. The body was held in the morgue for eleven days before being committed to Potter's Field.

With the body fresh in the ground, Jeptha Howe produced the insurance policy. He explained to company officials that B.F. Perry was an alias for Ben Pitezel, and that his widow would prove it. Carrie was unaware that the body in the patent shop was really her husband's. She was informed by Holmes that Ben was lying low in the East. The insurance company paid the claim to lawyer Howe, and the spoils were distributed to everyone except Hedgepath, who continued to stew in the St. Louis jail. When the money didn't arrive, Hedgepath exposed the plot to Major Lawrence Harrigan of the St. Louis Police Department. Harrigan immediately notified claims investigator W.E. Gary of Fidelity Mutual, who sent a team of sleuths to work the case. Aware of this latest complication, Holmes took to the road with the three Pitezel children, Georgie Yoke, and the children's mother. Carrie Pitezel and Miss Yoke traveled on the same train, each of them *unaware* of the other's presence. Carrie did not even know her children were on board. They were first seen in Cincinnati and then in Indianapolis on October 1. Nine days later, Holmes took young Howard Pitezel to an isolated farm house in Irvington, Indiana, where he was brutally murdered. The remains of the boy were later found by Detective Geyer in a cook stove.

Holmes moved his party to Detroit, where he intended to do away with the girls, Nellie and Alice. Mrs. Pitezel was sent east. From Detroit, the girls wrote poignant letters to their mother, which became exhibit A. But someone tipped off Holmes about the detectives. He crossed the border into Canada, locating the girls in a frame house at 16 St. Vincent Street in Toronto. In the basement of the house, Nellie and Alice were locked in a large trunk. Holmes ran a hose into the trunk and asphyxiated them. He borrowed a shovel from a neighbor, explaining that he had a sack of Idaho potatoes that he wanted to bury.

Back in Philadelphia, the body of Ben Pitezel, alias Perry, was exhumed and the correct identity established. Georgie Yoke was registered at a Boston hotel while Holmes made a peculiar side trip back to his boyhood home in Gilmanton. Did he suspect that the caper was just about up and that it was time to mend his bridges? Probably not. He needed some emergency traveling money.

Holmes found his first wife, Clara, in the little town of Tilton, New Hampshire. He told her of all the troubles he had encountered since he last saw her, five years earlier. He neglected to mention anything about Myrtle, Minnie, Julia, the inventions, or the Pitezel affair. He spun an amazing tale about a serious railroad accident that he was involved in while traveling on the Lehigh Valley Road. For weeks, Holmes said he lay in the hospital at the point of death, unable to remember anything of his past life. It was only through the patient understanding of a wonderful lady named Miss Yoke, that Holmes was able to regain his senses. He married his Good Samaritan before realizing that he already had a wife in New Hampshire. Clara showed galling sympathy, and the couple was reconciled. Holmes promised to return to her the following April. Before he left his family, he talked his brother Arthur out of $300.

Holmes returned to Boston, and finally on November 17, he was arrested, initially for the horse-swindling caper in Texas. Holmes didn't cherish the idea of being extradited to Texas, where a common horse thief could be lynched. So he decided to confess to the insurance fraud instead.

When asked about the Pitezel children, Holmes said that Minnie Williams took them with her to London, where she planned to open a massage parlor (the 1890s variety). He later amended the story to include someone named Edward Hatch. This person never existed, but the alibi gave him time to formulate his plans. On the train back to Philadelphia, Holmes offered his jailer a $500 bribe if he would agree to be hypnotized. He refused.

Mrs. Pitezel and Colonel Howe were both arrested. The lawyer's guilt was established by an incriminating letter that he sent to Carrie Pitezel.

> I hope never to have a case like this again, and as difficult a case. The insurance company claims many things about which I will tell you when I come, but I convinced them today at the grave. I cannot tell you the trouble I have had. I cared for them well, and am completely exhausted tonight. Several times I thought our case was gone. Burn this letter.

Detective Franklin Geyer of the Philadelphia Police Department made it a personal crusade to sift through all of Holmes lies to find some clues to the whereabouts of the Williams girls and the missing Pitezel children. He tracked across the Midwest, interviewing people in Cincinnati, Minneapolis, Detroit, and Chicago that had prior dealings with Holmes. Holmes pleaded guilty to a charge of fraud on June 3, 1895. One month later, a search of the Chicago castle began and so did the real nightmare.

Crews from the City Construction Department began excavation of the infamous cellar on July 20. It was damp and uneven, and the smell of gas hung low in the air. The men tore away the masonry on the alley wall, discovering a large tank that emitted noxious fumes. One of the laborers struck at the tank, and an explosion buried them in the piles of rubbish. Fortunately, Holmes's little surprise did not claim any more lives. The tank was a cedar- and zinc-lined casing, measuring fourteen feet in length. When asked by the police how it got there, the neighbors expressed total ignorance.

The men returned to work. One of them suggested that the ghosts of the Williams girls were lurking about. That was all the levity anyone could muster. Six feet below the surface they found the bones of a child. The ground was soft and mushy, clear evidence that someone had frequently turned a shovel.

The commissioner of public works and the loan agent decided it wasn't fair to the businessmen who rented the first-floor storefronts to raze the building. It was agreed instead to turn the upper floors into a *Holmes museum* and rebuild it at a later date (it would seem that the twentieth century does not have exclusive claim to vulgar display).

They found Minnie Williams's watch inside a cookstove, along with buttons from her dress and several charred tintype photographs. Faced with this kind of evidence, Holmes continued to deny his guilt. He kept a diary that expressed genuine concern over the children. His lawyer told the reporters that his client was more than willing to go to Toronto (where the crown attorney requested extradition) to prove that the charges were false. But then on July 15, 1895, Detective Geyer found the badly decomposed bodies of Alice and Nellie in the cellar of the house on St. Vincent Street. Suddenly, Holmes's bravado deserted him. The children were buried in Toronto before a private gathering that included the mother and two detectives. (The remains of Howard Pitezel were located by Geyer on August 27.)

The trial began in the Philadelphia courtroom of Judge Michael Arnold, on October 28, 1895. Holmes remained calm through the proceedings until Georgianna Yoke was called to the stand. He wept like a baby at this point but regained enough composure to cross-examine the witness himself. Miss Yoke spoke in a hushed tone, avoiding direct eye contact with her husband. The state asked her about the marriage to Holmes. She explained that he told her mother in Indiana that he would soon come into a land inheritance in the West and Southwest. His only other living relative was an elderly aunt in Africa. At no time, according to Miss Yoke, did Holmes ever admit to being married. She did know about a previous wife, but believed that they were legally divorced. She told of Holmes's assuming the name of Henry Howard in order to acquire the Denver property and how they were married by the Reverend Mr. Wilcox on January 17, 1894. She was obviously pained by the experience and no doubt retained some degree of feeling for him. But she was cooperative with the prosecution.

When all the evidence had been presented, the jury retired on November 2. Before they left the jury box, their minds were made up. Out of courtesy to the defendant, they remained in the room for several hours. A unanimous guilty verdict was returned, and on November 30, Holmes was sentenced to die. At no time during the trial, did Holmes's parents or brothers and sisters appear on his behalf. He was the disgrace of Gilmanton.

The killer proved to be as cagey on death row as he had been during his strange career. He confessed to his crimes on April 12, 1896, but recanted the very next day. A newspaper offered him $7,500 for the "real story" (he later wrote his prison memoirs). When police checked several of the names Holmes admitted to murdering, they found a few that were still alive and well.

Two Catholic priests visited Holmes in his cell the day before the execution. He accepted communion, asking them for their forgiveness and blessing. They wanted him to repent his crimes before God and man, but this he would not do. "I wish to state here, so that there can be no chance of misunderstanding hereafter, that I am not guilty of taking the lives of the Pitezel children or their father Benjamin F. Pitezel, of whose death I was convicted, and for which I am to hang today."

Holmes enjoyed a good night's rest before he died. Would Carrie Pitezel (who was left Holmes's entire estate—$30), Georgie Yoke, Myrtle Belknap, or Clara Lovering ever again sleep through the night? Did they wake up one night screaming in terror, a dream of better times interrupted by *him*? Did the surviving Holmes children lead normal lives? Would Miss Yoke ever take another husband without investigating his past? Their lives could not have been the same after this stain on their souls. We simply do not know.

The Englewood castle was destroyed on August 19, 1895, under mysterious circumstances. Three explosions woke the neighborhood shortly after midnight. In minutes the entire building was consumed in flames. A half-hour after it started, the roof caved in, taking with it the dark secrets within its walls. The police theorized it was the work of safecrackers. Fred Barton, owner of the first-floor candy store, told of two strange young men who visited the Holmes museum earlier in the day. They seemed to lose their way, remaining inside for a long time. A gallon can of gasoline was later found in the rubble. The insurance men arrived, and that, of course, presented a new set of impossible problems. An accident? No accident. Holmes had some wealthy clients in Chicago. Some of them may have participated in the orgies or may have known directly about the murders. For those reasons, they found it expedient to have agents destroy the gruesome castle before the police search reached the upper floors. Robert L. Corbitt, a neighbor of Holmes, published a book about his own private search of the castle. He claimed to have found letters postmarked from London, giving some credence to the theory that Minnie had re-located there. Corbitt did not consider that Holmes may have cleverly planted the letters to deceive the police. Whatever the case, the secrets of his true motives and what other persons had direct knowledge of the affair were buried in the rubble that day.

Once fashionable Englewood is now a sprawling slum, and the 63rd Street business district is a shadow of its former elegance. The whites abandoned the south-side neighborhood in the years following World War I. The tract of ground where the castle stood is unrecognizable today. With some imagination, the spirits of the Williams girls and Julia Connor may still be seen here. Perhaps one dark night when the moon is full and the shadows long.

It's easy to speculate about the macabre because history sometimes becomes folklore. Was Holmes a hypnotic demon? With what was described as a "low and puny voice," Holmes enticed dozens of intelligent women to betray their principles—and their lives. Another legend associated with the execution tells of a lightning bolt that ripped from the sky the very second the rope snapped Holmes to another world.

Was it a mere coincidence that the foreman of the Philadelphia jury, Linford Biles, was electrocuted by a live wire on his roof several weeks after the hanging? Or that Emmeline Cigrand's father died in a gas explosion? Or that a fire in the Fidelity Mutual office nearly ruined the company? William A. Shoemaker, a lawyer who worked for Holmes on the case, was later disbarred. Even the Catholic priest who administered to Holmes was found in the church courtyard with his pockets picked.

David Franke, a student of the Holmes case, tells us that his zodiac

A Summer of Gold

birthdate foretold of evil. Guided by some unearthly power, Holmes's terrible capacity to pervert and destroy seemed to extend past the grave.

The Victims (list includes *only* those confessed by Holmes)   **Method**

1. Dr. Robert Leacock (of New Baltimore, Mich.) .. *Poisoning*
2. Dr. Russell (no first name given) .... *Blow to head in castle*
3. Julia Connor (stenographer, mistress) .... *Abortion*
4. Pearl Connor (daughter) .... *Poisoning*
5. Mr. _____ Rodgers (of Morgantown, Penn.) ... *Blow to head during fishing trip*
6. Charles Cole (tenant) .... *Blow to head in castle*
7. Lizzie _____ (no last name given; domestic at castle)............................... *Suffocation in chamber*
8. Sarah Cook (a Holmes tenant from Hamilton, Ontario)............................... *Suffocation in chamber*
9. Her unborn child........................ *Suffocation in chamber*
10. Mary Haracamp (also from Hamilton)......... *Suffocation in chamber*
11. Emmeline Cigrand (stenographer, mistress)...... *Suffocation*
12. Robert Phelps?? (fiance of Miss Cigrand, perhaps fictitious) .... *Suffocation*
13. Rosine Van Jassand a.k.a. Emily Van Tassel .... *Poisoned in candy store*
14. Robert Latimer (attempted blackmailer of Holmes) *Imprisoned/starved*
15. Anna Betts .... *Poisoned in drug store*
16. Gertrude Connor (resident of Iowa)........... *Poisoned in drug store*
17. Kate _____ (resident of Omaha, no last name given)................................ *Suffocation*
18. Mr. _____ Warner (business associate of Holmes) .... *Burned alive*

19.	Unknown (banker from Wisconsin)	Chloroform
20.	Unknown (boarder in castle)	Chloroform
21.	Nannie Williams	Suffocation
22.	Minnie Williams	Poisoned in Momence, Ill.
23.	Unknown.............................	Killed at 74th & Honore Street
24.	Baldwin Williams (relative of Minnie)	Shot in Leadville
25.	Benjamin Pitezel.........................	Explosion
26.	Howard Pitezel..........................	Suffocation
27.	Nellie Pitezel	Suffocation
28.	Alice Pitezel	Suffocation

A Summer So Hot . . .

The wooden tenements, the brick office buildings, the streets, the city stables . . . were heated infernos that August. The killer heat wave began on August 3 and lasted over a week. People didn't fare as well during the 90° heat wave back then. There was no shedding of clothes, suits were dark-colored wool, and women's skirts continued to drag the ground. They escaped to the bathing beaches or took rides on grip cars to gain relief. The grip car took in the rushing air, making it the coolest spot in Chicago.

There were twenty-nine cases of heat prostration reported on August 5. Fruit sellers along Maxwell Street took advantage of their customers by hiding their sun-baked rotten fruit under a layer of the good stuff. But pity the poor horse. The noble steed was man's beast of burden. He was shown little compassion during the heat waves. Sixty horses collapsed on August 3. During an average summer day, there would only be ten to twenty horse carcasses to collect. The Union Rendering Company was assigned this lucrative contract by the city, but demands for their services was so great that it took twelve hours to answer a call. We can imagine what kind of traffic jams this must have caused. During the heat wave, the city offered $10 per-horse to anyone who would remove it from the street.

The delays in horse removal created an impossible situation at the county hospital, where a horse carcass rotted in the sun, just below the patients' windows. City temperatures reached 98 that day, but the windows at the hospital had to be closed tight because of the awful stench.

There were the usual share of horse accidents too. At the corner of Madison and Dearborn one afternoon, a dray owned by the A.C. McClurg Company and driven by Albert Thorsen negotiated through the traffic. A Madison streetcar passed alongside the wagon. It was at that moment that Thorsen noticed a four-foot manhole in the cobblestone street was missing its cover. Thorsen foolishly tried to squeeze the wagon between the manhole and the streetcar. He might have made it, but the grip car jarred the wagon and shoved the horse.

Thorsen shouted in fright. Ed Jansen, a city worker inside of the hole heard the commotion and backed into the tunnel. Lucky for him. The horse tried to clear the opening but failed. His front feet passed over the tip, but the rear of the horse fell into the hole. The terrified animal was half in, and half out. He tried to extricate himself from the trap, but couldn't. The horse's hind hooves beat a lively rhythm on some underground pipes that contained wire from the Chicago Telephone Company. Several other workmen freed Jansen a half block away.

There was a gaper's block, and everyone offered a solution. The police pushed the mob back, but it just regrouped around the trapped horse, blocking the streetcars. An iron pipe measuring fourteen feet in length, and three inches in diameter was passed under the horse's foreshoulders. Twenty-five men tried to pull him out, but the pipe bent into a "U" shape, and the animal could not be budged.

Finally, the hook and ladder truck No. 6 arrived. A piece of timber twelve feet long was strapped flatwise to their ladder to prevent it from snapping in two. The same procedure was repeated again, and this time nearly a hundred men assisted in the effort. He was lifted from the manhole, a dazed, scratched, but wiser horse.

The perils of summer affected the tenement dwellers the most. Their rickety shacks sucked in the heat, forcing them to move their belongings into the street. Twenty-two more people died of heat prostration on August 9. One man was driven mad by the heat. He slashed himself in the throat with a razor. In the Jewish west-side ghetto, people passed the nights sleeping in the gutters, using wooden paving blocks as their pillows. Exhausted mothers watched over their young from the doorways of slum houses. From Canal Street west to Halsted, the sidewalks were a sweating sea of misery. Family bedding was spread across the streets amid the garbage. In some cases the family dog stood guard over the sleeping youngsters.

On Barber Street, east of Clinton, a mother constructed a bed for her baby, using herself as a shield to block off the stumbling drunks who spilled out from the local tavern. Other children made temporary beds on top of pushcarts owned by peanut vendors, while their parents fought with neighbors in ten different languages over the scarce street space.

This was mean Chicago. Infant mortality was high because disease was everywhere. Women's long skirts dragged across the ground, picking up dirt and germs, which were spread to their young. Disease, pestilence, starvation, and crime were everywhere. But the saloon around the corner made them all forget the troubles of the day.

Neighborhood missions served the needs of the afflicted, but their survival depended on the donations of the high and mighty. Chicago millionaires were never averse to philanthropy. On Sundays, the missions would be visited by churchgoing people who discarded their little baubles for the benefit of the poor. Aprons with French lace, strings of beads, and belts were given to the missions. But these goods could not feed a hungry child.

Young missionaries wandered the slums, bringing greeting and small portions of food to the needy. Five days of the week were devoted to visitation, consultation, and relief work. Saturday was the day devoted to the filing of reports, and Sunday was the traditional day for religious observance. Frail and undernourished themselves, the missionary women would eat a midday meal in a neighborhood bakery that included tea and a roll served on a rough board covered by newspaper.

They dressed simply because there was no reason not to. Disease and poverty awaited them in the slum dwellings they visited. Frequently, they could not communicate with the families huddled together in their cellar apartments. Sebor Street was the home to newly arrived Italian immigrants. In a dingy hovel below street level, an Italian widow looked after her five children, supporting them as best she could by cleaning rags. The missionary inspected the youngest child's hands. "Let me see them just as clean next Sunday in church," she reminded him.

The missionary's joy came from knowing that in her small way she brought comfort to their lives. Up and down Jefferson and Forquer Streets the sounds of wailing infants from weather-beaten homes could be heard. There was still much for her to do.

Life before the turn of the century was both sweet and cruel. There were Fourth of July picnics at Lincoln Park, excursions to Sharp

A Summer of Gold

Shooter's Park (later Riverview), roasted peanuts for a penny, but the very poor slept among the garbage during heat waves. And still the daily press cautioned the workingman about union evils, why he needed a high tariff, and the godless Democrats. Who among them would answer labor's call?

Silver and Gold

For a short time they had their savior. Even though William Jennings Bryan was not really that, he gave them hope. He was on their lips; he was on their minds. They did not understand the issue he stood for, but he was refreshingly new and, curiously, something very old. Bryan came to Chicago that summer representing an agrarian ideal that would no longer be. His views were fundamental and harked back to Thomas Jefferson. But he was *new*, and that's why he was such a paradox.

Bryan appeared when America was caught in a political vacuum. Candidates for elected office were winded gasbags, still waving "the bloody shirt" of the Civil War, clinging to Republican views of high tariff and the gold standard, and committed to the bidding of the trusts. The Republican candidate for president, William McKinley, was a well-meaning, quiet statesman, who wore a red carnation in his lapel. He was nice but was manufactured by Ohio political boss Marcus Alonzo Hanna, who saw in McKinley a war hero, a capable governor, and, best of all, an ardent protectionist for American business.

There were several issues at stake in the 1896 election. The isolationist posture of American foreign policy was being challenged by Henry Cabot Lodge, Theodore Roosevelt, and Senator William Eaton Chandler, who were enthusiastic supporters of colonial expansion and the two-ocean navy. This was the thesis of Alfred Thayer Mahan, whose book *The Influence of Sea Power upon History, 1660-1783*, became one of the most important documents of the century. The book argued for naval buildup, saying that those who possessed it were undisputed masters of their hemisphere. The book was read and understood by the expansionists who sought to annex Cuba and by the Republicans who adopted an imperialist plank.

But this issue took a back seat to the great silver-gold debate, which dominated the American political scene for about ten years. Years later, the controversy seems pointless and remains one of those issues that is difficult to understand, even among scholars of the period. Basically it was a factional fight. Hard money versus soft money, East against West. Agrarian America supported the Democratic stand for unlimited coinage of silver to expand the currency in the wake of the 1893 depression. The gold standard had been in existence in the United States for sixty-two years. The Republicans naturally viewed it as a moral issue. Loose, fast money caused inflation, which would ultimately lead to socialism. The battle of the have-nots against special interests was on everybody's mind in the summer of '96.

At Bughouse Square and in the Loop hotels, the "Popocrats" (Populist/Democrats—it was all the same to the *Chicago Tribune*) stood jaw to jaw with the "goldbugs." Rag pickers and delivery boys asked each other: What fixes the value of gold? Union veterans patiently explained that England supported the free-silverites because they were sure that if one of their kind were elected to office, Confederate war bonds would finally be paid off.

The Democrats gathered in Chicago the week of July 1, bitterly divided. The eastern faction supported the gold standard and President Cleveland. They were the majority. Typical of the fighting among delegations was the case of Illinois. Governor John Peter Altgeld was elected chairman at the state Democratic convention in Peoria. His mission was to hold the forty-eight delegates together as a voting unit. Altgeld was hated and maligned for his opposition to the introduction of federal troops to the 1894 Railworkers Strike and for his unconscionable decision to free the Haymarket men. Altgeld was a free-silverite, dedicated to the election of Richard Parks Bland of Missouri as the next president. Bland was an old campaigner for free silver and one of the authors of the Bland-Allison Act, which called for the coinage of silver at a ratio of sixteen to one. Within Altgeld's delegation were silver factions. Mike McDonald and his henchman Asa Trude fought hard to elect Governor Horace Boies of Iowa. The delegations could not agree on a course of action, let alone what to do about the gold bugs, who rallied behind Senator David Hill of New York, an old Tammany Hall boss.

The other gold men put their stock in Senator William Vilas of Wisconsin and ex-Governor William Russell of Massachusetts. There was little chance for either of them, but the gold minority was hoping for an irreconcilable split among the silverites, who couldn't agree on a candidate. Bland was their favorite, but he had to compete against Boies, Governor Claude Matthews of Indiana, Senator Joseph Blackburn of

Kentucky, newspaperman John R. McLean, and Senator Henry Teller. Grover Cleveland's name was nowhere to be found . . . and neither was Bryan's. Bryan came to Chicago anonymously. He coveted the position of temporary chairman, but that was doubtful, since a power struggle between the Nebraska gold and silver men threatened to unseat him.

One-hundred laborers worked inside the coliseum for a week to get things ready for the Democrats. They hung bunting from the girders and positioned the largest American flag at that time on the south end of the hall. It was an enormous 72½' x 100' affair—put up in lieu of state flags, which had characterized the Republican convention. There were seats for 1,000 delegates in a space of 50' x 125' in the center of the hall. The speaker's stand was built on the east side of the hall, sandwiched between two sections of press row.

The Palmer House was the favored hotel for the state delegations. The south end of the rotunda featured a large portrait of Governor Boies, while the Bland men hung pictures of their candidate on the walls leading upstairs. The gold Democrats received the choice rooms, and the spacious clubroom was set up as their headquarters.

When the New York Tammanyites arrived, they found a gold framed portrait of President Cleveland hanging in their room. The next day a maid found the painting hidden in back of a bed. Senator Hill's picture was substituted.

The preconvention chicanery was put aside on July 6 so that the leading Democrat contenders could partake of Mrs. Palmer's hospitality during an afternoon tea given at the mansion. Bertha greeted Senators Blackburn, Vilas, Gray, and Daniel wearing a delecate chiffon dress of Nile green, embroidered with white silk and Strasburg pebbles. Recently plucked American Beauty roses were admired by Cyrus McCormick and Joseph Medill. Guests strolled leisurely about the garden sipping champagne and enjoying the view of Lake Michigan. William Jennings Bryan and all the constituents that these noble Democrats claimed to represent were not invited to the affair.

At the stroke of noon, July 7, 1896, William P. Garrity banged a gavel (that had once been a part of the oak timber of the Fort Dearborn blockhouse) to signal the start of the convention. The Seventh Regiment Armory band struck up a tune called "Just Tell Them That You Saw Me" when Senator David Hill entered the building. Poor Hill. He tried to lead a minority that was under instructions not to bolt the convention: He was assigned to hold them all together by giving the keynote speech. When asked why he never smiled, Hill said: "I never smile and look pleasant at a funeral." His supporters tried to nominate him as temporary chairman, but a role call gave the majority to Senator John Daniel of Virginia. Bryan lost this decision, but he considered it a major victory over the vested interests.

The coliseum was still part of a dry district in 1896, which presented a terrible problem to many Democrats. No problem at all. A blind pig saloon opened up directly across the street, guarded by two burly policemen who winked at the delegates passing by. "Saloon in the rear, sir! Just step right up," the proprietor touted. A Kansas prohibitionist walked by one day, noticing the lively traffic from the convention. "This is clearly illegal," he said. "Aren't you going to do something about it?"

"Sure," the copper said. "This is Chicago, and there's no law on State Street or Madison to keep a man from barking for trade for his saloon."

"But this is a prohibition district."

"What do we know about that, ye scalaboo? We don't belong out here any more than you do, see? Think we're going around and exceed our duties? We're told to watch for crooks and not to bother our heads about saloons."

The party planks were read. The Democrats opposed import labor, supported Altgeld's stance against federal intervention in local matters, were in favor of the free coinage of silver at a rate of sixteen to one, opposed a third term for the president, and reaffirmed their belief in the Monroe Doctrine. For two days, the silverites beat the gold bugs at every turn.

On July 9, the *Chicago Tribune* observed a groundswell forming for Bryan, after he succeeded in winning his seat in the delegation. "The Nebraska stable has entered a dark horse in William Jennings Bryan, who is of sound wind and believed able to go the distance." So sure that their favorite son had a chance, the Nebraska silver men ordered a bushel full of Bryan campaign buttons. After being seated, Senator James K. Jones of Arkansas asked Bryan to take charge of the platform debate between the silver and gold factions. It was a concession to Bryan's staunch support of silver and was thought to be a consolation for his failed attempt to land the temporary chairman's spot.

Bryan arranged a debate with Hill, Vilas, and Russell for July 9. By prior arrangement, Senator Ben Tillman, the "Pitchfork Man," would close the debate for the silver forces. However, his speech was

A Summer of Gold

fifty minutes long, and might Senator Hill object on principle? Tillman agreed, and the table was now set for Bryan.

Bryan was aware of the importance of speaking last, and perhaps he sensed that the time was right. At the Clifton House that night, Bryan laughed when he heard the noisy revelry of Bland supporters outside his window. "These people don't know it, but they will be cheering for me just this way tomorrow night. I will make the greatest speech of my life tomorrow in reply to Senator Hill."

A reporter for the *New York Evening Post* asked him the next day whether he thought he was "the coming man of the convention." "You're premature, you're premature," he said, waving the man off. Bryan appeared to be at ease with himself, but his stomach was really in a knot. He excused himself while Senator Jones explained the speaking order to the convention. Pitchfork Tillman spoke first. He spoke out against Cleveland, the easterners who subjugated his beloved South, and the liars and serpents in the hall now. He was booed and hissed.

David Hill was cheered as he took the stand, but his speech was void of emotion—though it was conceded that his defense of the president was well reasoned and thoughtful.

Vilas of Wisconsin was next, but his defense of gold was dull and lifeless. Governor Russell was scheduled to speak next, but protested to Hill that he did not have enough time. Bryan suggested that each speaker be given ten more minutes. Hill agreed, which again played into the Boy Orator's hands.

Russell objected: "The minority also feels that the report of the majority is defective in failing to make any recognition of the honesty, economy, courage, and fidelity of the present Democratic administration." What he said was probably true, but few delegates paid attention. A murmur of anticipation filled the hall because they heard about Bryan's oratory. Edgar Lee Masters observed Bryan from the gallery. He remembered that the candidate seemed to leap up from his chair and *glide* toward the podium. He wore a black Alpaca suit, baggy trousers, and a vest. He did not belong to any moneyed interest or political machine. His convictions may have been naive and overstated, but they were nurtured on the Illinois and Nebraska prairie. He believed in his cause, and his time had come.

Bryan was just thirty-six years old in 1896. He was the son of Judge Silas Bryan, a noted trial lawyer in Salem, Illinois. As a youngster, William had the religious fervor of both his parents instilled in him. Up until the time he was twelve years old, the boy attended Methodist services in the morning with his mother and Baptist church in the afternoon with his father. Strong religious convictions taught to him by Silas shaped Bryan's outlook on life.

As a young man, he embraced the Jeffersonian ideal while supporting the Granger and Greenback movements. His talent for debate surfaced while he attended Whipple Academy and, later, Illinois College at Jacksonville. As a prize for winning a debate, Bryan chose an Oxford Bible in place of cash. He believed in progress but only within the religious framework. He clung to Jefferson's view that America was a rural, homogeneous society. Those who attacked him in 1896 failed to see this. His support of silver seemed radical, but Bryan was anything but that.

He arrived in Chicago for the first time in 1882. Bryan did not like the city or the corruption of Carter Harrison I. But he attended the Union Law School (now Northwestern University) and clerked for the noted jurist Lyman Trumbull. It was reported that Bryan walked four miles to school each day to save a nickel. Trumbull's defense of Andrew Johnson and the Freedman's Bill further shaped Bryan's political view.

Upon completion of his studies, he set up his practice in Jacksonville, but found greater opportunity in Lincoln, Nebraska, which had all the characteristics of a Wild West town. The fact that Nebraska was a Republican state did not phase him. His judgments proved to be correct. There was room to grow, and soon Bryan won himself a congressional seat. He embraced the silver issue in 1890, after reading *Coins Financial School*, a book published in Chicago by William Harvey. As a congressman, he supported tariff reform, the income tax, and direct election of senators. His battles with Grover Cleveland over silver earned him the support of the Populists, while helping to pave the way for his 1896 coup.

And now he stood before them all. He held his hand up to ask for their silence. He threw back his head—and began one of history's most famous speeches. The moment, the place, the climate of the time helped Bryan, but so did the construction crews at the coliseum.

Buffalo Bill's Wild West Show recently finished an engagement. Seating capacity for the event had been expanded to 50,000 (the figure seems high but was repeated in the *Chicago Tribune*), the convention only required several thousand of those seats to be occupied. So that the speakers could be better heard, a floor-length curtain was moved

A Summer of Gold

up 200 feet from the north end. The unused space was turned into a lobby, while the curtain prevented echoes and kept Bryan's audience close to him at all times. Logistics played a small part of his success that night.

> Mr. Chairman and gentlemen of the convention. I would be presumptous indeed to present myself against the distinguished gentlemen to whom you have listened, if this were a mere measuring of hostilities; but this is not a contest between persons. The humblest citizen in all the land, when clad in the armor of a righteous cause, is stronger than all the hosts of error. I come to speak to you in defense of a cause as holy as the cause of liberty, the cause of humanity.

He likened the silver-gold issue to that of the Civil War, when brothers faced each other in mortal combat. He believed in his cause and so did the Democrats who were with him from the start. His powerful voice carried to every end of the hall, Buffalo Bill or no Buffalo Bill. He quoted Carlyle, spoke of pioneer vision, and during each pause, the crowd was on its feet roaring its approval. Bryan took great care not to offend the eastern wing of the party, which was about to be buried.

> If they dare to come out in the open field and defend the gold standard as a good thing, we will fight them to the uttermost. Having behind us the producing masses of this nation . . . we will answer their demands for a gold standard by saying to them: "You shall not press down upon the brow of labor this crown of thorns; you shall not crucify mankind on a cross of gold."

As he began his last sentence, Bryan brought his hands to his head, creating a tableaux vivant of the crucified Savior. First he showed them the crown of thorns, and then he spread his arms at right angles, taking a step back for effect. A man on the cross! There was a stunned silence. Bryan walked off the platform thinking his speech had been a failure. But when he reached the floor, the tumult began. The delegates were seated in five sections, with just four feet between each group of seats. When he returned to his seat, a mighty procession began. The other state delegations circled the Nebraska men, lifting Bryan to their shoulders. For twenty minutes bedlam reigned. They danced, they carried him around the hall, they pounded their feet and waved handkerchiefs.

Agents of Mark Hanna rushed from the auditorium, surely convinced that the madness of the world had been let loose. "The Chicago platform is filled with revolution!" Hanna said after hearing the news. For at least a half-hour the convention was out of control. Things finally quieted down, not because someone said they should but out of sheer exhaustion.

A note was sent to Bryan asking if he wanted his name put in nomination while the time was right. He declined, saying that if it couldn't be done the next day, then it would not be worth it. The convention adjourned, and Bryan returned to his room at the Clifton House, but not before Hill's minority report defending Cleveland was defeated 626 to 330. Governor Altgeld announced a 48-0 vote for his delegation against the president. He was booed and hissed, a reaction that he was accustomed to in his political career.

Bryan's instruction to his delegation was clear. If his name were to be offered in nomination, there would be no deals or promises. Twenty-thousand people filled the coliseum that night, and it was obvious that the Bryan boom had not diminished during the adjournment. Judge Henry T. Lewis of the Georgia delegation was the man who submitted his name. There was no time for a speech because the second Bryan's name was mentioned, another roar went up. Bryan received the news from a messenger boy at the hotel. He closed his eyes to contemplate the moment. "How, do you know I didn't know he was going to do that?" Bryan expected the Kansas people to place his name before the convention.

"Silver Dick" Bland commanded a lot of influence, and it would take five ballots before Bryan could secure his nomination. Altgeld stubbornly refused to surrender his delegates. At the outset, Bryan had only one admirer among the Illinois people—F. Regnier of Monmouth. Turning to Clarence Darrow, a man who would figure prominently in Bryan's future years, Altgeld said, "I have been thinking over Bryan's speech. What did he say anyhow?" Altgeld was the only one who held out till the end. He knew it was over when California and Arkansas went for Bryan. Visibly shaken, he released his delegates to the new candidate. Right after that, Bland withdrew his name. It took five ballots; the voting went like this:

First ballot	Bryan......137	Bland......235	Boies.......67
Second ballot	Bryan......197	Bland......281	Boies.......37
Third ballot	Bryan......219	Bland......291	Boies.......36

Fourth ballot	Bryan......280	Bland......241	Boies.......33
Fifth ballot	Bryan......652	Bland...... 11	Pattison.....95

When news of Bryan's nomination reached William McKinley in Canton, Ohio, he greeted his callers from his front porch before taking his customary buggy ride with his ailing wife. "No, I shall have nothing to say," McKinley told reporters, indicating the direction his future campaign would take. Mark Hanna told McKinley to relax and continue to keep giving his mild little speeches from the back porch, leaving the serious campaigning to him. The Ohio machine spent $7 million to elect the "major," twice that of Bryan. Hanna hired aging Civil War veterans to stump the country on behalf of McKinley, predicting dire consequences if the silver crowd got into office. There was strong evidence of Republican election fraud in at least ten states, making this one of the most depressing, vicious campaigns in American history.

The best days for Bryan were his first. Before the national press turned on him, the candidate enjoyed the love and adulation of his supporters. His first campaign promise was a pledge not to run for a second term. It was consistent with the party platform, but it prompted immediate ridicule. And how they loved to ridicule Bryan! They called him the "Prince of Anarchy" and the "Popocrat." John Hay referred to him as a "half-baked, glib little briefless, jackleg lawyer." Andrew Carnegie just called him the "conjurer." In 1896, the mainstream of politics was truly frightened by him.

He gave his first speech from the balcony of the Clifton House the night of the nomination. Appearing on the Monroe Street side of the hotel, Bryan was bathed in electric light and smiling radiantly. A campaign aide took the American flag that had been used as bunting for the grill work and draped it around his massive shoulders. Someone in the crowd asked him: "Must we keep off the grass when you are president?" The man was a member of Jacob Coxey's homeless army that had besieged Washington in 1894 in search of jobs and opportunity. "There will be no sign up to keep off the grass when I am president." The crowd roared again. The Bland marching band appeared in full force for Bryan—and he thanked them.

They wanted to touch him, shake his hand, and feel his presence. But he stood on a balcony, and it was impossible. So Bryan extended his hand into the open air. "Now you have all shaken hands with me," he explained. "A great deal of sentiment will be developed in this campaign. It will be a camp meeting campaign. We are going to have songs as well as speeches." He waved to the crowd and disappeared inside where another throng of hangers-on and well-wishers on the fringe of political life awaited him.

Bryan's last stop in Chicago was to Alfred Brisbois's photography studio at 125 State Street. In the wretched heat, the candidate sat stiffly for over an hour. The windows were kept closed for fear of ruining the camera focus. Bryan faced the camera, clutching a red bandana which he used to mop his brow between takes. "Can't you bring on a few windmills?" he asked. Bryan wore the same black alpaca coat that he wore for his speech, and it was adorned by a "16-1" button. An hour later, the campaign began. He left the Clifton House in the company of Willis J. Abbot who reacted angrily to a Chicago banker's offer of a private Pullman car for the trip. "Mr. Bryan! You should not accept this offer. You are the great commoner, the people's candidate, and it would not do to accept favors from the great railroad corporations." The analogy appealed to him, and till the day he died, William Jennings Bryan *was* the Great Commoner. He founded a newspaper in Lincoln, Nebraska, under the same name.

Bryan named old Arthur Sewall of Maine as his running mate. It was a sop to the eastern Democrats and an attempt to gain favor in enemy territory. The Populist Party and National Silver Party simultaneously named Bryan their candidate, but the Populists could not swallow Arthur Sewall's presence on the ticket. Against Bryan's wishes, the bitterly divided Populists nominated Thomas Watson of Georgia to run with Bryan. Watson was a compromise between the radical wing of the party, characterized by Eugene Debs, and the broader-based conservatives. He was an interesting, footnoted character in American history. In his earlier years, Watson commanded a rag-tag coalition of poor whites and black tenant farmers. As a rural southerner, it was a remarkable gesture for civil rights. In 1904, Watson actually secured the nomination for president, running on the Populist ticket. But when political opponents undermined his power by hiring city blacks to vote against him, Watson lost most of his liberal ideology. In 1904, he was a Populist. Just two years later, he was identified with the Ku Klux Klan, an amazing political transformation. He urged disfranchisement for the Negro in his newspaper, the *Jeffersonian*. His schizophrenic political tendency reached a culmination when Watson led an anti-Semitic campaign against southern Jews, following the lynching of Leo Frank, an innocent pencil company executive, in August 1915. When he died, Watson was eulogized by Eugene Debs and the Klan, both of whom saw fit to send flowers.

With the ticket "with two tails," Bryan gave them music and speeches as he promised. John Philip Sousa's "El Capitan" march became the theme song. There was no time for something as simple as a bath. While Bryan criss-crossed the states, covering 18,000 miles by train, he would overcome the problem by soaking himself in vinegar. McKinley stayed home. Bryan embraced the people and heard their hue and cry. But in the end, none of it mattered because the western support he received carried insufficient weight to defeat the big eastern bosses. Matt Quay of Pennsylvania helped organize the gold Democrats into a political force. They nominated Senator John Palmer of Illinois to run on a third (or is it fourth?) party ticket. Grover Cleveland was delighted that the "sound money" wing had remained true to its convictions.

Bryan was a righteous candidate. At night, he dropped to his knees and prayed to the tune of the clicking wheels beneath him. Frontier America was already dead in 1896, and so too was his Jeffersonian ideal. He came back to Chicago that fall, attempting to stoke the embers of those wild July days. Somehow it wasn't the same.

That fall, McKinley carried eighteen states north of the Ohio and Potomac rivers. He won 56 percent of the population and 64 percent of the wealth. Bryan received 6,492,559 votes—the most by any losing candidate up to that time. McKinley rewarded Hanna's devotion by appointing feeble old John Sherman of Ohio to the post of Secretary of State. This created a vacancy in the Senate, which was filled by Mark Hanna.

Bryan continued his quest in 1900, and again in 1908, but each time the vote spread against him grew wider. Populism died and so did the agrarian life that Bryan so desperately tried to represent. Even his Methodist/Baptist teachings were laid bare for public ridicule—by Clarence Darrow at the Scopes trial in 1925. It was a small irony of history that Darrow was there to witness the ascension and the fall. Bryan cannot be called a failure of history or an opportunist or any of the other things that his detractors have suggested. He gave the electoral process some hope and in his own way, helped usher in the era of reform known as the Progressive Era. And it began during Chicago's summer of gold.

4.
Close-up on the 1890s: Dawn of a New Century

THE CITY WAS FLOODED WITH LIGHT. ELECTRIC LIGHTS COVERED WITH red silk and paper shades glowed from the residences along Michigan Avenue. The Statue of Progress on top of Montgomery Ward's Building was the brightest beacon of the Midwest, reaching out to the prairie and farmlands. Even in the tenement districts the poor found time to celebrate. They put candles in their windows because they believed that the coming century would be something good, if not for them, then for their children.

It was Monday night, December 31, 1900. Hail to the new century! A heavy snow blanketed the ground that afternoon, and temperatures dipped to the low teens. But the New Year's celebration would be something special. A year earlier people were fooled into thinking that 1900 was the new century. This time they would not be misled. For weeks the newspapers listed the achievements of the old century and what could be expected from the new one.

> One may easily predict two events which are certain to happen and which, by judging the outcome of such events in the past, are to act as formative influences. I refer to the great war of which we can already see the opening moves, and the death struggle between capital and labor which will be fought out in America, and which will be for the 20th Century what the French Revolution was for the 18th and 19th.

Richard Legallicare penned that somber editorial for the Hearst chain on the eve of Christmas, 1900. It was a prophetic view of the future, even though the labor struggles were not as bloody as he imagined. Other predictions were wild and seemingly influenced by too much Jules Verne. In 1897, the *Tribune* polled civic planners for their views on where Chicago would be in the last decade of the 20th century.

> At the end of the next century, I believe that the city will take in all of Cook County, all of DuPage County, and the northern townships of Will County. Then the South Chicago county will have extended into Indiana as far as Valparaiso. If the state of Indiana will cede that valuable parcel of territory, then indeed will Chicago be the queen of the world.

The prediction that the "free and sovereign state of Chicago" covering 1,600 square miles with a population of 10 million, was based on the growth rate of the city since the Chicago fire and the influence of railroads. They failed to see the emergence of the sunbelt states as a new area of migration.

"Such a vulgar thing as a horse will never be seen upon the downtown streets of the city" (though vulgar by 1897 standards, nostalgic rides on a horse and buggy down Michigan Avenue are currently bringing added dollars to city tourism). Architect James J. Egan foresaw the building of "super structures," some as high as sixty stories high, dotting the Chicago skyline. It was not only possible, he declared, but probable because the modern elevator will be replaced by one powered solely by electricity. In the new structures people will live better. Wooden tenements will be a thing of the past, and coal will no longer be used as a home heating fuel.

A massive sports stadium seating 125,000 would surely be built, and it was. It was called Soldier Field but was not enclosed as the architect said it would be. Professor Henry Davies of Yale University saw an end to war because he believed that the superpowers would eventually disarm when they realized that there would be no new weapons left to invent. Astronomer Garrett Serviss pondered the notion of space travel. He concluded that the "air ship of the 20th Century may find one of its useful applications in carrying the astronomer and his instruments a little closer to the stars."

This speculation filled the newspapers for weeks. Most of the views affirmed the positive, confident attitude that Americans felt about their country. The past century had witnessed America's growth and dominance over the continent. People were unafraid because science and technology would rid the earth of its troubles. The problems of the day were solvable, if not tomorrow, then in fifty years by a stronger, healthier generation. What they failed to realize was that human nature does not change. But, as the *Tribune* concluded in its 1897 predictions, "to attempt to picture in fancy all that Chicago will be a century from now would be beyond the power of the 19th century mind."

Gaily, gaily, gaily, Chicago marched into 1901. Mayor Harrison promised to uphold a midnight saloon-closing law but privately told Chief Joseph Kipley to let the boys have a good time. Kipley went to bed early that night. State and Madison was alive with the shouts of Loop revelers. Men drank gin and fired their revolvers into the night air. Restaurants were filled, and in the distance, tugboats blasted their horns.

Religious services of a more reserved nature were held at the Chicago Coliseum, where the American Red Cross sponsored a midnight watch service for representatives of the nations participating in the Geneva Convention and members of Chicago clergy and society. Inspirational messages sent by Clara Barton, William McKinley, and William Jennings Bryan were read by William Penn Nixon. The faithful sang the "Old One Hundred" at 11:58 P.M. when an old man with a flowing beard and tattered clothes rushed to the podium.

"Hear me, brothers and sisters! I am the savior!" he shouted, as he threw his hands up over his head. His name was Fridrich Trostel, a German umbrella maker, but for a second, there must have been someone in that auditorium who thought that he *was* the savior. Trostel read passages from the Bible for several moments before the sergeant-at-arms rushed to the stage and threw him to the floor. No vagrant would be allowed to disturb this congregation, whose luminaries included Mrs. Pullman and Mrs. McCormick. "Praise God from whom all blessings flow!" was sung by the faithful as Trostel was led to an awaiting police wagon.

At 100 Lake Shore Drive, the lights dimmed in the grand ballroom of Potter Palmer's "castle," a solitary trumpet blared to announce the arrival of the new century, while an electric light illuminated "1901" on the wall. Mr. Honore Palmer and Mr. Adrian Honore were gracious hosts to 175 guests. A toast! Mrs. Palmer looked splendid in her black velvet gown with diamonds and pearls about her neck and wrists. This was her famous New Year's Ball, this time in honor of her dear friend, Mrs. Griswold Gray of New York. In attendance were Robert Todd Lincoln, Richard T. Crane, and future governor Frank Lowden.

Earlier in the evening, a light supper was offered to twenty-five swells of the younger generation. The other guests were instructed to arrive after nine, but they did not feel slighted. To be invited to the Palmer mansion on New Year's Eve was a cherished social honor. Ever since Henry Ives Cobb designed the gray-stone castle with turrets near Banks and Lake Shore Drive, it had become the favored gathering spot for Chicago society.

Palmer. The name suggested ambience and luxury. If Astor represented New York society, then Palmer came to symbolize the Chicago of the Gilded Age. Potter Palmer and his young wife Bertha Honore established the social trends. The others just followed.

It was Palmer who recognized that the Prairie Avenue district could not last as a quiet area for Chicago's merchant princes to raise their families. He looked to the north side as a possible site to build a new mansion. The neighborhood at the edge of Lake Michigan was a soggy marsh, a challenge even for the most imaginative city planner.

Palmer went ahead with his plans, buying up lake-shore property from the city at reasonable prices. From the ashes of the Chicago Fire, he rebuilt his famous hotel and assisted in the redevelopment of the downtown district. Seen in this light, his choice of the virgin territory bordering the lake was not so surprising after all. By purchasing the surrounding lots, Palmer was in the enviable position of *selecting* his neighbors. The Gold Coast was born when the first spade of dirt was turned by workmen who began to erect his $1-million castle. That was in 1882, and three years later Bertha crossed the sandstone walkway for the first time. The interior of the mansion defies modern imagination. Regal, excessive, gaudy—it was all those things. But the white-and-gold drawing room done in Louis XVI style, the Oriental rugs, imported mosaics, billiard room, and oak floors were consistent with the age. Soon, they were joined by the Herman Kohlsaats, the George Meekers, the Franklin McVeaghs, and the Hempstead Washburns, who had left Prairie Avenue.

In 1893, Palmer invested $40,832.75 into general improvements on the castle. The picture gallery, cabinet room, butler's pantries, and milk-and-butter room were expanded and improved. The lavish expenditures sometimes overshadowed the owner's penurious nature. Chicago's most famous innkeeper would force employees to sign agreements that would release him from any liability in the event of on-the-job accidents. When Palmer got wind of a laborer cheating him out of several hours worth of pay during the remodeling phase, he interviewed him at length, forcing him to sign a transcripted confession.

On New Year's Eve, 1900, the ballroom was canopied with white silk and twined with evergreen. Bouquets of American Beauty roses were in all the parlors, with holly berries added for the extra Christmas touch. Johnny Hand's orchestra provided the evening entertainment while guests compared the party favors that were catered in from Paris. At one-thirty in the morning, guests retired to a smaller room where they were served a light supper. Then the coachmen appeared at the driveway to take them all home, so that they might prepare for the traditional New Year's Day reception.

While the landaus and broughams clip-clopped through deserted north-side streets, the State and Madison celebrants headed for the streetcars. Earlier in the evening, detective P.F. McLaughlin was making his rounds when a pedestrian waiting for a streetcar stopped him. "I saw somebody come out of there in a big hurry; you'd better check," he said, pointing to the subway tunnel at Randolph and LaSalle. McLaughlin, a veteran of the Haymarket troubles, went down to investigate. Underneath an arch of a colonnade, he found an upright metal object resting against the concrete. It was a three-and-a-half-inch pipe bomb, similar to the ones used by the labor movement. The detective removed it just in time. The next Lincoln Avenue car that passed by would have detonated it, and the force of the Chicago River that ran directly overhead would have collapsed the system and would have made escape for the passengers impossible. But the bomb was exploded on a secluded portion of a Chicago beach the next day. It was said that the force of the bomb jarred buildings a half-mile away.

P.F. McLaughlin prevented a major Chicago disaster that would have been remembered for a hundred years. He was the first hero of a new era and helped get the "age of miracles" off to the right start.

5.
Levee Low Life

The recruiting grounds of the bagnio are the stores where girls are often cast, still unknown to sin, but in want and without shelter; in a word, places outside the levee, where distress and temptation stand ever present as a menace to purity and rectitude. Behind every effort there is a cause.
—Madame Dora Clafin, keeper of a house of ill repute, 1893.

First we counted the voters, then the votes.
—Alderman Michael
(Hinky Dink) Kenna, boss of the old first ward.

GAMBLERS, PICKPOCKETS, OPIUM PEDDLERS, FOOTPADS, SLUGGERS, MADams, pimps, panders, and plug uglies roamed Chicago streets in 1907. Despite some notable attempts at reform (mostly around election time), Chicago, that "Gem of the Prairie," continued to be America's wickedest city.

There has always been a red-light district (so named because of the red beacon light outside many of the houses). The location shifted since the 1850s, when incensed Chicagoans took matters into their own hands and burned out the Sands one night. Little Cheyenne (when Cheyenne finally developed its own vice district, they called it *Chicago*), Hell's Half Acre, and the Hair Trigger Block along Randolph Street came and went. But none lasted as long as the levee. The name suggested a genteel southern tradition of riverboats, gamblers, card sharps, and their ladies.

There were no riverboats, but there were lots of card sharps and women. In the annals of Chicago vice, there existed two levees. The first was spawned in the shadow of the Loop office buildings and within view of the Union League Club members. The old tenderloin sprang up before the World's Columbian Exposition. It existed on the southern tip of the Loop, bounded on the east by Dearborn Street, with Clark on the west and Harrison on the north. This was known as the wicked Custom House Place Levee.

Within the confines of the first levee stood thirty-seven houses of prostitution (which had the famous "dipping houses," narrow little closets which allowed a victim to be mugged and robbed by the girl and her pimp), forty-six saloons, eleven pawn brokers, an obscene book store, and a shooting gallery. This was the area ruled by Carrie Watson (who entertained only the best Chicagoans) and Vina Fields, a large black madam who fed the hungry and destitute during the 1893 panic. Chicago's red-light district provided sporting entertainment, good wagering, a drink or two, and was the proving ground for "Chicago May" Churchill Sharpe, queen of the criminals, who later recalled those times: "The mere mention of the details of some of the circuses is unthinkable. I think Rome at its worst had nothing on Chicago during those lurid days."

Into this cauldron of iniquity came William Stead, the bearded editor of the English journal, the *Review of Reviews*. He came to Chicago in November 1893 to see firsthand the prevailing conditions. He visited the Custom House Levee and, by chance, wandered into Hank North's saloon on Clark Street between Harrison and Polk. North was an ex-minstrel who sheltered unemployed vagrants in his bar, men left destitute by the Panic of 1893. A man of Stead's refinement and dress proved an inviting target. The bums rushed him, but North took a bottle of seltzer water and doused them before they could get to Stead. "Back away, boys! This is Mr. Stead from England!" he said. One of the vagrants was Frank Brown, an ex-vaudeville performer known as "Brownie, King of the Bums." Brown talked with Stead at length about the real Chicago—not the Prairie Avenue Chicago of Marshall Field, but the real city, where the bums flopped at the Harrison Street lockup. That was the prison with floors of stone with one gutter providing its only sanitation. The insane were mixed with street walkers, pickpockets, and homeless children.

Hank North provided Stead with lodging at the St. Lawrence Hotel. His conference in the Central Music Hall in November aroused the sensibility of Chicago. It stirred the first step toward meaningful reform. Each night, he returned to the hotel where he was joined by the barkeep and the vagrant. Together they wrote *If Christ Came to Chicago*, a shocking view of the city that listed the addresses of the whorehouses and who collected the rents. Stead claimed that only two of Chicago's sixty-eight aldermen were not boodlers. He even named the millionaires who chose to avoid paying their taxes. When the book appeared in the spring of 1894, 100,000 copies were sold in a little more than a week.

The levee existed in the crooked first ward, bordered by elegant Prairie Avenue on the east and the southern fringe of the Loop on the north. This was the third precinct, controlled by a swaggering Irishman who wore a green waistcoat checked with white. In 1892, Bathhouse John Coughlin took his place in the city council, and Chicago politics was never the same. He was fond of horse racing, poetry, and the political sharps he met while working as a sauna "rubber" at the Palmer House. Coughlin was a real dandy of the pearl-button era.

He was born in a tough Irish section known as Connelly's Patch in 1857 (located west of the Loop near Adams and Monroe). In his day, Coughlin marched with the precision-drilled First Ward Democratic Marching Club, paying 50¢ for each vote that came his way. When William Jennings Bryan won his unflagging support in 1896, Coughlin inlaid silver dollars into his bar to promote the "16 to 1" campaign. (Or in Coughlin's view, sixteen parts whiskey, one part water.) The Bath was a living caricature of a political era that spanned the Civil War to World War II, when most of the big-city machines collapsed. (In Chicago, the era was considerably longer.) His larceny was so blatant, his style so outrageous, his charm so infectious that even Lincoln Steffens was inclined to forgive him. In July 1903, Steffens arrived in Chicago to investigate the city for his monthly reports on municipal government in *McClure's Magazine*. After pronouncing Pittsburgh "a city ashamed" and Minneapolis "downfallen," Steffens interviewed the Bath. For days Coughlin was not himself. He feared what the journalist had to say about Chicago. The city escaped his wrath. Conditions would never be perfect, but Chicago was managed well.

> Chicago should be celebrated among American cities for reform, not moral fits and political uprisings, not reform waves that wash the "best people" into office to make fools of themselves and subside, leaving the machine stronger than ever; none of these aristocratic disappointments of popular government, but reform that reforms. Slow, sure, political, democratic reform, by the people for the people. That is what Chicago has. It has found a way! I don't know that is the way. All that I am sure of is that Chicago has something to teach every city and town in the country, including Chicago.

Coughlin was pleased. "I found him a square, honest man, who seems to know his business. What we talked about is a personal, not a public matter. I would be the last to besmirch the fair name of Chicago. But I will say that I took a liking to Mr. Steffens."

George "King" Cole of the Municipal Voter's League earned Lincoln Steffens' praise. When Cole outlined the Bath's various schemes, he earned *his* permanent scorn. "In this here report, you said I was born in Waukegan. I was born in Chicago and am proud of it," he said.

"If the MVL ever endorsed you, John, I'd sue 'em," added Michael "Hinky Dink" Kenna, the real brains behind the bluster. He was the "little fellow," a tough Irish saloon keeper who was the first-ward committeeman from 1891 to 1897, at which time he took his place in the city council.

He called his saloon the Workingman's Exchange. For many of the unemployed vagrants who would not find work after the World's Fair closed, the second floor of his saloon was the only home they knew. Kenna spent $30 a day feeding his hungry army, while serving up beers to thirsty patrons in a beaker with two handles. The glass held a full quart. Hinky Dink explained to the French writer Jules Huret that "Politics is business. This is where we make voters. They drink 12,000 glasses of beer a week in my place." Huret toured America in 1904 to observe American culture. Where else but Kenna's place?

For several minutes, Huret watched a slow trickle follow a lazy path down the length of the bar. He asked Kenna the rationale for leaving a faucet on when no one was using it. "The running water makes 'em thirsty. That makes better business." When prohibition finally closed the building, it was estimated that Kenna sold 175,000 barrels of beer in his time.

There was money to be made in the first, so Kenna aligned with Coughlin to form a powerful political machine that lasted in one form or another for 45 years. The voting lists contained 40,000 names. In the early 1900s, the MVL pushed for an ordinance to expand the ward southward to 31st Street, adding 22,000 more names to the list. The aldermen of the first successfully fought this measure, preserving and controlling the voting lists till *they* decided to retire.

Open vice was not only tolerated in Chicago but was sanctioned by those in power. Through operatives like Dennis "The Duke" Cooney, the tribute was paid each month while the cops looked the other way. Cooney ran the Rex Cafe at 2138 S. State Street, while directing the police of South Clark Street, and Cottage Grove Avenue. In later years he served a new master—Al Capone. Cooney was Kenna's bag man. While the little fellow may not have actually handled the resort money, Cooney did.

When Carter Harrison the younger was re-elected in 1903, the reformers urged him to clean up the Custom House Levee. There were reports of respectable girls being led to an immoral life in the vice dens along Plymouth Court. It took two years, but in 1905, State's Attorney John J. Healy pushed most of the brothels and winerooms south. A city ordinance defined a wineroom as "an interior shut off from the general public by doors, screens, curtains, portieres, or other devices." The code forbade the dining and drinking of persons numbering less than four in a room connected to a bar. The barkeeps paid lip service to this code by moving potted palms into the doorways.

The city council curbed the activities of the dance-hall operators by passing a strong measure on March 1, 1905, that banned sales of liquor after 1 A.M. Sales of alcohol in a public hall where men and women mingled were also forbidden (but rarely enforced). The dance hall was popularized by newly arrived immigrants, all the more reason for the council to take action. "These foreigners bring their native customs over here and inject them into our society. Everything here ought to be United States and in conformity with our customs and laws," Alderman Dunn said.

A new and more open levee sprung up between 18th and 22nd Streets. The change was slow to occur, and when it did, the neighborhood organized. Vivien Palmer, a resident of the Prairie Avenue section which stood directly east of the levee recalled that the first disorderly houses appeared during the World's Fair. Before the vice lords arrived, Armour Avenue, Dearborn, and 19th Streets were dotted with pleasing little cottages. But these houses were "built over" with glazed brick with new additions. Real-estate agents welcomed the encroachment of the wealthy vice agents, and so did the landlords.

Citizen's vigilance committees from the first and second wards engaged an attorney, Louis J. Behan, who pressed for grand-jury indictments in 1903. Securing an indictment and winning a conviction were two separate issues. In May of that year, twenty-four resort keepers were paraded before Judge Mack, and twenty-three were summarily disposed of. Ike Bloom, proprietor of the notorious Freiberg's Dance Hall was the only case the state attorney was sure would result in a conviction. Bloom had violated the 1 A.M. closing five dif-

The Why Not, Bucket of Blood, House of All Nations, Bed Bug Row, and the Old 92 were but a few of the bordellos that comprised the old levee.

ferent times in 1903, but this time the state lined up nine witnesses who agreed to testify against him.

Bloom reached the witnesses. He took them to his dance hall, bought them all dinner, and coached them on their testimony. When they got into court, they all suffered severe lapses of memory. Judge Mack instructed the jury to return a verdict of not guilty.

Attorney Behan quit the committee because of a row with a private detective employed by the citizens. This was pretty typical of the reform movements that fought the levee from 1900 to 1915. They succeeded in arousing public support but could never agree on principle. Internal bickering frequently doomed their best efforts. The grand jury of July 1903 recommended the indictments of the property owners and landlords of the district, but took no personal action in that direction. Conditions in the district were that way because the police were ignorant of the true situation. Why was that? A juror refused to comment, but he put his hand behind him with palm upraised. "Although we don't say so, I think it is like this. No, I don't lay that sort of thing up against the patrolmen. They would do their duty if they were permitted to do so," the man said.

The fashionable Prairie Avenue section was bounded by 16th Street, Calumet, Indiana, and Michigan Avenues. Their way of life, their insulated community, and leisurely paces were permanently disrupted by the coming of the vice district. The vigilance committee could do very little if the police would not cooperate. They were instructed to arrest any prostitutes who ventured past the elevated tracks along Wabash Avenue and into Prairie Avenue. As the levee district grew between 1902 and 1912, this became increasingly difficult. It took several years of resistance, but the residents finally abandoned their neighborhood for more tranquil suburban settings.

The newly arrived Custom House gang included Frank Wing, Roy Jones, Ed Weiss, and George Little, who managed Jack Johnson's affairs. During this changing time, the two vice factions remained at peace with each other as the 22nd Street regulars welcomed the interlopers to the district.

This was the cocksure era, where Americans felt good about themselves and their country. America was becoming a colossus. The prairies and farmlands were surrendering influence to the growing cities. The promise of love and romance was a strong one for the shop clerks and domestics who looked for their release in the promise of the night. The city beckoned the nation's youth, so the doors of the levee swung open.

Inside the Levee

Thousands of girls came to Chicago each year in search of the ideal life denied them in the small towns of the Middle West. "Should a girl marry a man who makes fifteen dollars a week?" the *Chicago Tribune* asked its readers in 1907. The answer was yes, of course!

Like Theodore Dreiser's *Sister Carrie*, thousands of nameless, faceless girls stepped off the train at Dearborn Street to find such a man. They did not find the streets laden with gold, but rough cobblestone dusty in the summer and a hopeless muck in the winter. Overhead, the imposing clock tower of the train station signaled the advent of another Chicago day. Chicago welcomed each new addition, but in the mad scurry to make money, it did not take the time to help the newcomer negotiate her way.

Girls found their way to the garment district sweat shops. They were hellholes with a solitary light bulb swinging overhead, without windows and proper ventilation. Imagine the summer of 1901, a time when July temperatures reached 118 in the Loop. Ice chunks that were cut in the winter from Lake Michigan ice floes were being depleted. Some hospitals and public places used air convection over this ice to cool the air, but the system was not widely used till years later.

Public buildings were not yet required by law to provide screened windows, so flies and bugs flew in, bringing disease. Luckier girls found employment at the big department stores like Siegel-Cooper, Marshall Field, the Fair, and the Boston Store. Here they were robbed of their dignity and earnings by floor walkers who imposed fines for every minor infraction.

Department stores paid the girls just six dollars a week. Further down State Street stood Whiskey Row, a thriving vice district temporarily closed by Chief John Collins during the 1905 cleanup. By 1907, the area between Van Buren and Polk was tenanted by a curious assortment of winerooms, penny parlors, dime "museums," nickel theatres, and arcades. There was the Senate, the Little White City (where Little Egypt danced in the window), the Grand Palace, and Andy Craig's Tivoli. Craig was a syndicate bondsman at the Harrison lockup, the head of the infamous Pickpocket's Trust, and a keeper of a disreputable house. Most of the low dives had since abandoned Whiskey Row by 1907, but the nickeloriums remained.

Small boys hustled pedestrians for nickels so they could go inside to watch the flickers. These early movies were nothing more than two-act sermons with such titles as *Jealousy into Madness, Mary Dear,* and *Retribution*. They were heavy handed, violent, and sometimes racy. *Jealousy into Madness* was called a portrait of "real life" by its producers. A peasant wife in France is kissed by a handsome stranger who enters her kitchen while her husband's back is turned. She warns the impertinent stranger to mind his manners, but she later steals out of the kitchen to meet him in the forest. The husband follows his wife to an isolated spot, where she kisses the stranger. The sight turns him stark raving mad, and he returns from the forest a maniac. The wife and her lover have him committed to a local asylum. The pair then come to visit him in his cell, and together they *mock* him. The crazy man is locked in a basement cell where he is attacked by rats. He manages to escape, returns to his old house, and finds his wife and the stranger. He strangles his wife, kills the man, and shoots a policeman who tries to subdue him. He then kills himself, thus ending a *Jealousy into Madness*.

Reformers called for suppression of these films, but the real danger was not in their content but the type of people who frequented the theatres. Here the cadet (or pimp) cultivated with a limited amount of charm would stand outside the saloons and nickeloriums recruiting girls for work in the levee. An "early warning" system was devised in the district when a constable strolled by. The cadet would tip his hat and press a doorbell cleverly concealed behind an awning or electric sign. The inmates inside would scatter through a maze of secret panels and tunnels.

Honest cops faced a real dilemma during the vice crackdowns. Discerning between a legitimate cafe and an illegal wineroom was not the easiest task. Sometimes the levee vice mongers sneaked into the heart of the downtown business district and operated under the noses of the law.

George Silver was one of the 22nd Street pilgrims. In 1903, he opened up a $20,000 levee showplace called the Maxim. He neglected to secure a liquor license for it, bragging of his "pull" with Mayor Harrison. When Captain William O'Brien visited the place, Silver told him that things were squared "by the boys downtown." The next day, the city collector called O'Brien to tell him that Silver was being granted a license and that he should be left alone. It's one thing to have clout, but quite another to flaunt it to the people who can take it away. Silver printed invitations, asking his customer's to visit "the mayor's place." Three days later, the mayor revoked the license.

"My pull is all right," Silver said. "It's them folks in the city hall that don't understand it. This is a bad, bad business." Harrison charged Silver with having violated the midnight closing and for advertising his place in a "disgusting fashion." Undraped females were painted on the outside signs. Not even Kenna or Coughlin was willing to help. Silver's mouth had got him into trouble. "I can't stand for this fellow any longer," Kenna said. "He isn't satisfied with running a straight business like the rest of us, and he must suffer for his nonsense."

Silver took his case to the courts. He found a friend in old Judge Gary, who restored his license. "I take it that it is the custom for employees after their nocturnal labors to drink a glass of beer before going to bed," Gary said. "That is sometimes the practice in private families." Silver promised to behave, but he was probably the only levee dive keeper to be turned out of the district on his ear.

Silver opened a new place at Clark and Randolph, in the heart of the Loop. The notorious tenderloin could not stomach him, but the downtown businessmen tolerated his presence. But then, Carter Harrison was no longer mayor. Fred Busse, the ex-saloon keeper, allowed Silver to run his Rialto as he pleased.

The *Chicago Tribune* of August 18, 1907, described Silver's place as "a bar and wineroom in comparison with which many of the saloons and winerooms of the levee district would have no cause to blush." At any hour of the night, ragtime music was heard from the basement wineroom. Silver built a polished mahogany bar facing Clark Street. Above the bar were stiffly posed photographs of actors, pugilists, jockeys, and the same Jezebels that helped close his Dearborn Street dive.

From the lower level, mixed sounds of laughter and rousing songs filtered upstairs. Business was up. Women of various ages cavorted from one table to the next, enjoying a man's company only as long as he bought drinks. Most of the girls were still in their teens. As the hour of closing approached, Silver enjoined his patrons to move "further back" into the secluded wineroom area. When the 1 A.M. closing drew near, Silver evicted the people he did not know. The marquee lights were dimmed so the police would not notice. In the wineroom, intimate little coteries sipped champagne, told ribald stories, and enjoyed Silver's hospitality. This was a typical wineroom. And despite his protests, it was exactly the kind of place where the "cadet" (or pimp) took his new girls for a drink and a song.

Such a man promised her love, a good time, and sometimes marriage—before her final downfall in a "breaking-in house." Here she was raped repeatedly and kept under guard. Sometimes the new inmates were introduced to cocaine and morphine. Some of them passively accepted their surroundings without the use of drugs.

The tales of the white slavers filled the daily papers. Maude Van Dusen, a thirty-five-year-old school teacher from Falls City, Nebraska was obsessed with the notion that they were out to capture her. Clutching her Bible to her breast, the fearful woman jumped twenty floors to her death from atop the McCormick Building on Michigan Avenue, November 25, 1912. On her body, they found a 35,000 word typewritten autobiography. She described her sister, who was lured into prostitution. She also implored Mayor Harrison and Chief McWeeney to do something.

Though stories about them were exaggerated, white slavers did ply their trade in Chicago. A 1910 survey conducted by the vice commission showed that most girls entered the life of their own accord. Poverty, drink, and weariness of the work drudge were some of the more common reasons given. Thelma and Robert Chrisman traveled the department stores to discuss with the sales clerks their "future."

The vicious clique that captured Caterina Bressi was not as inclined toward gentle persuasion. Caterina must have been beautiful. Santina Pizzi, a refined Chicago lady who visited her home in the vineyards outside of Naples apparently thought so. The sixteen-year-old girl was the daughter of simple well-meaning peasants, who listened to the stories about this magical place in America. A girl could have a chance there. Santina Pizzi wore fine clothes. She spoke Italian. And now she was willing to give their daughter an opportunity. Caterina was given $100 for third-class steerage on the White Star Line by the kindly lady. Through the mist, her first view of America was the Statue of Liberty. Optimism and hope must have filled her soul. At dockside, she was met by two ropers, and her image of America suddenly changed. They took her by train to Chicago, careful to sit on each side of her in case she made a dash. The ropers delivered her to 407 Clark Street, the domain of Baptista Pizzi, Italian whoremaster.

On the second floor of his bar, she was broken in by several men. Her clothes were taken, and she was given expensive finery to entertain clients with. The garments were valued at $600, and she was told that she had to "earn" her keep to pay back the debt. She tried to run, but was slashed across the face. When the house physician was unable to control the bleeding, she was taken to the county hospital where she was guarded by the two pimps. In a few weeks she was released, but her face was disfigured for life. Later, a vice raid led by reformer Edwin Sims rescued her from the house. Caterina was locked in jail, afraid to tell her story. When it leaked out, the U.S. Government paid her fare back to Naples. Pizzi was found guilty of pandering on June 3, 1910.

Maurice Van Bever and his wife Julia were among the first levee bosses found guilty of white slaving. They operated two adjoining dives at Dearborn and 21st Streets. Theirs was a life of relative ease. The Van Bevers were frequently seen motoring around the lakefront in a brougham with footman.

Van Bever's white slave ring was broken up on October 13, 1909, when federal agents arrested him outside the Chamber of Commerce Building in the Loop. "Are you Van Bever?" federal agent Clifford Roe asked him. "I am." "You are under arrest." He was taken to the Des Plaines station, where he posted a $2,000 bail while telling reporters about his sterling past.

"I have always lived up to the order of the police department in having all the girls registered at the station. I was never arrested before." This followed the revelations of Mollie Hart, wife of Michael Hart, a bartender at Van Bever's Paris resort at 2101 Armour Avenue. Dick Tyler (also a bartender at Van Bever's White City Saloon) and Hart were sent to St. Louis to procure girls for levee employ. When the victim was selected, she would be taken to East St. Louis, where she would be fed some golden lies about the excellent employment prospects in Chicago. This meeting would usually take place in a quiet hotel, so the police wouldn't be suspicious. When the girl agreed to leave with them, she would be taken to another small town further down the railroad line. At that point, she would board the train for Chicago and get off in Englewood. Julia Van Bever would meet the party at the train station, and from there the girl would be driven to a downtown hotel where she was picked up by a resort keeper. Elaborate precautions were taken because the police routinely watched the downtown train stations for cadets soliciting single women.

"A man can't hold a job in the south side levee unless he is willing to go out and get girls," Mike Hart admitted under direct examination. "It is the practice of those who manage to get any girls, and owing to the reformers, that is becoming more and more difficult every day to get off the train with the girls at some suburb of Chicago and either place them in a hotel or take a cab and drive them into the city at once."

These facts came to light when a nineteen-year-old St. Louis girl named Sarah Joseph was released from Van Bever's resort. The girl was known to Julia Van Bever, and at her insistence, Mike Hart was sent to procure her. He was promised a new suit of clothes if he could bring the girl back with him. "See that Jew girl and make sure she comes back with you," Maurice said. But Mollie found out about a police inquiry into the St. Louis connection, so she wrote him a note of warning.

> Dear Mike: Take the first train and come right home. Come by yourself. Tell your brother that if he can get a few girls he can send for anything he wants. It would be better for them to come by themselves just now.
> Mollie

Remembering that new suit of clothes, Hart wired Julia Van Bever. She sent him $20 and two train tickets. Mollie picked her up at the train station, and on the way to the resort, she coached the girl on how to answer the policeman's questions. Realizing her plight, Sarah told them she wanted to return home. When they arrived at the Paris, Van Bever told her that a girl that looked that good ought to do well for herself. Clifford Roe later brought the girl to the stand, and she told of her misfortunes at the hands of the ring.

Q—What did Maurice Van Bever tell you when he saw you that afternoon?

A—He said to tell the police I had been in a resort before I came here.

Q—Did you say whether or not you wanted to stay there after you saw the place?

A—No, sir, I did not.

Q—Did you tell Van Bever this?

A—Yes. He said I would like it once I got used to it.

Q—Did you tell him you wanted to leave?

A—Yes. He said that he wanted to get me some clothes and then I could go. Later he said I couldn't go until I had paid him what I owed.

Q—Didn't you tell the police you were 21 years old?

A—Yes, because I was told to. I am only 19. I told the police too that I had been in a place like that before, but I had not.

Q—Didn't you know that was a resort when you went there?

A—No, sir. I realized it the first night and wanted to go home.

Q—Why didn't you?

A—I had no money.

Q—But men gave you money.

A—I didn't see any. I got checks.

Q—Didn't you get any money for selling drinks?

A—No, I got checks.

In a similar case, Van Bever and his wife were accused of bringing a girl named Maud Grace from St. Louis. Van Bever, alias W.H. Clark, and Julia, alias Madam Maurice, were sentenced to one year in the Bridewell and a $1,000 fine. David Garfinkle, a twenty-nine-year-old connection in St. Louis was given six months for aiding and abetting the illicit traffic. "We have thoroughly cleaned up our docket along this line," Clifford Roe beamed. "In this Van Bever conviction we have put an end to a regularly organized traffic in girls between Chicago and St. Louis."

However, Van Bever found some loopholes in the law. He was arrested again in November of 1910. The couple brought *another* St. Louis girl named Pearl Sypher to the Paris. They were arrested shortly before they were to depart for an extended European vacation.

Van Bever was not the only call-house operator who attempted to disguise his occupation. In early June of 1907, a police tip led to the arrest of Leona Garrity, proprietor of two houses at 75 and 83 Peoria Street, in Mike Heitler's district. It seemed like just another white-slave arrest at the time. Garrity lured a fifteen-year-old girl named Belle Winters to the resort.

After she was arraigned on a charge of pandering, her true identity was revealed. In her "other" life, she was Mrs. Lemuel Schlotter, resident of Green Bay Road in Glencoe. Her husband was a wealthy jewelry merchant, but her fancy neighbors quickly disavowed any association with her. Madam Schlotter was a levee woman with high ideals, but now her hopes for a respectable life was dashed. Her husband took their son George to the West Coast, while she sold all her furniture to a second-hand dealer on the west side. As she stood in the train station in Glencoe waiting for the train that would take her back into Chicago, her neighbors hooted, jeered, and yelled profanities at her.

Before 1907, the term *white slave* was virtually unknown to mainstream America. Federal laws protected immigrant girls from the dockside ropers, but there was little that could be done for the girls transported across state lines. Wiley J. Phillips, chairman of the White Slave Traffic Committee, reported that 278 girls under the age of fifteen were rescued from levee dens during a two-month period in 1907. Chicago was the midwestern corridor of the illegal traffic, with Seattle as the departure point for girls shipped to Europe and the Orient.

Direct pressure from Rufus Simmons and Reverend M.P. Boynton of the Midnight Mission resulted in the passage of the Mann Act, sponsored by Chicago Congressman James Mann. President Taft signed the bill into law on June 26, 1910, after months of bargaining and trading off. At the heart of the issue was whether Congress had the authority to regulate interstate commerce of persons, not commodities. The law was challenged by those who had an interest in commercial vice, but its constitutionality was upheld.

When Van Bever made the move to the 22nd Street district, he found himself in direct competition with "Sunny" Jim Colosimo, a robust paisano fond of paper suits, a pot of his own spaghetti, and the melodic operas of Caruso, Tetrazzini, and Titta Ruffo.

Colosimo was just one of thousands of "white wings" who carried pails of water to railroad section hands during the early 1890s. He landed a city job as a street cleaner, catching the eye of labor racketeer "Dago" Mike Corrozzo (who was arrested for complicity in the Moss Enright murder in 1920). During those lean and hungry days, Colosimo met the gamblers at Pat O'Malley's saloon at Polk and Clark. He acquired his tastes for pugilism, politics, and pinochle, not necessarily in that order. When he lost his money, O'Malley allowed him to flop for the night in the back room. Through Corrozzo, he organized the street sweepers into a formidable political organization. Colosimo recognized the power of Kenna and Coughlin and worked with them when he opened his own levee dive.

In 1902, he married Victoria Moresco, one of eighteen children born to a stonecutter's wife. He was a street inspector; she was a sales clerk. She was older than he and more experienced in the ways of the new land. Each night she read the classics to him while Italian opera droned in the background. Victoria was fat, homely, but devoted to her man. Together they opened their own place at Armour Avenue and 21st Street, appropriately named the Victoria. Colosimo acquired culture while he made himself rich. Enrico Caruso was a personal friend who always insisted on adjoining suites for Colosimo while staying at New York's Knickerbocker Hotel. Colosimo opened his famous cafe on Wabash Avenue in 1910. It became a premier Chicago night spot, which was a favorite of the literary, show, and criminal sets. On any given night, it was not unusual to find Clarence Darrow, George Ade, and Barrett O'Hara rubbing elbows with "Loving Putty" Julius Annixter, "Monkey Face" Charley Genker, and Mont Tennes. The daring nature of Colosimo's attracted the young thrill seekers who were out to see something. Big Jim's growing affluence also caught the attention of the Black Hand.

When Frank Razzina, member of the secret society known as the Comorra, was sent to jail in 1907, he made the sign of death when asked about Colosimo. For these reasons, Johnny Torrio was brought in to oversee things in 1909.

Suggestive songs, a street lit by gaslight, and young boys hawking newspapers and selling chewing gum from a street corner. Such was the south-side levee in 1910, and the House of all Nations, the Little Green House, Bed Bug Row, the Bucket of Blood, the Everleigh Club, Freiberg's Dance Hall, and Ed Weiss's Capitol were the principal attractions. Isaac Gitelson, better known in the district as Ike Bloom, converted his German Weinstube into a dance hall and wineroom in 1895. It became the command post of the levee, the one place considered "untouchable" by the cops. From the back room of Freiberg's, orders were issued by Coughlin and Kenna, who operated through Sol Friedman, Ike Bloom's brother-in-law. Friedman handled the whiskey, taxicab, and clothing concessions in the levee, while the dive keepers were required to take out their insurance from Coughlin's own firm. Payoffs were made in the private office of Freiberg's, and each service carried a precise fee. To stop an indictment for pandering, it would cost $1,000. But the district was segregated from the central city, and there was some attempt at regulation.

Two plainclothes detectives were assigned to the levee to "book" the names and addresses of the girls who lived there. The information was kept in a file at the 22nd Street station. Underaged girls were "coached" on how to answer the police questions by the keeper of the house. When the new prospect arrived at the bagnio (interviews were always conducted on the premises), she would invariably say that she was from out-of-town, had always led an immoral life, and was of the legal age. The booking system worked nicely for the resort keeper. When a girl was found to be underaged and an arrest was made, the dive keeper would say that the booking agents allowed her to stay. (Birth certificates and photographs were not required by the police, so the abuses of this system and graft potential were obvious).

Within the levee, there were extremes of good and bad taste. The California was a dollar-a-girl resort, built with sliding walls and a waiting room attended by a rotund black woman who urged the men on by saying, "Pick a baby, boys! Don't get glued to your seats!" The house was run by "Blubber" Bob Gray and his wife Therese McCafey. "Blubber" Bob's considerable girth got in the way, when he tried to escape Federal agents on August 27, 1909. Five women of Belgian, Canadian, and French extraction were arrested along with Gray, who was found protruding from the rear window, hopelessly stuck.

The Casino at 21st and Dearborn featured a wineroom that adjoined the private rooms. They were attended to by a woman who wore a ring of keys around her waist, admitting only those men who had paid the cover charge. The Capitol belonged to Weiss. White-vested waiters dashed about the barroom yelling the orders to the barkeeps. "Two pints at four!" Pasty-faced professional escorts sat against the wall, inbibing with their scarlet women, available for a price. A waiter greeted each new patron entering from the street. "Well, what do I see? What do I see?" signaling two girls, who escorted him to a table. The waiter slipped a "percentage check" on the table, while the girls got to know the man better. Each of them received ten cents on the dollar for all drinks served at the table. A mechanical piano played a lively song in the background, accompanied by a young black singer whose job was to encourage his customers to buy more beer.

Every house on the levee employed a "professor." Sometimes he worked as the roper or head cashier. Most of the time he was the piano man or balladeer, commonly known as the "coon shouter" to white America. These young blacks received $10 a week plus a percentage of the drinks. The songs they played and sang were suggestive in nature; a fusion of Caribbean black music and popular ballads. The music was "ragged time" or "ragtime" as it became known to the prewar generation. Ragtime's origins were in St. Louis, but quickly spread to the northern cities, where the bawdy houses accepted the black performers who were denied opportunity in the legitimate concert halls and theatres.

Ragtime was the first popular music art form of the new century. The mechanized rolls inside the player pianos were cheaply produced, which helped establish Scott Joplin, Tom Turpin, and the great Jelly Roll Morton as the virtuosos of the art. White America condemned the music, before Tin-Pan Alley sanitized it for John Philip Sousa. The quality was diluted, but classic ragtime, with its steady beat and syncopated melody, dominated the music scene for twenty years. On warm summer nights, the strains of the "Maple Leaf Rag" and Joplin's operatic "Guest of Honor" could be heard from the back alleys and streets of the south-side district.

It was estimated that 7 million bottles of beer were consumed in Chicago in 1910. Booze was the reason for everything. It was bought by the resort keepers for four-and-a-half cents a pint and was sold for a quarter to one dollar per bottle. Customers frequently received their beer laced with morphine, a drug all but impossible to detect in an autopsy.

Drugs kept girls in the life. Four levee druggists sold four pounds of morphine and six ounces of cocaine each month, while another peddled 500 tablets a week of morphine sulphate. The girls were called "air walkers," a comotose state brought on by an insidious cocaine imitation known as encaine.

Since syphilis was an obvious hazard of the trade, the houses relied on their own doctors to administer confidential cures for the girls. In the years before the passage of the Pure Food and Drug Act, patent medicines claiming to cure all forms of social disease were advertised in the most respectable papers. Who can forget Hood's Sarsaparilla and the One and Only Wizard Oil? Both were advertised as a cure for gout and venereal disease. Confidential cures for V.D. would be tacked to the bathroom walls of levee houses. One reported "cure" could be found at the house doctor's office for charges that often reached $400. The cure was usually a vile red mouthwash laced with alcohol and morphine that may have cured the outward symptoms at least.

More drug addicts roamed city streets of Chicago in 1900 than at any other time in the city's long history. The patent medicine companies knew no regulation, but at least they cannot be accused of not having a conscience. An 1895 advertisement in the *Chicago Tribune* proclaimed that there was a sure cure for the morphine habit. Just write to Doctor Carlos Bruisard at 439 Race Street, in Cincinnati for the remedy. For a small fee, of course.

When the sad tale of a drug-related death or a wayward girl's plunge into prostitution hit the morning papers, people traced it to a weakness of character or some natural badness in her. When the story included the scions of wealth, the idle sons of the prominent families, shame and disgrace often brought on reform.

In 1905, they whispered about the suicide of Marshall Field, Jr. The night before, he allegedly spent a night at the Everleigh Club. The next morning he put a bullet in his head while sitting alone in the study at the Prairie Avenue mansion. The *Tribune* concluded that he was examining his gun, and it had been an unfortunate accident. (There were rumors that Field had been involved in some gun play and had been dragged from the levee to the mansion.)

On January 10, 1910, they found Nathaniel Ford Moore, the twenty-six-year-old heir to the Rock Island Railroad fortune, dead at Madam Victoria Shaw's place at 2012 S. Dearborn. Moore led a riotous life. He spent his fortune doing what he did best—loafing. A golf pro at age twenty, Moore was one of the upstart rich of Chicago that so offended the more respectable families of New York. In 1905, Moore staged an after-theatre party at the New York restaurant, Rector's, that cost $20,000. Diamond sleeve cuff links were given to the gentlemen, and a string of pearls were offered to the ladies. Moore hired a full orchestra, and while they played a lively tune, the host slipped $20 dollar gold pieces down the dress backs of chorus girls who dined at the table. The gold pieces had been frozen on ice by the chefs at Moore's request.

This scandal was too much for the gentle Helen Fargo Moore, the suffering young wife he left behind. She vowed to leave him, but a reconciliation was made at the Moore's country estate on the shore of Lake Geneva. Nathaniel promised to change his ways. "I want to lead a better life. Loafing makes one very tired, you know. I'm going to try some hard work," he said. So Moore went to work in the freight department of his father's railroad. Daddy was impressed. He rewarded his son with $100,000 on his twenty-first birthday. But Moore went back to his old ways. Along with J. Ogden Armour's son, Nathaniel hired a train and commandeered it across the California wilderness at break-neck speed so that the young man would not miss a fancy Santa Barbara dinner party. Guests were amused when Moore and friend appeared in coat and tails at the required hour.

But James Hobart Moore and wife were taking their winter retreat when Nathaniel met his death at Vic Shaw's place. Moore spent the evening of January 8 at the College Inn before repairing to the intimacy of the Everleigh Club.

Since Moore paid for his entertainment from checks drawn from the First National Bank of New York, the keepers were anxious to receive his business. The hidden side of Moore, perhaps unknown to his wife, was that he was a morphine addict. After leaving the Everleigh resort around 1 A.M., a sottish Moore staggered over to the Shaw place in the company of his chauffeur Frank Fitzgerald.

Moore liked his morphine by syringe. After a brief tête-a-tête with the girls, he went to bed, assisted by Nina Webster, Hattie Harris, Minnie Miller, and Pearl Dorset. Victoria Shaw and Roy Jones returned from the Studebaker Theatre at 3 A.M. but saw nothing unusual about having Moore as their overnight guest.

At 5 P.M. the next day, the body was discovered. Jones told the girls to scram while he thought about what to do next. One idea was to unload the body on Minna and Ada Everleigh. But the sisters were tipped off before they could do that. So Lieutenant Kelleher and Captain Cudmore of the 22nd Street district were summoned along with Moore's doctor.

"Nat Moore was a fine fellow," Vic Shaw told reporters. "He was here a month ago with an actress, and that's the last I saw of him." Jones said that he sent all the girls packing to China and that he and his wife had quit this business and were now leading better lives. The heat was on again.

A coroner's jury backed up the examining physician by concluding that Moore's drug-related death was due to some heart problems. Dr. C.M. McKenna, who had treated Moore in the past, made the diagnosis. A watch, a pen knife, two rings, and $2.50 in cash were found on the body.

A hysterical Helen Moore secluded herself at the couple's apartment at 1104 Lake Shore Drive. They had just moved in, after spending $50 a day living at the LaSalle Hotel. A guard was put around the place to keep reporters away, while the vacationing Moores sped home.

There would be no more lazy golf afternoons at the Exmoor Country Club, no more motor trips through the capitals of Europe, and no more New York theatre parties. Nat Moore, all-around good sport, was dead. The widow had only one request. She wanted her late husband buried in the old purple robe he had so loved.

Levee Low Life

The First Ward Ball

Vice and reform are Chicago traditions. Stricken with a dash of guilt, the city has made efforts to purge itself of the corruption that extended from the corridors of city hall to the lowest levee dives. They believed that the answer to wide-open vice was segregation. Police regimes controlled the Loop winerooms and swept out the gamblers when prudence demanded it, but the south-side levee remained untouched. Since there seemed to be no way to rid the city of vice, why not confine it to one district?

But there was one yearly event that seemed to offend the reformers the most. It was the annual First Ward Ball, ostensibly held to raise money for the political war chest of Kenna and Coughlin. During the 1890s, the ball was staged at Freiberg's for the benefit of "Lame Jimmy," Carrie Watson's crippled pianist. There was a profit potential in this, as well as an open invitation to debauch. Madams, call girls, and sluggers sat in the private boxes alongside of politicians, businessmen, and society slummers.

In 1892, a Harrison Street detective shot another officer named Louis Arado, over $1 while reveling at Freibergs. The public clamor that followed forced a temporary end to the ball. But a great scheme like this wouldn't die that easily. The site was shifted to the First Regiment Armory, and then the Chicago Coliseum on Wabash Street. It was here that the ball attained its legendary proportions.

Plans for the ball began in the fall. The social committee was a who's who of Chicago vice. Gambler Pat O'Malley, an early ally of Mont Tennes in the 1907 gambler's war, and Ferdinand Buxbaum, owner of the after-hours Marlborough Hotel, where the levee girls took their customers, belonged to the committee. Other ball planners included the convicted pickpocket Andy Craig (whose Tivoli lured the downtown salesgirls to a disorderly life), John Dineen, the State Street saloon keeper, George Little, Jim Colosimo, Sol Friedman, and Ike Bloom.

The rental fee for the Coliseum was $1,000. That was secured through Alderman Charles Gunther, who headed the board of directors of the hall. Gunther's most significant contribution to Chicago culture was that he proposed the first State Street mall. He visualized a downtown mall free of livery, horse carriages, and trucks. The idea was far-sighted in 1897 but really happened in 1979.

Tickets were sold in the levee and every gambling den on the north, south, and west side. Attendance was required of everyone operating in the first ward. A dollar was the standard admission fee, but private boxes that circled the main floor were $5. To stimulate attendance, Coughlin and Kenna passed out free passes. But when the recipients got past the front door, they had to pay a 50¢ hat-check fee.

In 1907, Sol Friedman handled the booze concession. He told the waiter's union that a condition of employment for waiters would be a series of fees they had to pay, ranging from $5 for those serving the private boxes to a dollar for those serving those in the basement. The Chicago Federation protested, and an alliance with the cabbies union failed. When pressed for an accounting, Friedman explained that he needed the extra money to get "the price of a good set of clothes." The surcharge was tacked on because the ward organization needed extra cash for the upcoming 1908 spring elections.

And finally the great night arrived. The ball was usually held the second week of December. The 1907 affair was the tenth annual get together, and this one was a masquerade ball. There were 2 bands, 200 waiters, and 10,000 bottles of champagne being chilled in the ice house. The city council adjourned early after passing a resolution complimenting Coughlin on his dapper suit. Joining Coughlin at the ball was Tim Sullivan, New York boss of Tammany Hall, two congressmen, and the mayor of Kewanee, Illinois. The 22nd Street doves appeared in full force as Indian maidens, geisha girls sans skirts, and queens of the Nile. At midnight the Grand March commenced, signaling an abandonment of good taste and restraint. Masks were tossed aside as Coughlin led a parade around the dance floor with Minna and Ada Everleigh on each side. With the strains of the Bath's own arrangement, "Dear Midnight of Love," playing in the background, the levee's leading citizens held their heads high and paraded around the smoke-filled auditorium.

Women in silks and laces, diamonds and jewels cast aside the masks, and the real orgy began. The private boxes that surrounded the dance floor were immediately besieged by waiters carrying full cases of ale. Behind the boxes was a promenade, and in the annex next door a bar extended the length of the room.

It is hard to imagine what the First Ward Ball was really like, though President McKinley's head of secret service remarked that the Thieves Ball of London was a Sunday School party compared to this. Drinks were served till 3 A.M., by which time people were slumped over in their seats in a hopeless stupor. In the small hours of the morning, the women collapsed in their dancing partner's arms, while an army of pickpockets rifled the wallets of the unsuspecting.

The 1907 Ball netted the organization $40,000. Plans were made for a bigger and better 1908 event—but the next one would be the last. Arthur Barrage Farwell, the guardian of Hyde Park morals, issued strong protests to Mayor Busse and Police Chief George Shippey about the 1907 orgy. He was joined in the crusade by the congregation of the Grace Episcopal Church, which stood next to the coliseum. But Busse did not want to hurt his valuable political alliance with the Democrats, so the ball went on as scheduled the night of December 14.

But the night before the big event, a two-story frame shack that stood on the south side of the hall was dynamited by Dominick Ciago. It was the twenty-seventh bomb to be hurled in six months and probably had something to do with the gambler's war. The place was used as a storage facility by the coliseum operators and was the home of a vagabond known as Pietrowsky the Junkman. Bathhouse telephoned Hinky Dink, in whose honor the 1908 affair was to be staged. A statement was issued that blamed the reformers, but Coughlin vowed that the "Grand March will go off if it has to be under a tent."

It never got to that because Inspector Wheeler of the Harrison Street detail stationed 100 cops on the Wabash Avenue side. One-hundred-fifty ushers, decked out in blue satin ribbons and evening clothes, prodded people into the packed auditorium.

Cable cars rumbled past the coliseum, as mustachioed cops wearing stiff collars vainly tried to control the skittish horses they rode. Sidewalks were jammed with an amazing throng of people seeking access to the hall—madams in daring costumes, fuzzy-cheeked young men trying to look tough chewing a wad, city-hall hangers on, and the usual assortment of levee thugs pushed and shoved their way in. Standing in front of his flock and enjoying perhaps his finest moment was the Bath. In his familiar green suit, with the Dink at his side, Coughlin welcomed the prominent guests as they alighted from their hansom cabs.

Trying to capture their images for posterity, *Record-Herald* photographer Lyman Atwell and cartoonist Wyncie King set up a tripod and camera in the middle of Wabash Street. The photos would make good scandal in the morning papers. Coughlin's face suddenly took on a sour look. He pointed at them, and immediately a group of hired sluggers descended on King. Two burly cops from Harrison Street restrained Atwell while the sluggers pummeled him in the face and stomach. The camera was hurled at the cable car tracks, and it shattered to pieces. The film was quickly snatched and given to Coughlin. The order was given to clear out, so the beaten newsmen retreated before giving the cops a chance to arrest them.

All exits from the hall were padlocked, except one. That was used for ejections. The outside doors were locked when it was decided that the crowd inside violated existing fire laws. The mob outside beat on the doors, and a near riot ensued in which the *Tribune* reported that hats, bracelets, scarves, and furs were scattered about the ground. Inside it was even worse. Women who passed out from the lingering stench of cigar smoke were lifted over the heads of the crowd and passed from hand to hand until they were placed safely outside the only exit.

While the early evening was "spiritless and dull," the final part of the night was "a riot of unbridled license," the *Record-Herald* reported the next day. Girls cavorted in pink and blue tights, bathing suits, and costumes unfit in society. Reformer Dean Sumner was shocked to observe a levee whore wearing a nun's habit. Bathhouse slapped him on the back and offered him a round of champagne. But Sumner was gathering evidence and so refused.

"Hail, Hail, the Gang's All Here," was played as Coughlin and Kenna led out the final grand march. The smoke was so thick that it was hard to see the aldermen from the other side of the room. Eight men and three women were arrested that night, several of whom committed the unpardonable crime of sneaking in without a ticket. Champagne flowed like the Chicago River in April. Minna Everleigh ordered enough wine to start her own saloon, but the end soon came, and the First Ward Ball lapsed into memory. Wyncie King and Atwell brought suit against Coughlin and his bullies. But five ballots finally returned a verdict of not guilty against the Bath. "I would have gladly paid the 100 bucks to keep my friends out of the papers," he said. The same judge then sentenced a nineteen-year-old youth named Albert Frazer to four months in the Bridewell. He had stolen $1 to pay for the admission fee to the ball.

The ball was called off by Mayor Busse in 1909. In its place they staged the First Ward Concert, held December 13, 1909. Two-and-a-half hours of chamber music provided by Tony Fisher's band failed to inspire 4,000 snoring levee patrons, who were required to remove their hats and refrain from smoking. They heard "Annie Laurie" and "The Watch on the Rhine." Kenna looked sadly about. "Hell, this ain't like no First Ward Ball." Somehow, things would never be quite the same after Gipsy Smith stormed the ward. The First Ward Ball was the first thing to go.

Reform, with Regrets

He stepped off the train in October 1909, this wandering preacher who was part Elmer Gantry and part Harold Hill. His name was Rodney Smith, and he wore a fashionable handlebar mustache, had wavy dark hair, but was mostly malarky. He was born a gypsy near the forest of Epping, England, in 1860. Epping was a long way from the Sinai, but he said that, "I myself am inclined to believe that we are one of the lost tribes of Israel." Smith tried to imitate William Stead, the globe-trotting pacifist who believed his divine mission was to rescue levee bums, Congo slaves, Siberian convicts, and wayward girls. But Smith was an effective orator, and he had the backing of sixty Chicago churches when he promised to "shake the foundations of this city and move it forward to a better life."

"Gipsy" Smith planned to invade the levee with old-fashioned gospel and fire-and-brimstone preaching. He organized his forces during month-long meetings at the Seventh Regimental Armory. With a choir of 1,500 backing him up, Smith met Chicago for the first time the night of October 3. He gave an impassioned speech, and Chicago was aroused. A persistent crowd stood outside the hall unable to get seats. Mind you, this was no sporting event, horse race, or dance. In those days people attended lectures, and nothing was more captivating than an effective orator.

> You women are to blame. You are too afraid to risk your white reputations to help the woman that has fallen, but the demon that ruined her you will take into your homes, to your dinners, to meet your daughters. You will marry your daughter to a scoundrel if he can dress well and drive in an automobile.
>
> A man who visits the red light district by night has no right to associate with decent people in the daylight even though he may sit on the throne of a millionaire.

And when he was done preaching, Gipsy told the good folk that "if you don't like me, keep your mouth shut anyway." The *Tribune*, which spearheaded the Clean Chicago campaign, applauded. Big business that talked about reform gave Gipsy their support.

Gipsy wore a tricolored sash around his waist and a slouch hat. He was backed up by the Salvation Army band, mounted police, society swells, reformed drunks, and women in furs, when the procession left the armory at 9 P.M., October 18, 1909, bound for the levee. The *Tribune* claimed that no stranger crowd had gathered since the Haymarket Riot. It took nearly an hour to reach the 22nd Street district, by which time the mob swelled to an estimated 40,000. The bands played "Nearer My God to Thee" and "Where Is My Wandering Boy Tonight?" Answer: seeing the levee for the first time. As Minna Everleigh observed, "It's a shame to see all these nice boys down here for the first time."

Men and women stood shoulder to shoulder while inmates of the bagnios poked their heads out of the windows to watch the curious procession. Mounted police had all they could do keeping order as Gipsy walked backwards imploring the crowd to cast out Satan. But when Gipsy reached Armour Avenue, he was in for a surprise. The Everleigh Club, the California, the Jap House and all the rest were locked tightly and the shades were drawn. The word was out to lay low. But the saloons were legal, and they were operating full tilt. Barkeepers reported record earnings.

Incredibly, parents brought their young ones down to the district. One lad who sneaked out told a reporter that he wanted "to see it all so he could tell the other fellows who weren't so lucky." Only one arrest was made. A black woman named Mary Chase fired three shots over the head of the crowd.

And then it was over. The procession continued on to 34th and Wentworth where Smith held a revival meeting. Gipsy left Chicago confident that he had ridded Chicago of its social evil. There were other souls to save along the whistle stop.

Back in the levee, the doors swung open. Automatic pianos played their tunes. Extra beer was stocked in the ice box, and the busiest night in levee history began. Lieutenant Enright of the 22nd Street detail reported that every resort on the line was filled and that people were being turned away. "Far be it for me to moralize," said one woman. "We're here to make money and certainly it's coming in fast. If Gipsy Smith would lead a few more parades down here, I would soon make enough money to retire and live on the interest of my wealth." All agreed that the revival meeting was a good distraction, but with the

Talley-Ho coaches, Langhams, Dog Carts, Double Suspension Victorias, and their elegantly attired coachmen surround the clubhouse north of the grandstand just before Derby Day. To see or be seen was the question. (Courtesy of the Chicago Historical Society, William T. Barnum photo.)

An artist's depiction of the Haymarket Riot. Note the presence of "anarchists" and how they fired upon the police column. In fact, it was the men in blue who did all the shooting. (Courtesy of the Chicago Historical Society, copyright (c) by Paul Morand.)

Photo at left bottom shows the spot, facing Crane's Alley, where the prosecution claimed the bomb was lit and thrown from. In the distance, behind the elevated tracks, stands Zepf's Hall. It once housed the first-floor tavern where Albert Parsons and his family were when the bomb was thrown. Today it is the Grand Stage Lighting Company. (Photo by Bob Deckert.) Top: Spot where the bomb landed, directly across the street from the alley on the west side of Des Plaines Street. (Photo by Richard Lindberg.) Above: The corner from which the Haymarket bomb was thrown. The vestibule and the building are gone, however. (Photo by Bob Deckert.)

Left: A campaign spearheaded by the *Chicago Tribune* resulted in the erection of the police memorial in 1889. Only the base of the statue remains at the sight because of repeated acts of vandalism by young radicals during the 1960s. (Photo by Bob Deckert.) Above: Grace Street, looking east toward Broadway. William McGarigle once lived here. His house has been replaced by a three-story apartment building. It stood directly across from the home on the right, only one of two buildings on the block that date back to the turn of the century. (Photo by Richard Lindberg.)

Top: The vacant property near 53rd and Wallace, where the Holmes Castle once stood. To the visitor or curiosity seeker, it is all but impossible to locate the precise location of the building. The area is a shadow of its former greatness. Englewood has succumbed to urban blight. Above: Another symbol of Chicago's past industrial age—the stone entrance to the Chicago Stockyards District along Halsted Street. (Photos by Richard Lindberg.)

Two photos of the Chicago Coliseum in 1904 (top) and today (above). Built from the bricks of Libby Prison in Richmond, Virginia, the Chicago Coliseum hosted four Republican conventions and William Jennings Bryan's 1896 nomination. The older photo was taken during Teddy Roosevelt's nomination. Streetcars, children criss-crossing the streets, and horse-driven carriages contrast with the current scene of quiet desolation. (Old photo is courtesy of the Chicago Historical Society, Charles R. Clark photo; new photo by Bob Deckert.)

A close-up shot of Freiberg's Dance Hall, seen from the elevated platform that stood next to it. Ike Bloom's place was the command post of the levee, but he disguised its true purposes by advertising it as Freiberg's Dance Academy—note the sign on the front door. (Courtesy of the Chicago Historical Society.)

The "world famous" Everleigh Club in 1924, nine years before it was demolished. The two adjoining buildings lent grace, ambience, and culture to the often vicious, tawdry character of the district. (Courtesy of the Chicago Historical Society.)

Top: The once-opulent Lexington Hotel stands east of the levee at 22nd and Michigan. It is deserted today, but Al Capone once held sway from his luxurious fourth-floor suite, which he paid $18,000 a year to rent. Above: Heart of the south-side levee today. Nineteenth Street is overrun with weeds, junked autos, and broken sidewalks. The cycle of its history is complete—from residential district to organized vice to junkyard. (Photo by Richard Lindberg.)

The Dearborn Station as it looked to Theodore Dreiser and the nameless people who passed through its doors. The massive copula was destroyed by fire in 1922. (Courtesy of the Chicago Historical Society, Barnum and Barnum Album.)

Above: There's nothing left to show that Frances Riccollet once lived in a rooming house on this corner. This drugstore at Augusta and Western was built years after her suicide. Now it too is old and weather-beaten. (Photo by Richard Lindberg.) Right: The Black Sox. (Photo courtesy of George Brace.)

Above: For thirty years, "Shoeless" Joe Jackson, the greatest of them all, maintained his innocence. In 1951, a move began to clear his name of wrongdoing. Just weeks before he was scheduled to tell his side of the story on a national TV show, Jackson died of a heart attack. The movement continues. Right: Ed Cicotte called Charles "Chick" Gandil the "master of ceremonies" of the 1919 Black Sox conspiracy. Chick was as tough as they came. A former prizefighter out of St. Paul, Gandil refused to report to the Sox in 1920 because he wanted more money. He didn't realize that his holdout would be permanent after the scandal broke. (Photos courtesy of George Brace.)

The Illinois National Guard stands watch over a building ransacked by rioters. Chicago, 1919. Note the presence of neighborhood boys, prepared to "defend the turf." (Courtesy of the Chicago Historical Society.)

passage of the Mann Act and other legislation, the era of the segregated vice district was rapidly coming to an end.

It was March 6, 1910, when Mayor Busse and the council appropriated $5,000 for the formation of a vice commission to explore the relationship between the police, resort owners, druggists, the beer halls, and the methods of procurement. Walter Sumner, dean of the St. Peter & Paul Cathedral, took charge of a group of thirty clergymen, businessmen, and civic leaders whose conclusions were printed in a book considered too hot to be mailed by the city postal system. Edwin Sims, U.S. district attorney, Julius Rosenwald, executive of Sears, Roebuck, and Ellen Henrotin (the only woman on the panel) of the Federation of Women's Clubs were other prominent figures who had a hand in the preparation of the vice report. The post office routinely censored the mail. Drugstore owners who sold French postcards were frequently arrested for pornography. Yet a wide open vice district was allowed to thrive for years.

Urban America continued to contradict itself, as it attempted to define its morality in the new century. The vice commission promised to avoid implicating local politicians into their work, almost an impossible situation since graft was the handmaiden of all levee operations. Among the other things the commission recommended was the closing of the beer halls, the formation of a home for indigent girls, and some attention given to the working conditions of downtown sales clerks.

The levee lost one of its strongest allies when Mayor Carter Harrison, Jr., a long-time supporter of vice segregation, attended a St. Louis convention. There he was handed a pamphlet published by the Everleigh girls describing the pleasures to be found at their club. Harrison was aghast. It was a modest little book that did not picture any unclad girls or obscene acts. It did show a few stuffed sofas, gilded chandeliers, and told of a good time to be had upstairs. A directive was given to Police Chief John McWeeney to immediately close the Everleigh Club and some of the notorious hotels scattered along Michigan Avenue from 12th Street to 31st. McWeeney was reluctant to do this because he had one hand in a downtown saloon called the Delaware and the other in Bloom's payoffs. McWeeney told the vice commission that his district commanders maintained a card file listing every saloon, resort, and gambling den in their precinct. Thirty-six lieutenants were called before the civil service commission, and thirty-six denied any knowledge of a card file. Harrison's orders were carried out, but McWeeney lasted only one more year. Captain Nicholas Hunt of the Harrison Street district accused the mayor and McWeeney of collusion while the gambling parlors remained open. Hunt was fired by the chief, who in turn was fired by the mayor. All this, after McWeeney had been awarded a diamond-studded police star by the corporation counsel for a job well done.

The Everleigh Club was padlocked for good on October 24, 1911. Ed Little told the girls that they would be allowed to reopen after they paid a $20,000 tribute. They refused. "I never was a knocker, and nothing the police can do to me will change this disposition," Minna said on the last day. "I'll close up the ship and walk out of the place with a smile on my face. If the ship sinks, we'll go down with a cheer and a good drink under our belts."

In their time, Ada and Minna conveyed a sense of grace within their building, compared to the snake dens run by Vic Shaw and Zoe Millard (who thought the girls were too uppity). The Everleigh Club at 2131 Dearborn was constructed in 1890 for a cool $125,000 by Lizzie Allen and Christopher Columbus Crabb. Crabb was a fortunate man. He was Carrie Watson's lover but took up with Lizzie Allen when Carrie died.

The building was leased to Effie Hankins in 1895. When Allen died, Crabb inherited $300,000 and the title of the property. He leased the club to the Everleigh sisters in 1899 for $500 a month. The sisters were refined Kentucky girls, who had fled their brutish husbands for a stage career. They called themselves "Everleigh" because a grandmother once signed her letters "everly yours."

In 1898, they made some fast money by opening a bordello in Omaha, catering to the Omaha Exposition. They realized this was a temporary situation, so they looked about for a new opportunity. Conditions seemed right in Chicago. When they signed their lease, the girls went to work improving the building. They hired their own chefs, porters, and servants. The parlors were stocked with expensive furniture, and a library was built to improve the girls' reading habits. The young prostitutes were required to wear evening gowns in place of the usual skimpy chemises. They were taught elocution and manners because, as Minna said, "We only serve the best people." The Everleigh Club opened its doors on February 2, 1900. They made several thousand the first night. There was a scandal in 1908 when one of Minna's girls ran off with the black heavyweight Jack Johnson. Belle Schreiber left a stenographer's job in Milwaukee to make some fast money on the levee. Minna barred Johnson from the club, but the champ continued to pursue white levee women. He divorced Belle Schreiber and then opened his own saloon at 41 W. 31st Street. He named it the Cafe de Champion, and it was here in August 1912, that he met a nineteen-year-old Minneapolis girl named Lucille Cameron. Her story is a sad one because of the anguish she caused her family. Jeannette Dorr was a levee procuress who induced the girl to flee to Chicago. Lucille got to know Johnson well, and the two of them were seen dancing to dawn in the south-side cabarets.

The mother came to Chicago to claim her daughter. But the girl had no intentions of returning home. Mrs. Cameron-Falconet charged the fighter with abduction when the charge should have been *seduction*. Johnson was arraigned on a Mann Act charge. Angry whites hung his likeness in effigy from a lamppost at State and Walton and hate mail poured in from all over the country. When he posted his $25,000 bail and stepped into the street, an inkwell was hurled at him from the upper floor of a skyscraper. These were some of the milder reactions to Johnson's escapades. Booker T. Washington said that the champ caused "grave injustice to his race."

Lucille was transferred to Rockford, where her mother engaged a psychiatrist to find out if she suffered some affliction of the mind. When they could find nothing wrong, she was released to her mother, who sequestered her in a hotel room while she made arrangements to return to Minnesota. But she escaped and returned to Johnson. He made Lucille his third wife on December 3, 1912, at a private ceremony on Wabash Avenue (Johnson's second wife committed suicide after leaving him in 1911). Mrs. Falconet was informed of the marriage while in seclusion in her Minneapolis home. She swooned and passed out.

For the next two years, life on the levee settled into familiar patterns. Johnny Torrio managed his Uncle Jim Colosimo's affairs but soon found private enterprise more to his liking. He opened his own house at 2118 Federal Street. Torrio was a newcomer with ambition and style. He uplifted the neighborhood character of the gangs into the modern "mafiosi." But at this time, the levee was at peace with itself. Julius and Charlie Maubaum aligned with Ed Weiss, and together they changed Buxbaum's into the W & W Catering Company, which was a blind operation.

"Dago" Frank Lewis was one of the levee independents who operated outside the trust. In 1910, he introduced an exotic dance known as the "grizzly bear." It was popular in the days of the San Francisco Barbary Coast with the jack rollers and their women. Indecent in 1910, the style was called "bear catting," and Kenna would not allow it at Freiberg's. Waltzes and two steps were the preferred styles.

The police were active again in August of 1912. Frank Lewis and Harry Cusick were arrested for harboring minors in their resorts. Mayor Harrison ordered the raids after he got tired of waiting for the 22nd Street commander to do something. The district was the most corrupt in the city. The names of the captains changed after every election, but the new replacements continued the old traditions.

Fred Busse cleaned out the police force when he took over as mayor in 1907. Chief John Collins was replaced by George Shippey, who made wholesale changes in the politically sensitive first ward. Captain Patrick Harding, a political ally of former Mayor Dunne, was transferred to the Attrill Street station. With him went the entire force, including Lieutenant John Bonfield (patronage continued through several generations of Bonfields). Harding was then replaced by Edward McCann of the Englewood station (McCann was moved *from* 22nd Street during the previous election). McCann was a robust Irishman who was the father of nine. He wore a handlebar mustache and a small gold cross pinned to his vest. A most respectable man.

"This is the beginning of a new era," he told the patrolmen assigned to the district. "I have worked many hours in picking out the men I wanted for duty here. And I will say right here from now on, any person in the red-light district who claims to pay graft to any member of the department will be summoned to name who that officer was. Presents to policemen will avail them nothing, and it will go hard with the patrolmen or resort keeper whom I get evidence of the passing of tribute." These words were spoken by McCann on May 22, 1907.

McCann lasted in the levee just ten months. He was transferred to the Des Plaines Street station on March 10, 1908, with the rank of inspector. Conditions along Madison, Halsted, Carpenter, and Curtis Streets were only slightly better than in the levee. This was the domain of Mike "de Pike" Heitler, "Monkey Face" Charley Genker, and two brothers named Louis and Julius Frank. When McCann established himself in the new district, he informed the Frank brothers that if the resort keepers wanted to stay open, they had better come up with some of the tribute that he had once warned the 22nd Street cops about accepting.

The dive keepers were anxious to cooperate with the inspector. So each month, they would enter Frank's saloon on the corner of Halsted and Madison with a $20 bill pinned to a note. The name of the resort was printed on the paper so there would be no mistake. The payments were delivered the second day of each month and were presented to McCann by Louis Frank. Sometimes Frank would have to hand deliver the money in a satchel directly to McCann's home.

The resort keepers were accustomed to paying protection, but one day McCann discovered that some of the houses in his district were disguising the true number of inmates they kept. When he found out about their scheme, McCann informed Frank that the deal was off. They would have to pay $40 a month if they wanted to stay open. "Here's their money! Give it back to them," he said. "This isn't dealing squarely with me, and they will have to deal squarely with me or not at all!" The price of protection went up from $450 a month to $550. But there were those on the west side who could not afford the prices. Morrie Shatz, a dive keeper at 108 Peoria Street, exposed the payoff system to State's Attorney John Wayman, who began a probe. Among other things Shatz told of were McCann's race horses. He used his graft money to purchase a stable of prized steeds. McCann's picture was spread across the front pages on July 24, 1909, with details of the payoff system.

Dean Sumner, the pious reformer, stood by McCann all the way to the penitentiary. Wayman rounded up the known informers to build a strong case against McCann. A conviction was secured on September 24, but there were those in the reform movement who maintained that McCann had been railroaded by an ambitious politician. This simply does not seem to be the case.

McCann was not forgotten by his friends and admirers. Theodore Roosevelt urged Governor Edward F. Dunne to issue a pardon. This was done on May 5, 1911, shortly before McCann's pension eligibility was scheduled to expire.

George Shippey resigned as police chief on August 5, 1909, in the face of the McCann revelations. His attempts at reform were mere smokescreens. After "cleaning out" the 22nd Street station, Shippey quietly transferred many of the old faces back. LeRoy Steward's priority as the new police chief was to install someone in the levee who would see to it that liquor sales were banned in the resorts.

Captain William Cudmore was given a chance to see to it that intoxicants were prohibited, but he was a passive, live-and-let-live type of man. When Steward's agents reported that bartenders in the resort would slip out the back door and up to the second floor to fetch the booze, Cudmore found himself out of a job. The second great levee shakeup took place on August 25, 1910, when Cudmore was sent to the Warren Avenue district, and John Halpin was brought in.

But no one remained on this job very long. Captain Harding was brought back to 22nd Street, but he couldn't resist the lure of graft either. In 1912, Harding and two of his lieutenants were exiled to Des Plaines Street after his cleverly concealed bookkeeping system was uncovered. It accurately accounted for the profit margin of the dives and winerooms. Replacing Harding was "White Alley" Michael Ryan, probably the worst of the bunch. He was a twenty-two-year veteran of the force who passed all the required civil service exams. He was the hand-picked lackey of Mike Kenna. When Ryan moved into the station on February 1, 1912, he hung a portrait of Ike Bloom above the desk.

Then in September of 1912, the long-hoped-for victory over levee vice began to take shape. The grand jury began a probe of the district with the assistance of Arthur Barrage Farwell and the Committee of Fifteen, headed up by its attorney Carl Walderon. It started promising enough for the reformers. Ten-thousand welfare paraders marched down Michigan Avenue, compelling the mayor to ask for a referendum on closing the district. Meanwhile, Carl Walderon secured indictments against "Dago" Frank, Harry Cusick, Sam Hatch, and Kenna's bag man Al Harris. This followed months of undercover investigation by U.S. deputy marshals, who were hot on the trail of Mike "de Pike" Heitler, who tried to strong-arm Morrie Shatz when he found out that he was about to blow the whistle on Edward McCann.

Late in 1911, federal agents arrested three of Mike's girls at the Union Station, just as they were preparing to board a train to Pittsburgh. Heitler routinely shuttled girls across the country. Salt Lake City was his preferred drop-off point. Information received from these probes helped pave the way for the Wayman investigations.

What set back the reform movement was the apparent jealousy and lack of cooperation between church and state organizations. Assistant State's Attorney Charles Barrett was personally miffed at Walderon for slighting his boss, State's Attorney John Wayman. Barrett then stopped the prosecution of Louis Weiss for lack of evidence. The vice lord was released on a $200 bond, while the reformers waged a war with each other as to who would have the right to reform.

John Wayman was elected state's attorney in 1908 when he was

The embattled estate's attorney John Wayman. Was his death a suicide or an accident?

only thirty-six years old. He is one of the lost figures of Chicago history, a man who was both a Greek scholar and expert criminologist. He was a small-town boy from Glen Easton, West Virginia, who overturned the old political order. In 1908 he defeated John Healy for state's attorney in the primary and survived two recounts. As state's attorney, he advocated changes in the parole system and sent labor slugger Mossie Enright to the penitentiary. Indeed, Wayman showed no bias in his dealings. He counted among his admirers Bathhouse John, who nominated Wayman as his choice for handsomest man in Chicago in a 1912 poll.

The state's attorney justifiably believed that vice suppression was not his job. He believed that a segregated vice district was preferable to the wide-open city and expressed this view to civic groups across the city. In September 1912, reformer Virginia Brooks accused Wayman of coveting levee real estate as a potential investment. Wayman had worked closely with the Santa Fe and their adjoining property. He was further accused of collusion with Mayor Harrison and Chief McWeeney, a real blemish on a term that was scheduled to end in January 1913.

Wayman fought back with an attack against Walderon. An issue was made out of Municipal Judge Dolan's dismissal of a case involving mortgage broker Adolph Leibman, a friend of Walderon's, whose only crime was attempted seduction. Liebman tacked a note in the women's washroom at Marshall Field's that read: "Please call me up at RA-3304. I am a fine man, and call me if you are a nice looking girl." The note was discovered by a Chicago debutante who turned it over to Gert Brittner of the Juvenile Protective Association. Undercover policewomen visited Liebman's office, where a host of anxious women waited to see him. Improper photographs were discovered in his desk, intended for private viewing with his girls. Liebman was arrested, his honor compromised. It was interesting gossip for the LaSalle Street crowd who knew him. Wayman was stung by the insinuation of wrongdoing. He was a man of some principle, a rugged individualist who was a follower of the Theodore Roosevelt doctrine.

Wayman declared that he alone would wipe out the bawdy houses in the vice districts. From Edgewater on the posh north shore to distant Hammond, he would give them their reform but cautioned that he "will close the districts, but let the cops keep it closed in January."

He launched a two-pronged attack. The state's attorney set up "levee court," open from nine to ten o'clock in the Criminal Courts Building. While informants told all, Chief McWeeney's men patroled Whiskey Row, arresting unescorted women and closing down the saloons that violated the one o'clock closing. Meanwhile Wayman's men searched the county records for the name of the property owners but found the names of dead people and bogus holding companies. The old respected firm of Chicago Title & Trust was named as a trustee of an Armour Avenue resort, but the threat of a libel lawsuit sent Wayman scurrying back to the books. Retractions were printed the next day.

Other embarrassments awaited the crusaders. Wayman's men burst into Phyllis Adams's resort on October 7 with a fistful of warrants. "Get your clothes on, girls, we're goin' downtown," detectives Shea and Lynch said. From the rear emerged Arthur Barrage Farwell as well as Lucy Page Gaston of the anticigarette league. Miss Gaston had just told the girls to repent their sin—puffing a cigarette in public. Saving souls or slumming was the question posed to Farwell. "We are saving souls," Farwell said. Detective Lynch took them downtown.

Levee Low Life

The hoped-for victory in the courts occurred on October 12, 1912, before Judge Kickham Scanlon. The judge upheld a motion by Philo Otis, when he sued Cora Abbott of 2136 Armour Avenue for keeping a disorderly house that bred disease and retarded property values. Jurors got an earful when informants told of $100 payoffs and all-night wine parties with local policemen.

Wayman made good on his promises. Raids began October 4, and they continued night and day. Ike Bloom, the most determined vice lord, organized his own "Committee of Fifteen." The leading vice mongers then decided to send the girls out into respectable society, to convince Wayman's people that segregation wasn't so bad after all. The sallow-complected girls wore extravagant amounts of powder and makeup and daring outfits. They strolled through Hyde Park, Edgewater, and up and down Michigan Avenue, smoking cigarettes scandalously. This move caught Wayman by surprise. Bloom and his pals rubbed their hands in glee. In effect the syndicate said, "Here: You want 'em, take em!"

Welfare worker Kate Adams opened the doors of the Florence Crittenden Anchorage Home at 2615 Indiana Avenue and the Lifeboat Home on Cottage Grove Avenue. Most girls spurned this plea and returned to their former habitués. But Wayman raided them as fast as they reopened. The elections were held that fall, and the Bath and the Dink were swept into office despite a valiant fight by the anti-saloon suffragette Marion Drake. Mysteriously, the voting rolls of the first ward had swelled for the election.

Maclay Hoyne succeeded Wayman as state's attorney on December 3. Hoyne did not list vice cleanup as a priority. He was more interested in jury tampering, leaving the levee in the lap of the police chief. The doors of the Royal Burlesque Theatre swung open on Whiskey Row. Eager crowds shoved their way downstairs and pushed a quarter in the doorkeeper's hand to get a seat in the "Turkish Theatre" to see the *real* show. "Reformers got to be greased the same as bulls," Ike Bloom said.

Gunfight at the Levee

The winerooms, the dives, the bookie joints, and the hotels reopened cautiously. Big Jim Colosimo let Johnny Torrio run the Saratoga while he spent much of his time at his plush new cafe on Wabash Avenue, entertaining a nineteen-year-old choir girl named Dale

Winter. Aware of his opportunity, Torrio gave a good accounting of himself. He opened his own place at 2118 S. Federal Street, but found a new foe in the form of a morals squad headed by two new levee reformers.

William C. Dannenberg was a retired secret-service agent and Metellius C. Funkhouser was a major in the Illinois National Guard when they were assigned the task of heading up an agency loosely called the morals squad. In a separate move, Funkhouser was appointed second deputy of police. Two hundred more levee bagnios were closed immediately.

"They're running us into a hole," Torrio moaned. "I'm gettin' tired of payin' dough to get a chance to run, and then havin' these guys bustin' me and my friends every day or two. I'm tired of havin' my women yell to me about gettin' no dough. We got to take a couple of 'em into an alley and kick 'em up some . . . so's the others will wise up to the fact that they're not wanted around here:"

Colosimo told his nephew to settle down. He called a conference of the leading levee bosses, including detectives Ed Murphy and Johnny Howe. "Chicken" Larry Cullett, another former cop, approached Dannenberg with an offer of $500 a week to lay low. The morals inspector answered them by publishing the pictures of men arrested in the call houses in the morning papers.

Dannenberg found no allies in the 22nd Street district station either. Captain Ryan regarded the morals cops as "green" interlopers, and he resented the stoolies planted in his district. During the nights when the 183 beat cops could find nothing going on, Dannenberg's five men made raids. Meanwhile, Michael McFadden and John Cook of the 22nd Street detail circulated pictures of the morals men at Swan's Billiard Parlor on 22nd Street so everyone knew whom he was dealing with.

A smear campaign followed. Colosimo allegedly paid off several newspaper cartoonists to lampoon Funkhouser in the papers. When this scheme failed, Colosimo tried to have Funkhouser declared legally bankrupt. It was a bizarre plot involving a legal claim that the major's partner held against him. What Colosimo's people did was buy up the claim and press for immediate settlement.

Wild tales of gangs of hitmen brought in by Torrio gripped the city. The gunmen reportedly were hid in a labyrinth of tunnels that connected the 22nd Street houses. Vic Shaw even armed herself with a revolver as the levee prepared for a war to the finish. It was the long summer of 1914. Troubles in Europe were a distant rumble, growing louder each day. The Stevens-Duryea (America's most luxurious automobile) was on display on "automobile row" on Michigan Avenue. A new hit play called the *Elopers* had just opened at the LaSalle.

Enter one Rocco Venillo, alias "Roxy Vanilla," cousin of Johnny Torrio and proprietor of a Federal Street call house. He had just finished an abbreviated eight-year stretch in Deer Lodge, Montana, for shooting his roommate through the heart in 1908. In the spring of 1914, the governor of Montana reduced his sentence so that he might be given a chance for a parole, which he secured. Venillo drove his flashy red touring car to Chicago, arriving just in time to witness Isaac Henagow's murder on April 7, 1914, in Roy Jones' saloon at 2037 Wabash Avenue.

James Franche was known in the district as "Ed Duffy" or "Duffy the Goat." His hangout was above Dago Frank Lewis's saloon, popularly called the Goat's Place. Henagow was a San Franciscan who dropped into the Jones place for a drink. Franche and his girlfriend Kitty Fitzgibbons, an aging prostitute from the old Custom House district, entered the saloon at 8:30. Henagow requested a song from Zella Ingram and then engaged Franche in a conversation. Witnesses told of Duffy the Goat's anger over Henagow's assertion that a woman was entitled to universal suffrage. There was a shouting match before Franche shot him in the chest. Zella Ingram was singing "When I Lost You" at the time.

Franche was another one of the rich men's sons who found their thrills in crime. His brother Cyril ran the family varnish business, preferring to disassociate himself from James. Roy Jones was in a real pickle this time. His license had recently been restored by Harrison, and one more violation would be tough to fight. To protect his license, employees were instructed to tell the police that the shooting took place outside the cafe. Just as they had done in the case of Nat Moore, the police were not told about it until several hours later. Captain Ryan appeared at the cafe. And even though the newsmen had already poked holes through Roy Jones story, Ryan believed him.

"I don't believe that Henagow was shot while seated in the cafe," he said. "It would have been impossible for him to walk after the bullet struck him, and it is foolish to think that he came down the stairs unaided. The shooting could have happened in the city's best places. I believe the man was shot while out in the street." Several days later, Franche surrendered to authorities and was capably defended by Charles Erbstein.

But the tragedy that really marked the passing of the levee occurred on July 16, 1914. It was a senseless mishap caused by the warring factions of vice and reform. That night, Dannenberg dispatched four men to 28 W. 22nd Street to raid the Turf, a three-story bagnio on the north side of the street. Three men and one woman were arrested in a second-floor apartment, but Funkhouser was unaware that Dannenberg was even in the district. Detectives Fred Amart and Joseph Merrill were two new members of the morals squad. The raid was their first practical experience in the district, Dannenberg left the men there, telling them to wait with the prisoners while he left for another raid. A police wagon was summoned, and a hostile crowd of vagrants, vice patrons, and hecklers gathered outside the Turf.

Amart and Merrill grew restive. Unsure of what to do, they left the Turf, walking east on 22nd Street. The mob trailed them, hurling insults and jeers. "There goes Dannenberg's stoolies!" someone yelled. They crossed 22nd Street and headed cautiously under the elevated tracks for what they believed would be a rendezvous with Dannenberg. Amart and Merrill made a motion to draw their revolvers. The mob dropped back. A few seconds passed. There were shots, and a crush of bodies sought shelter. The conflicting stories made it impossible to make an accurate determination as to what really happened.

Just east of Wabash Street a brick was hurled at Amart and Merrill. The missile hit an elderly woman in the crowd, and a burly man wearing a straw boater and a gray suit appeared. He brandished a nickel-plated revolver. "I'm going to shoot you, you stool pigeon!" he said, before firing three shots, one of which hit Merrill. The man was Roxy Venillo, who had been riding in the red touring car with Maurice Van Bever and Mac Fitzpatrick. The car was parked by the New Brighton, at 2002 Federal Street. The car slowly trailed the mob down 22nd Street.

Merrill commandeered a passing auto and had himself taken to the hospital. Hearing shots, detectives Stanley Birns and John Sloop of the 22nd Street station crossed 22nd to see what the problem was. They confronted Amart, ordering him to halt. But Sloop (who had been reinstated to the force after being suspended for police brutality) was not known to Amart, and more shots were exchanged. Birns lay dead in the street, while Amart fled into Swan's poolroom where he was arrested.

At that very moment, Colosimo had just finished a pasta dinner at his namesake cafe, in the company of his lawyer Rocco Stefano. Both men walked toward the elevated station next to Freiberg's where they were joined by White Alley Ryan, Solly Friedman, and William Schubert. The fact that Schubert was in the district that night is one of the interesting sidelights. The police inspector was in O'Malley's saloon when Mossie Enright killed the slugger, William Gentleman, and was there when Ike Henagow's murder was reported. Minutes earlier, a "Main 13" distress call (an early version of the 911 exchange) was placed to the 22nd Street station. A policeman on duty tipped the press that the call was sent through to Ryan just before he left the station. It was from someone who had inside knowledge of the pending attack on the morals squad. Ryan ignored it, and the desk sergeant denied ever receiving a call.

Meanwhile, the first cops arrived on the scene. Detective Ed O'Grady saw Torrio and Fitzpatrick help Venillo into the car. He was taken to St. Anthony de Padua Hospital, where the bullet was removed from his right ankle. The attending doctor was watched over by Torrio, who said, "I'll take that!" when the bullet was removed.

The usual inquests were held. Amart, a former mail carrier, streetcar conductor, and Navy veteran, was held accountable and held on a $5,000 bond. Ryan blamed the "green" morals cops, but the truth was otherwise. The bullet extracted from Birns was the "dum-dum" vari-

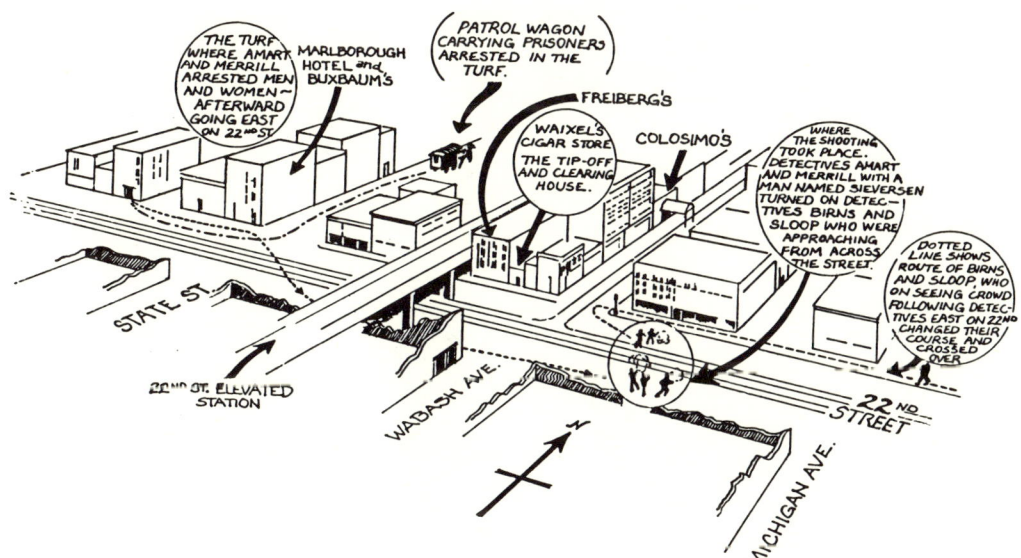

The path the special vice-squad detective followed the night of the gunfight at the levee, July 26, 1914.

ety, not the long cartridge commonly called the ".38 special" that the police used.

The levee was scoured for suspects, informers, and suspicious characters. Captain Ryan came up with nothing, but Dannenberg's next raid netted seventy people. State's Attorney Maclay Hoyne arrested Colosimo, his brother-in-law Joe Moresco, Harry Cusick, saloon owner William Leathers, and policeman J.A. Carey. Venillo was taken in, but Torrio escaped to Cedar Lake, Indiana.

"I'd sell all this for $10,000 even though it cost me $40,000," Colosimo said. A few minutes later, Kenna's lawyer Aaron Andrews appeared with $5,000 bail bond money.

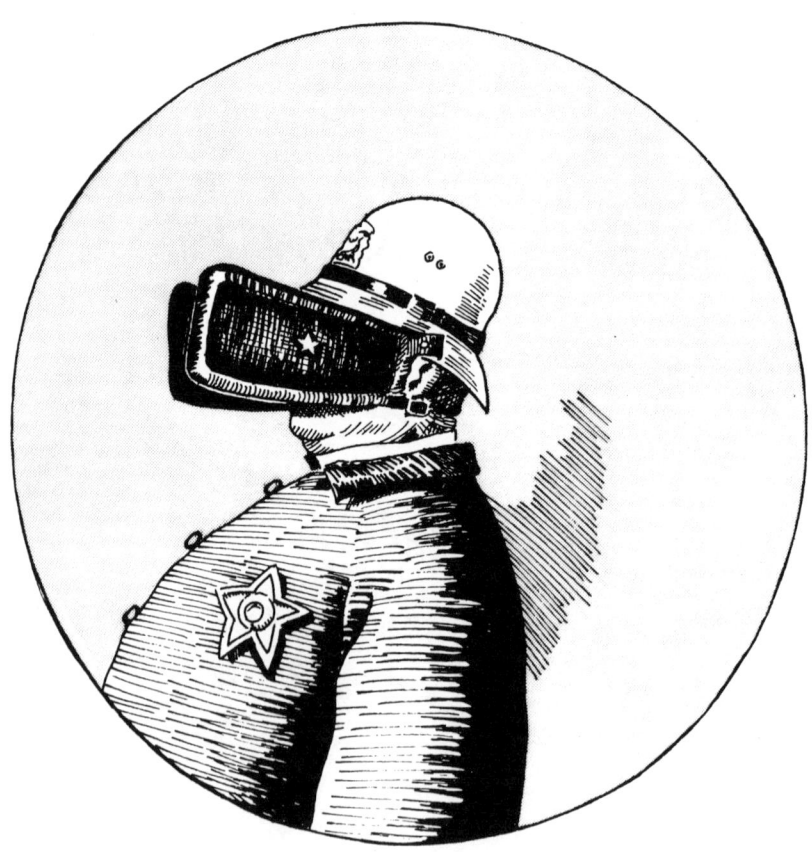

"Who Puts the Blinders on Him?" asked *Tribune* cartoonist Sidney Smith, following the shooting at the levee in July 1914. (Reproduction by Bob Deckert.)

Levee Low Life

The forces of law and order, not necessarily working for the same goals. Left to right at the Birns inquest are Mettelius C. Funkhouser, Detective Fred Amart, Chief James Gleason, and William C. Dannenberg.

Hoyne tried to center his case around the testimony of witnesses. Chauffeur William Peterson identified Venillo as the man who followed Dannenberg's cops. A pair of convicts named Ollie Mullenbach and Ted Sherman refused to testify, even after being promised immunity. Michael Kenna appeared before the grand jury, telling them that "conditions existed in the first ward before I was born, but they're better now!" The case collapsed.

There were internal repercussions in the police department. The civil service board interviewed Ryan and Lieutenant Morrissey. Among other things they wanted to know was why Ryan allowed levee habitués to bother the church people in the Midnight Mission. Rotten eggs sprinkled with ammonia were being tossed into the mission vestibule, while hot rodders raced their motorcycles up and down the street while meetings were in progress. Under direct questioning, Ryan maintained that Ike Henagow was killed on the sidewalk, but reporters did some investigating and found the bullet still lodged in the wall of Roy Jones's saloon. Ryan told of the payoff system and which saloons were exempt from the 1 A.M. closing.

Chief James Gleason (who replaced McWeeney) transferred Ryan to the West Lake station. The businessmen of Austin issued a protest to the mayor about the character of the new captain. This was the first of twenty-six interdepartmental transfers on the north and south sides. Ryan quit five days later, following the outcry from the Austin neighborhood. He also avoided a possible criminal indictment. Mayor Harrison interrupted his vacation to the upper peninsula of Michigan to return to Chicago. When he came back, he announced his opposition to organized vice. Unflagging support withered away to doubt and finally to resistance. "I have reached the conclusion, finally, that my idea of the vice question has been wrong. For many years, I did not view segregation as an alarming development in the treatment of the problem. The investigation conducted by the Rockefeller Foundation in Europe has converted me. I have no hesitancy in subscribing now to the general indictment of the segregation plan. Segregation means protected vice, and you can't have protected vice without running the big risk of seeing your law-enforcement officials corrupted," the mayor said.

His opponents charged it was another case of Harrison jumping on the bandwagon of public opinion. But he was not the same corrupt big-city mayor his father had been. The younger Carter learned *realpolitik* early on. When he faced the gray wolves of the city council for the first time in the 1890s, he quickly understood that he would have to work within *their* system to affect real change. He practiced give and take with Kenna and Coughlin, and when the time came to defeat the really dangerous Charles Tyson Yerkes, the aldermen cooperated. Through the years, he allowed them to run their games because he believed that it was better to confine prostitution and gambling to a centralized area where those who wanted it could go to. When he saw the unreality of his former position, he admitted it was wrong and pursued another course. By 1914, Harrison was in a position where he could dictate terms to Kenna and Coughlin. And one of them was clear. It was time for the levee to disappear.

Captain Max Nootbar, a graduate of Heidelberg University and a police instructor, was given the command of the 22nd Street district. In former days, Nootbar had served a brief stint as district captain but was quickly transferred out of the district when he tried to enforce the 1 A.M. closing at Freiberg's. Despite being former chief George Shippey's fair-haired boy, Nootbar was an honest cop, cut out of the same material as Herman Schuettler. His first line of attack was to close Freiberg's. It was the last impregnable fortress following the closing of Roy Jones's Cadillac by Carter Harrison.

Vagrants were given just fifteen days to leave the area or face criminal arrest if they could not show visible means of support. Nootbar tossed Ike Bloom's portrait into the garbage, reaffirming his pledge to close the dance hall. Bloom appeared before Nootbar, protesting that his hall was respectable. It was an "academy." Business cards were placed on empty tables by waiters in the hall each night. They read, "FREE INSTRUCTION IN MODERN DANCE TO OUR GUESTS. Hand this card to the head waiter and he will send you one of our competent instructors. Respectfully, Freiberg's Dance Academy." Nootbar sent men in to observe the proceedings. They reported that the "instructors" were known prostitutes, and affidavits were filed saying that whiskey highballs, beer, and wine were served long after 1 A.M.

Madam Georgie Spencer, who organized her fellow resort keepers into a private association known to the levee as the "Friendly Friends," was not quite as patient with Nootbar. "Listen to me, Mr. Policeman!" she said, pounding her fist on his desk. "I own a $45,000 hotel. I own a flat worth $40,000. I'd like to see you interfere with my business!" The Friendly Friends were organized several years earlier to help chase out the Everleigh sisters, who cut into their profits. Georgie Spencer and her friends Vic Shaw and Zoe Millard succeeded in chasing out Minna and Ada, but the captain was another story.

Bloom showed up in his hall on July 26 to inform his customers that the place was closing. It was three minutes before one, and the band played "Home Sweet Home." "That's the first time *that* tune has been played before daybreak," someone said before the lights went out.

As promised, Mayor Harrison closed Freiberg's and Colosimo's on August 14. But the wide-open administration of William Hale Thompson began on May 15, 1915, and a new and bolder era of vice was about to begin. Ike Bloom's license was restored on December 25, 1915, under a dummy company known as Hop Ling. Colosimo was back in business on January 28.

Duffy the Goat was sentenced to hang, but slips in the defense got him a second trial that resulted in acquittal. Roxy Venillo never went to court. The tragedy of the levee faded from the public eye, as the troubles on 22nd Street seemed unimportant compared to the larger drama unfolding in the war rooms of Europe's capitals. It was now August 1914, and things were changing quickly.

For all purposes, the old levee was finally dead. It didn't die because some high-minded reformer decided it was the right time. Chicago's segregated vice district was one of the last resort districts to depart, and it went on its own accord because of the changing fabric of American society. America was becoming a society on the go. The automobile was changing the customs and lifestyles of the nation. The high cost of graft and the customer's willingness to travel to remote locations to find wine and women compelled the Torrio-Colosimo combine to relocate to the suburbs (Colosimo chose to remain).

There was one last police scandal that convinced the levee thinkers that the wide-open suburb was the only recourse. Mayor Thompson signaled a new tolerance to the 22nd Street vice trust. He replaced Chief Gleason with his own man, Charles C. Healey. Healey had served as the head of the mounted police and then as a traffic coordinator. It was an election year, and Maclay Hoyne was running against the Thompson candidate, Harry Miller.

Hoyne, who wasn't interested in vice in 1912, suddenly made it a campaign issue when he charged Healey with graft, bribery, and malfeasance of office. Captain William P. O'Brien of the detective force had written a letter to Healey on March 20, 1916, detailing the conditions at a "black and tan" resort known as the Elite, on 3030 S. State. A separate letter recommended the closing of Sam Hare's Schiller Cafe at 320 E. 31st St. Both cabarets (winerooms were no longer in vogue; a new American musical form, jazz, was being played by blacks up from New Orleans, and the cabaret was a hybrid of the old beer hall, wineroom, and bawdy house; the attraction was the new music) featured the social mixing of whites and blacks. Black civic leaders complained that the white overlords of vice had moved south into their neighborhoods and corrupted their youth's morals.

Hoyne got hold of the letters and seized Major Funkhouser's personal records to make a case of it. Why were these resorts allowed to stay open? The worst elements of the first ward had infiltrated the second ward, the black belt along Cottage Grove Avenue and 31st. It was the domain of Alderman Oscar DePriest and State Senator George Harding. DePriest was the city's first black alderman, a hero to his constituents, but he had conspired to save Sam Hare's liquor license against O'Brien's strong objections. The alderman later admitted to a grand jury that he had received $1,000 from Henry "Teenan" Jones, owner of the Elite, for keeping the cops away.

Thompson's ally, George Harding, was a forty-six-year-old real estate millionaire who used his extensive influence to secure licenses at the Beaux Arts Club at 27th and State. O'Brien was suspended by Healey on October 7 but turned state's witness for Hoyne. Thompson characterized Hoyne's and O'Brien's charges as "brainstorms," but the facts proved otherwise. Healey, his secretary William Luthardt, and Charles Essig of Sportsman's Park were indicted on October 23,

1916. With Ring Lardner covering the court proceedings for the *Chicago Tribune*, a tale of graft and spoils was told. Thompson refused to suspend the chief until the famous little black book was discovered. In January 1917, Lieutenant White of the Lake Street station revealed the existence of a notebook that listed the transient hotels, cabarets, call houses, and gambling dens that "could not be raided" because they were the "chief's places," and the resorts that "could be raided" because no tribute was being paid to Mike "de Pike" Heitler and Billy Skidmore (Skidmore was a bail bondsman and syndicate fixer). Together they shared in the payoffs with the chief. Finally Thompson acted. He replaced Healey with Herman Schuettler, who had risen to prominence in the Haymarket era and later during the anti-gambling crackdown.

DePriest and Healey were acquitted but suffered severe blows to their careers. It was an expected anticlimax to the history of the levee. The old vice trust saw quicker profits in Burnham, Illinois, a town located eighteen miles south of Chicago. At the time, it was run by a twenty-five-year-old mayor named John Patton. He presided over his little town of 1,000 and came well suited to the job. His early years were spent working in a saloon. Jim Colosimo and Johnny Torrio purchased the Arrowhead Inn for $15,000 on October 15, 1917, establishing the first "road house."

The other 22nd Street bosses quickly bought up property in Stickney, Burnham, and Cicero. "Jew Kid" Grabiner ran Torrio's Speedway Inn in Burnham; Harry Hopkins and Jakie Adler of the old Silver Dollar moved south; Dago Frank Lewis opened the Columbia on Ogden Avenue. When Ed Weiss and his nephew Louis joined them, the old vice combine was reunited.

Back in the levee, Colosimo became soft and lazy. He was lulled to complacency by a fetching young songbird named Dale Winter. The aging gangster and rising young actress has been standard Hollywood fare over the years, perhaps inspired by Big Jim.

Dale Winter was a nineteen-year-old Grand Rapids girl when she was introduced to Colosimo in 1915. She had a stage-door mother, good looks, and some talent. Arturo Fabri, orchestra leader at the Livingston Hotel in Grand Rapids, recognized her possibility. He gave her a break. Not one, but two. Fabri later regretted taking her to Chicago to meet Big Jim, but her career in Grand Rapids already reached its peak. Through *Tribune* writer Jack Lait, she was given an audition at the cafe. "That's some girl you got. You're a lucky man,"

Big Jim told Fabri. Several months later, Colosimo said something different. "You don't have to worry, Art. I'll take good care of *my* girl." Fabri loved Dale, but he could not compete against a man as wealthy and powerful as Big Jim. He returned to Michigan and joined the army.

Colosimo gave Dale star billing. She received voice lessons from Octave Dua, Victor Arimondi, and Désiré DeFrere. The great Flo Ziegfeld even offered a part in one of his shows, but she turned him down. Big Jim wanted her to be a star of the Chicago Opera Company, where he had season tickets. Whatever Jim wanted for her was okay. But Victoria was wise to her husband's tricks. She told Fabri of his attentions to his former girlfriend. "There's nothing I can do," was his sensible reply.

Victoria secured a divorce from Jim on March 31, 1920, taking $45,000 of his levee money to the West Coast. With Victoria finally out of his hair, Colosimo married Dale at West Baden, Indiana, on April 17. "He had a heart of pure gold. If I hadn't loved him before, I loved him then. I just couldn't help it," she said of those moments they shared during their West Baden honeymoon. It was at this time that Miss Winter said she received death threats from the former Mrs. Colosimo.

Big Jim enjoyed his happiness for only three weeks. There were seven patrons in the cafe on May 11, 1920, when a lone gunman entered the vestibule and fired two shots. A waiter found Big Jim lying face down, dead. A hastily scribbled note that said "so long vampire" was found on one of the tables inside the cafe. Who shot Big Jim? Suspicion was cast on Victoria, who had arrived back in Chicago just two hours before the shooting. Crazy Frank Razzina was out of jail and was said to be asking for Jim. But the police had another suspect they were looking for. A man was seen fleeing the cafe wearing a derby hat and patent leather shoes. He was short, pudgy, and dark complected. The man was never found.

It was probably Al Capone, brought in recently from New York by Johnny Torrio. It was only ten months after the passage of the Volstead Act, and perhaps Big Jim had become an appendix to the young Turks who saw new sources of revenue besides women and gambling. They gave him a big send-off though. Eight aldermen, three judges, and two Congressmen attended what became gangland's first great funeral. Bathhouse John Coughlin brought a tear to everyone's eye with his stirring eulogy. The procession wound its way past the restaurant, with such shining lights as George Silver, Ike Bloom, Committeeman "Diamond" Joe Esposito of the bloody 19th ward, Hinky Dink Kenna, Mike Merlo, and the terrible Genna brothers trailing behind. It was a nice mixture of old-line vice and the young bloods who became famous in the twenties. The $2,500 casket was laid into the ground of Oakwoods Cemetery, after being denied access to Mount Carmel. The Catholic Church wanted no part of Big Jim in their cemetery. "Ah, they're just a bunch of pikers," someone from the organization said.

Ike Bloom returned to Freiberg's and continued to operate his hall under the name of the Vienna and the Midnight Frolic until 1924. When he attempted to open a speakeasy in the Loop called the Deadville, the federal liquor agents chased him out. The man who was generous with two-dollar gold pieces for his regulars met a sad end. He lost his fortune paying for a series of painful operations that deprived him of both his legs. Bloom died December 15, 1930. On that very same day the Chicago papers printed a page 2 story that reported that Victoria Colosimo was seeking a divorce from Antonio Villano, a young hood that she had taken up with after her divorce from Jim. Villano had threatened to kill her and all of her seventeen brothers and sisters.

The Everleigh sisters had since retired to New York under assumed names. Still bitter over being squeezed out by Bloom and Colosimo, Minna wrote a series of articles for the *Herald-Examiner* exposing the bribe system within the levee. This was the last the public heard of them until Charles Washburn decided to write of their life and times in his book *Come into My Parlor*.

Under assumed names, they visited Europe, attended theatre, wrote some poetry, and entertained old friends. Minna, the assertive one, passed away on September 16, 1948, at the age of 70. Ada followed her in death on January 5, 1960. She was 93. Through the years, Ada allowed her sister to make the important decisions. After Minna died, Ada moved to Virginia and, true to her vows of secrecy, requested that her burial site be kept secret.

Big Bill Thompson did everything in his power to abolish the morals squad in March of 1916. He called Funkhouser to his office to explain why some church ladies were permitted to view the censored film clips that were entrusted to the squad. The city finance committee ended the row very quietly by refusing to renew the morals squad budget for another year.

William Dannenberg began his own private-detective business, but was drawn back to the levee in 1923. In September of that year, millionaire New York publisher W.E.D. Stokes revealed that his beautiful young wife had once worked as an inmate of the Everleigh house in 1911. Stokes charged in his divorce suit that his wife Helen used the name Helen Norwood while working for Georgie Spencer and the Everleigh sisters. He circulated a photograph, allegedly showing young Helen holding her illegitimate child inside the Dearborn Street bordello. He linked Helen to various levee characters who worked at the Pekin and Beaux Arts Club, but all of this was just a frame.

Dannenberg located Anna Johnson, Minna's housekeeper, who testified that Stokes tried to bribe her with money to corroborate the story. A trunk of false affidavits found by Dannenberg revealed what was (then) the biggest frame-up in the history of jurisprudence. Despite Torrio's death threats, Dannenberg passed away very peacefully on August 10, 1955.

Of all the people who formed the levee tapestry, John Wayman was the least understood and perhaps the most tragic. He was boxed in by the do-gooders and politicians, but he closed the district as they wanted. When he sent McCann to the penitentiary, there were those in his party who touted him for governor. After this, he went after the grafters with zeal. When Moss Enright's gang escaped from jail, they vowed to come to Chicago and shoot him dead. He refused a bodyguard.

There were no reported acts of violence perpetrated against Wayman; rather, his death came at his own hand. Wayman was examining a gun that was being used as evidence in a murder case he was working on. He was alone in his study at the family residence at 6832 Constance when he pumped two shots into his chest. Suicide or accident? Wayman was taken to the hospital and issued a statement before he died: "I am sorry, old man, if I caused you any trouble. I didn't mean to do it. I guess I had a little sand in my gearbox when I did this thing." He had suffered a nervous breakdown following his unsuccessful bid for governor in 1913. The shots were probably self-induced.

Those two first-ward rogues, Bathhouse and Hinky Dink, retained their aldermanic seats until 1923. The ward was split up that year, and the Dink gave up his seat in favor of the Bath. Prohibition came, and the Dink cheerfully donated his one-pint beer mugs. When he closed the Workingman's Exchange, he gave Arthur Barrage Farwell one of the famous schooners. Farwell used it as a goldfish bowl.

Levee Low Life

In 1939, a weak and aged Michael Kenna took his place in the city council again. He replaced Coughlin, who had died a year earlier. Most of the time, the nimble Hinky Dink remained closed-mouthed, returning each day to his home at the Blackstone Hotel but still very much in control of his ward's destiny. The end came on October 9, 1946. He was eighty-nine years old, and his estimated worth was $2 million. Kenna's wake at St. Mary's at 9th and Wabash was an extravaganza that rivaled Jim Colosimo's. Seen at the funeral was former Democratic Senator James Slattery chatting amicably with Capone overlord Jake "Greasy Thumb" Guzik. Also in attendance were Mayor Daley's mentor Jake Arvey, gambler Frank "Chew Tobacco" Ryan, and Edward McCann. Resembling a Prussian military advisor, old McCann appeared in shiny knee-high riding boots.

Kenna was frugal by nature. Those who knew him maintain that his connection to the panders was nominal. This view was shared by John Kelly, the *Chicago Tribune* newsman who was a close friend during the heyday of the "front page" era of journalism. Kelly ghost-wrote all the ballads of Bathhouse Coughlin. The Bath's "Dear Midnight of Love" was the hit song of the First Ward Ball of 1900. May DeSooza's touching rendition was so popular, the public demanded more. Kelly gave them the "Bathhouse Opus." On the subject of Kenna's connection with the prostitution rings, Kelly's letter of July 10, 1942 explained that: "Hink was always my friend, and I still stick for him. His closest friends assert emphatically that he never handled a dime of sporting house money, and I believe it. He was in on the gambling end of it, but that is considered clean money."

The years were not as kind to Coughlin. Kenna tried to keep the young mavericks in line, but they couldn't help but chuckle when Coughlin proposed an ordinance to regulate women's skirt lengths. In later years the Bath was a tragicomic figure. He continued to maintain his horse farms near St. Charles, a costly investment that left him $56,000 in debt when he died at the Lexington Hotel (Al Capone's former headquarters) on November 10, 1938, at seventy-eight years of age. The funeral procession down 18th Street attracted thousands. There were ten cars bearing flowers, and the First Ward Marching Club wore black badges. The boys smiled when they recalled one of Coughlin's musical pieces, "They Buried Her Beside the Drainage Canal."

Coughlin and Kenna upheld the Chicago traditions of boodle and graft. Their legacy was continued later in the century by Otto Kerner,

Richard J. Daley, Jake Arvey, and Paddy Bauler. But beneath the larcenous exteriors of each of them beat the soul of the common man. When the suave but ruthless traction financier, Charles Tyson Yerkes, attempted to gain a ninety-nine-year franchise on streetcar lines, it was Coughlin and Kenna that cast the decisive votes that foiled the scheme. Where Yerkes allegedly said, "Let the strap hangers pay the dividends," Kenna reminded the Bath to "always go after the little stuff."

The south-side levee no longer exists. The black exodus from the south, increased mobility, and affluence led the pleasure seekers first to the southern suburbs, then back into the north side for their diversions. The southern tip of the levee is now Chinatown. If you walk along 22nd Street, on a summer night, it is still possible to retrace the steps of Inspector Birns, but it would take more than imagination because there is nothing left to indicate that this area was a part of Chicago's lusty past. The Everleigh Club became a transient hotel for blacks before it was demolished in 1933. The façade of the Chicago Coliseum was built from the remains of the Confederate Libby prison. Today, that is all that stands on Wabash Street. The other three walls were demolished in 1980. The wall was left as a concession to the preservationists, along with the tattered and crumbling door where Bathhouse John welcomed his guests. A sign warns trespassers not to tamper with the building. But they have already tampered with a landmark of Chicago history.

Chicagoans visiting other cities are often asked about that wide-open time that began in the nineties and ended with Capone going to jail. Rather, they point with pride to the city parks, the museums that dot the lakefront, and their ivy-covered ballpark on the north side. Nobody talks about the levee, the girls that made easy riches there, the reformers who tried to abolish it, or the politicians and cops whose careers were shaped by it.

The call houses, opium dens, gambling joints, winerooms, chopsuey houses, hotels, and cigar stands have all been leveled. Today, portions of the levee along Dearborn Street are overgrown with weeds, junked automobiles, and housing projects. The Dan Ryan Expressway bisects the area, whisking commuters to and from the central city. Nobody bothers to look, for there is nothing left to see.

6.
Close-up on Chicago in the 1900s: Virtue and Betrayal

IT WAS A MAN'S WORLD. MEN OWNED THE PROPERTY, ELECTED THE PRESIdent, and, for all intents and purposes, reared the children. Growing numbers of women were finding employment in the bustling factories and offices of Chicago, but the very idea of wage-earning women was contrary to the grain in 1907 (the year this story takes place). Women were, as George Bernard Shaw observed, ". . . all the same. The only thing to be said for them is they are well dressed and extraordinarily good looking."

Romantic fiction spewed forth from the pages of *Ladies Home Journal* provided a handy guide on how to achieve the ideal love state. Chastity, fidelity, and virtue were the tried-and-true path the American girl of 1907 followed. Anything less would result in shame, disease, degradation, and even death. Their scarlet sisters in the levee served as an example of the unprincipled life. So the romantic fare became an ideal escape from harsher realities. Unless they happened to be the privileged daughters of the old society families (and thereby assured of an arranged marriage to the bankrupt English nobility), the road through life was a somber passage for the anonymous women who attained adulthood in the early 1900s.

Frances Riccollet and Maria Sexton never attended glittering Prairie Avenue parties and never took the European tour that all young persons of culture and refinement were required to do. They wore simple dresses of broadcloth purchased from the Sears Roebuck Catalog or from one of the sale tables at Siegel-Cooper.

Perhaps they enjoyed reading about Evelyn Nesbit Thaw, the

femme-fatale wife of Harry K. Thaw of Pittsburgh. The young, handsome (and crazy) Thaw gunned down her lover Stanny White in faraway New York. It was the scandal of the decade. Evelyn Nesbit was the ice-cool image of womanhood created by Charles Dana Gibson and found in the advertising popular culture of the day. The indifferent stare, delicate coiffure, and strength of character disguised by outward fragility was the role model girls tried to adopt. It was a myth, but a viable one, used to attract the rising young man who might provide them with home, hearth, and family. Except for a small minority of activists who visualized a time when women might gain equal footing with men, most girls aspired to little else. And in fact, most of them achieved their goals.

But what of those who didn't measure up? What about those caught in the web of society's pretenses about proper conduct for young women? And what about the poor unfortunate who betrayed her virtue for a future prescribed by *Ladies Home Journal*? At the end of each calendar year, the chief of police submitted his report to the general superintendent detailing the street crime of the past year. Included in this listing were the numbers of arrested swindlers, drunkards, horse thieves, loiterers, and keepers of houses of ill fame, as well as the year's suicide victims. Suicide was a nuisance—and an illegal one at that. But each one had to be listed in vital statistics. Looking back at those early years, we see there was no pattern. There were 387 fatal attempts in 1906, and 382 in 1907. No names, just numbers.

It is not known how many were men, but the tragic stories of a young woman's misfortunes spread across the front page in six-inch type. People wanted it that way.

There were some sensational suicides in 1907. Anna Normoyle's death leap on July 17 from the fifteenth floor of the Masonic Temple created a near riot among Loop workers streaming through the spacious rotunda at 5 P.M. It was a daring, dangerous tableau vivant; screaming, fainting women and ashen-faced men. The young woman broke away from a luncheon companion because of depression over a lingering illness. The force of her impact caused sections of the marble floor to crack.

The very next day, a thirty-year-old housewife named Anna Scott strolled into Washington Park wearing a diamond tiara and lily-white dress valued at $37. She drank a near deadly dose of carbolic acid, swooned, and collapsed in a heap. She lived but had to face an unforgiving husband who had found out about a 3 A.M. meeting with a strange man on Madison Street a fortnight earlier. Her suicide attempt was the only way she knew of dealing with the divorce papers that were about to be served on her.

In the larger news stories of that year, Maria Sexton and Frances Riccollet would not earn a mention. Their lives merely became numbers in Chief Shippey's report to the superintendent. They were not counted among the forty-seven destitute women sent to the county agent in 1907 or the thirty-one poor souls sent to the Home of the Friends. Maria and Frances were not street walkers, vagrants, or Apple Annies. They were two single women left in Chicago by men lacking in honor. Theirs is a story of two women in their mid-twenties who saw youth slipping away; a story of virtue and betrayal in Chicago.

Maria Sexton worked a drab job at the Chicago Box Factory located at 241 Jefferson Street, when she met Joseph Gillespie. She lived in a miserable little flat at 950 Robey Street (now Damen Avenue). She met Gillespie nightly. In him she saw a man who might rescue her from a life alone on the west side and the fears of old age and spinsterhood. She was only twenty-three years old on the night of October 3, 1907, when she visited Gillespie's house at 57 Augusta Street to make one final plea to him to make good on his marriage vow. Maria Sexton was with child, a situation Gillespie did not find to his liking.

"At one time I was engaged to marry Miss Sexton," he said at the inquest the next day. "But I found out some things which caused me to change my mind."

He rejected her plea, so she returned to her flat to write two poignant letters that in a more enlightened age seem overdrawn and cloaked with Victorian sentiment. But they revealed the betrayal and the shame. Clutching a leather Bible, a small pistol, and the letters, Maria Sexton returned to Gillespie's street. Several doors away from where he now slept, she discharged a shell into the right side of her head and collapsed in the alley. It began to rain.

At five o'clock the next morning a newsboy named Joseph Zevertnick was making his rounds. The skies were still black, but a bolt of lightning momentarily illuminated the shape of a body lying in the alley. The boy ran screaming to the West Chicago Avenue police station. The police came with lanterns. They examined the body to see if it was a murder.

She clutched a prayer book in her left hand and a pistol in the right.

The pages were streaked and water-logged, but the book was open to the litany of the saints. In her handbag they found a few coins, a key to the flat, and some dime-store items used for personal grooming. Then

Abandoned in Chicago, Maria Sexton was with child when she committed suicide on October 3, 1907. When they discovered the body lying in the alley outside the house of her intended, her Bible was open to the litany of the saints.

they found the two letters tucked in her shirtwaist which laid bare Gillespie's betrayal.

> Dear little boy: I know you feel bad, but you have a comfortable home and relatives and friends to help you pass the dreary hours of your life; a good position and you earning enough money for any man to be satisfied with. You have no worry for the outcome of the future.
> What have I? The cold shoulder from every one, no home and the little place I now call home I'll have to part with, for I can't stay here any longer. Clothes to be bought for myself and the baby. Then to a hospital to work for my board, and God himself only knows what treatment I will get there.
> And yet you can desert the girl you love or once loved. Joe Darling, you know I was as true to you as any girl could be. I told you the truth before you ever took me to your home. Why did you not leave me then?
> It is not one that you are harming, but two. Oh, may God forgive you shall be my prayer night and day.
> Joe please, for God's sake return to me again for it is killing me. I can't stand it if you don't return sweet-heart, and you will regret it the longest and last day you live.
> Darling, please return to me and be my loving little Joe. I will never again do anything to offend you as long as I live. My heart is broken and my life is a wreck.
> Marie Sexton

The letter was concluded with a verse.

> Ah truly those are the saddest words of tongue and pen—
>   It might have been! It might have been!
> Everybody is loved by someone. Everybody knows that to be true.
> Some have a father and mother dear, and brother and sister too—
>   All this I remember since I was a babe so small.
> I have seemed to be the only one nobody loves.

Gillespie was arrested that morning and brought before a coroner's inquest. He assumed a remarkable indifference under questioning and a coldness to his girlfriend's misfortune. Deputy Coroner Andrews remonstrated him about his sense of values before releasing him from jurisdiction. Gillespie stepped out of the courtroom and on with the rest of his life.

A face of innocence—innocence compromised because a half-hearted promise of love was broken. Frances Riccollet was just one of a thousand nameless, homeless girls who came to Chicago at the turn of the century seeking a better life, but she found the gay city lights to be a mere illusion.

In some ways Frances Riccollet's story has no beginning, just an end. She died on March 11, 1907, but nobody knew when she was born. For three weeks she lived at 483 Western Avenue (now 1000 Western). She was another without a home, family, money, and options when she fired a bullet into her head at the rooming house owned by Elizabeth McDermott and Mrs. Charles Davis.

Francis Riccollet was a French-Canadian girl, born and reared in Sault Ste. Marie, Michigan. Following the death of her parents, she went into the world, turning up in Kenosha, Wisconsin, as a domestic. It was here that she attracted the attentions of Nicholas P. Neilson, an older, wealthy saloon keeper at 16 Main Street. For two years Frances worked her job and continued to believe in Neilson's half-hearted promises to marry her. So much so, she agreed to go with him to Chicago on February 11, 1907.

They lived together as man and wife in the Davis's rooming house on the west side for several days. Then Neilson left Frances with three weeks' of rent money for a job prospect in St. Paul. Then for many days, she did not hear from him. Finally she received a postcard that was postmarked Seattle, which read; "I am gone from Chicago forever —Nick." Apparently the landlord did not take Frances's suicide vow seriously; at 3 P.M. two revolver shots were heard from the upstairs bedroom.

She was found lying face down on the floor, barely alive. A police ambulance was summoned, and the girl was admitted to St. Elizabeth's at 3:45. There she died. Police officials returned to her room and found a trunk full of letters received from Neilson that spanned the previous two years. They also found her suicide note left to the coroner and to her sisters in Sault Ste. Marie—sisters that later did not see fit to claim her body.

> To the coroner: Not knowing that my folks can take care of my body, I ask you to lay me away the best you can. I have no money, only $12.50. My health has been poor, and I have waited in the hope that P.N. Neilson, 16 Main Street, Kenosha who has trapped me for two years would marry me. He has made me many promises and now to know that he has left me has killed me. I see in the card just sent me he is going east. I am completely helpless and in tears and completely broken down.
>
> Frances

> To my sisters: It is with a broken heart that I write these few lines that I have fallen away. I cannot longer resist the temptation to end it all. In tears I am left alone, forgotten and forsaken. I see no other way but to kill myself, as I am tired of knocking about the world homeless. I am set back in my future happiness and I do not care for anything. I am now dying in sin; don't despair. Pardon me for taking my life, but my troubles are hard to endure. I have been dying by inches a long time. Goodbye to all my sisters and brothers.
>
> Your sister, Frances.

The body was held at the morgue the required nine days. Frances Riccollet, previous address unknown, was denied the decency of Christian burial at Potter's Field. Robbed of her dignity, her body was given to the Northwestern University Dental School at Dearborn and Lake. She began her life in rural America and ended it anonymously in a cold city. The death certificate was signed by Coroner Peter Hoffman who summarized her life and death as such: "From shock and hemorrhage caused by a bullet wound in her right temple from a revolver held in her own hand with suicidal intent while despondent."

A rebuilt St. Elizabeth Hospital stands several blocks from Western and Augusta Avenues where Frances killed herself. The rooming house has been gone for many years. In its place stands a drugstore, grimy and gray from years of Chicago winters. But Frances's arrival in a police wagon is dutifully noted on March 11, 1907, buried deep in the hospital's microfilmed medical records. Nicholas Nelsen, barkeep at 72 Main Street, appears in the Kenosha City Directory for 1906. There is no record of Nicholas Neilson at 16 Main Street. Perhaps these persons are one and the same. After seventy-eight years it is impossible to tell.

And that is all there is. Maria Sexton and Frances Riccollet were among Chicago's homeless unwanted class. Except for a few scintillating paragraphs in the afternoon papers, their lives and times have vanished, together with the society that gave all its advantages to men. Maybe Nicholas Neilson's and Joe Gillespie's lives were stained by these two tragedies, but then, probably not. Perhaps these men later raised families of their own and became respected business leaders in their community. Most likely, they never told their wives about what transpired in Chicago in the spring of 1907, before they died sometime in the 1950s, tranquil and uncaring.

Nine days before Frances Riccollet penned her last letter, the Salvation Army opened its anti-suicide bureau at 399 State Street. General William Booth himself visited the site and praised the fine efforts of Mary Stillman and Alexander MacMillan who took credit for saving thirty-five friendless souls from a ghastly fate. "Before you preach to them, fill their stomachs," Mary Stillman said, explaining her amazing success.

7.
... Of Bombs, Gamblers, Racing Wires, Newspaper Wars, & Mont Tennes

WHO WAS MONT TENNES? BY HIS OWN ADMISSION HE WAS A "NEWSPAPERman distributing sporting news." Another account called him the perfect Chicago criminal—that is, he got away with it. The Mont Tennes story begins sometime around the turn of the century when he trimmed a bunch of suckers in a State Street crap game. He wandered into the illegal gathering with a few dollars and emerged with $3,800. Two days later Tennes went back to the same crap game to bet higher stakes, this time on a prize fight. Tennes bet the whole wad and won $7,600. And so began the checkered, mysterious career of the German immigrant's son. The trail Mont Tennes blazed, stretched from the poolrooms of the north side, to the federal courtrooms downtown, to the bloody prohibition and gambling wars of Alphonse Capone. It is a trail of bombs, comedy, crooked cops, mayors on the take, ruthless publishers, sluggers, and hustlers. In the end Mont had the last laugh on them all. He lived to tell the tale, and he kept his money.

His early life is a mystery. He was born in Chicago on January 16, 1874, but there is no record of the event in the city records. His real name was Jacob Tennes, a concession to his father. But everyone began calling him Mont, a nickname given to him as a lad by his mother. "I don't believe I ever heard a name like that," crusty old Judge Landis told him in 1916. "Is it short for Montmorcy?" Some of the wiseacres who frequented his handbooks laughed at the judge's question. Landis cleared the courtroom.

Jacob Tennes the elder was a clerk who resided at 203 Chicago Avenue. His son's name first appears in the city directory for 1897. His occupation was listed as bartender, but young Mont had brains and guile. The next year he bought his own place at 287 Center Street. Into his billiard hall and saloon wandered the scions of the old gambler combines. Mont got to meet the safe blowers, confidence men, and the mustachioed whist players in tweed suits and derby hats. They concealed tiny derringers and "sleeve holdouts" (a pulley device sewn into a jacket to produce a winning hand in the palm when needed). They included Harry Kavanaugh, Ed Brennan, and Daniel Dee; but they got careless. Brennan ran Hyde Park but skipped out to Ireland during one of the police shakeups. Kavanaugh's switchboard was ripped apart by Herman Schuettler's "flying squadron," so he fled to England. Daniel Dee left his interests in the capable hands of Jim O'Leary, the "Gambler Boss 'iv th' Yards," an arch enemy (but occasional ally) of Tennes during the Chicago gambling wars. O'Leary (the contrary son of Catherine O'Leary of the cow-and-the-Chicago-Fire controversy) ran the stockyards in direct opposition to Tennes. He went into partnership with Rod Laverty and opened his saloon and handbook across from the transit house of the Chicago stockyards.

A large advertisement attached to the building said, "Why go downtown? Everything in the city brought right here for your enjoyment and comfort. Do you want a Turkish bath? Here is the place. Shave? Come in. Bowling alleys? The best in the city. Restaurant? We serve anything that can be had from land or sea. A little wager on dice or the ponies? We might be persuaded to take your money." O'Leary ran an honest game. He would bet on anything and anyone, but the other gamblers admitted that Big Jim was no piker. O'Leary was an accomplished bowler who regularly participated in the national tournaments. During these trips, he would stuff $30,000 in a satchel and put it under his bed for safe keeping. Inside his Halsted Street Palace, there was an eighty-foot marble and mahogany bar. O'Leary the old "art collector" even sold paintings displayed prominently along the walls.

O'Leary's place was rigged with a warning system that when sounded, activated heavy iron doors that prevented police raiders from entering the gambling rooms on the second floor. It was truly the showplace of the Chicago bookmaking parlors.

West-side interests were dominated by Johnny Rogers of the nineteenth ward, who made his peace with Tennes. "Blind" John Condon opened up the Roby Racetrack in suburban Harlem in 1899, thanks to O'Leary's financial backing. Tom McGinnis was a former ally of Big

. . . Of Bombs, Gamblers, and Racing Wires

Jim as well as the proprietor of a saloon at 311 Clark Street and a link to Aldermen Kenna and Coughlin, who had their hands in everyone's pie.

There were three powerful gambler combinations vying for control of the Chicago betting dollar in 1900. Mike McDonald's interests were being protected by Frank McWhorter, his old bookkeeper Harry Holland, safeblower "Paddy" Guerin, Dan Brown, and John Ryan. The most influential gambling syndicate was headed by Charles "Social" Smith, Harry Perry, Bud White, and McGinnis, who ended his connections with O'Leary.

Jim O'Leary stood alone against the two combines, while Mont Tennes remained on the sidelines prudently waiting for an opening. For years, the three syndicates battled each other over territory and spoils, the same way Al Capone conducted his beer wars a quarter of a century later. It was never clear to the cops which gambler was working for O'Leary or Bud White. Loyalties frequently shifted. Retaliation for perceived treaty violations did not come in the form of bullets or the one-way ride. Hired constables would secure arrest warrants against a rival, and a raid would be conducted. The Chicago police welcomed the assistance of the "private cops" because when the syndicates were at war, the town was generally "closed," which reflected well on the chief.

In 1901, the representatives of the three syndicates met in Evanston to agree on some common objectives and to hammer out an agreement that would end the petty bickering. It was decided to abandon handbooking in Chicago during the winter and to confine gambling to one suburban poolroom. Several of the older poolrooms that had been constructed alongside of the drainage canals in Evanston and Indiana were closed by mutual agreement. During the summer racing seasons, handbooking was allowed as long as no syndicate tried to gain an upper hand. In 1902, the first of several costly wars broke out when O'Leary violated existing agreements by pushing his influence back into the central city and at the racetracks.

The gambling combines operated their poolrooms (which were nothing more than off-track betting parlors) in opposition to the sanctioned races at Hawthorne, Roby, and Washington Park. Racetrack entrepreneurs were not anxious to lose their business to the poolrooms, which provided results from *all* the tracks as well as games of faro and roulette. When the poolroom operators weren't fighting each other, they competed against the tracks, sometimes violently.

Arsonists torched the Hawthorne Race Track on May 30, 1902, following the conclusion of the fourth race. Two men were observed loitering near the base of the cupola. Nobody thought it was unusual for someone to stand on top of the roof to watch a race, but a few minutes later there was a puff of smoke and then a burst of flame. The structure was made of wood, an easy tinder. The paddock, considered to be the finest in the west by professional horsemen, was also leveled. Hawthorne was rebuilt in just seven weeks, this time with concrete and steel. But who would do such a thing?

The gamblers accused Jim O'Leary, who had an interest in Condon's Roby Track. It was also a chance to retaliate against Smith-Perry-White, who conducted their handbooks inside Hawthorne. A year later, agents set fire to a can of oil underneath the grandstand at Washington Park. Inspector Nicholas Hunt of the Chicago Police Department stood idly by while other men doused the flames. Hunt was from the stockyards district and a loyal friend of O'Leary.

"The fight that is in progress is not an effort to force anyone to give up a portion of their (sic) business," explained Frank McWhorter, who engineered the revolt against O'Leary. "It is a fight to force compliance with the terms of a contract that is going to be enforced. Two years ago [1901] all the bookmaking interests of Chicago entered into an ironclad agreement extending over a period of nine years by which there was to be no handbooking or poolselling in Chicago whatever." Nobody seriously believed that the gamblers planned to stay out of the city. The *Daily News* offered a more realistic appraisal of the situation on August 30, 1903.

> The trust gamblers call out the police one day. The anti-trust gamblers call out the police another day. There is no attempt on either side to disguise the fact that it is a fight to determine which set of gamblers shall control the city, or that part of the city which may be controlled by the influences that do not always make for good. Our mayor [Harrison] is in Yellowstone; our chief of police [O'Neill] is composing melodies; all the rest of them are afraid to move lest they move the wrong way. And so the gamblers are compelled to settle the matter between themselves.

Armed with axes and shotguns, constables headed up by Dickie Dean, a paid agent of Smith-Perry, raided O'Leary's fortress on August 27. "I can stand raids as long as you can," O'Leary said to Bud White's people, when he appeared in court to post bond for his men. "I

. . . Of Bombs, Gamblers, and Racing Wires

am willing to follow my profession on the proposition and bet that I will be up when the 'gambler's trust' is a back number."

The very next day, O'Leary's agents busted into Tom McGinnis's Clark Street resort to arrest a group of Chinese playing a game called "bung-loo." While this was going on, Smith-Perry men raided Mont Tennes's place at 123 Clark. Tennes refused to join the trust, and his independence was considered to be an acknowledgment of a partnership with O'Leary. This was not the case, however.

Inside Mont's place, betting sheets that showed $1,000 worth of wagers placed at Hawthorne were seized by Dean. Despite the setbacks, O'Leary vowed to sweat it out, even though his telegraph direct to Hawthorne was cut off.

O'Leary's war against the trust was also a war against Kenna and Coughlin, who sided with Bud White and Social Smith. All O'Leary got for his troubles were nine indictments handed down by the grand jury, and his prestige in gambling circles was diminished by the 1903 war. Mont Tennes had wisely distanced himself from the stockyard boss.

Before the Tennes syndicate expanded its sphere of influence, much of the power still rested with the racetrack owners. In July of 1904, a special grand jury indicted sixty-four gamblers, including Mont Tennes and his brother Peter. Mont pleaded guilty to a charge of bookmaking and paid a $200 fine. He would not suffer the same kind of indignity again, until 1922.

The latest drive to clean out the Hawthorne Racetrack of its bookies was spearheaded by Louis Seeberger, president of the Citizen's Association. At his behest, the grand jury ordered Sheriff Thomas Barrett to arrest known bookies on sight. The jury also summoned Victor Lawson of the *Daily News* to explain why his paper persisted in listing the betting odds and racetrack dope. The answer was simple. There was good money in it.

Barrett told the jury to mind its own business. The sheriff consulted attorney Levy Mayer, who offered the opinion that a grand jury had as much authority to direct Barrett as the man in the moon. It was obvious he was shielding the powerful racetrack owners, and Bud White did not like it. "It looks to us, what is sauce for the goose, is sauce for the gander," White said. If this legal opinion were true, then it held that their poolrooms should be allowed to operate without interference.

O'Leary cautiously opened his resort on Blue Island Avenue, while the Citizen's Association sought relief from State's Attorney Charles

Deneen, who offered the usual stock reply. He sympathized with the reformers, but there was nothing he could do. The statutes clearly left it up to the sheriff to police the racetracks. So the Citizen's Association of neighboring Harlem *drafted* Barrett as a posse for their gambling squad. He was a resident and private citizen of the community and, therefore, could not be exempt from duty. Before it got to that, the indictments against the Hawthorne gamblers collapsed when the key witness, Detective Otto Schubert turned up missing. He had gone undercover to place bets with the track bookies.

Up to 1905 the territories were still in dispute. Tennes expanded his interests by purchasing several saloons, one known as the Turf at 499 Lincoln Avenue. His saloons were just fronts for the gambling operations in the back room.

Mayor Edward Dunne's election in 1905 signaled a return of the wide-open town. The new mayor took one positive step by reappointing Police Chief Francis O'Neill on June 26, 1905. It was a first for Chicago politics. Up to that time, no police chief had ever survived a mayoral change, but it was short-lived. The relatively honest O'Neill was retired by Dunne on July 26 in favor of an old political crony named John Collins.

Like many other high-ranking officials in the department at the time, Collins was a veteran of the Haymarket troubles. In fact, he stood in the third column of patrolmen who were dynamited that night. (Curiously, another notorious grafter stood right next to him. His name was Patrick Lavin. Both men escaped injury.)

Collins caught the attention of Edward Dunne's father in 1889, after his work on the Cronin case. Dr. Cronin, a wealthy physician, was involved in Irish nationalist politics. A secret organization known as the Clan-Na-Gaels murdered him for his opposing views. For years, the Clan-Na-Gaels exerted influence over prominent members of the police force. Collins was transferred to Simon O'Donnell's west-side district by Joseph Kipley, a Clan-Na-Gaels sympathizer himself. (Even in 1900, O'Donnell's 12th Street district was still the political graveyard for cops who fell from grace.) When Kipley was ousted as chief, Collins made a belated comeback.

On the surface, Dunne's choice appeared to be a sound one. O'Neill was a sentimental old man fond of the Irish ballads of his homeland. He would frequently sing them to anyone who cared to listen.

The *Tribune* applauded Collins when he said that "gambling in this

. . . Of Bombs, Gamblers, and Racing Wires 183

town is a disgrace. We have handbooks, poker, craps, slot machines, and every gambling device known. Men are waylaid on their way home from work and solicited by barkers and touts. We can drive every

Sentimental old Francis O'Neill, chief of police from 1901 to 1905. O'Neill was the first chief to survive a Chicago mayoral change. He was a noted balladeer of Irish folk songs and was more honest than his successor, John Collins.

damned one of them out of Chicago, and we'll try to do it." A series of spectacular raids the next day convinced the reformers that Collins was a man of his word. "Chicago's got a live one now. It's off the map for you, fellers," someone said as gambling inmates from the Madison Street Calhoun Club were led into patrol wagons. Detectives armed with sledge hammers turned the betting tables into kindling, while poker chips were crunched under foot. Five raids in the downtown district filled the Harrison Street station. Men identified as city-hall employees were given bonds supplied by Andy Craig, who was waiting for them. While the bonds were being written, the gamblers were instructed to report back the next day. Craig shook his head sadly. "Just about sixty-five forfeitures and fines for me tomorrow," he said.

Telephones, wheels of fortune, and city directories were seized at thirteen more gambling parlors and were brought to city hall as evidence. Most of the paraphernalia was taken from Tennes's establishments at 123, 165, and 214 Clark Street. The Gem Cigar Store at 123 Clark was a favored target of the raiders during every reform movement. It was said that the place was raided so many times that a bondsman was kept on the payroll full-time.

Collins was satisfied with his day's work. "I don't want to talk any more until I have done something. I am determined to drive out every gambler in the city."

Perhaps that accounts for why he removed competent Herman Schuettler from the gambling detail and placed himself in charge. The Collins raids caused the gamblers a minor inconvenience. A bail bondsmen had to be summoned, and gambling fines ranging from $1 for visiting a handbook to $100 for keeping a house were paid. And that was it. They reopened just as quickly and continued to operate until the next wave of reform gripped the department. During this time, Tennes became the big fish among Loop gamblers.

Faro, roulette, and the handbooks yielded up to 50 percent of their gross to the Tennes syndicate. Certain police officials were allowed to bet free and keep whatever winnings they accumulated. It was good public relations and smart politics. In this way, no cop would dare arrest J.E. Ackerman, Mont's business solicitor, who stood outside the poolroom at 14 Federal Street. Each day during the noon hour, Ackerman handed out business cards that said "Pool & Billiards."

"It's a fine place. Tennes, you know. Nice big rooms. Pleasant play, and the right sort of crowd." Inside, a group of thirty men hud-

. . . Of Bombs, Gamblers, and Racing Wires   185

dled around a billiard table turned into a dice shoot. The stakes were a quarter a throw.

It was about this time that Tennes announced the first of several "retirements." The cops placated the reformers by closing several of the North Clark Street handbooks. The reality was that Tennes operated a poolroom inside the board of trade and another across the street from the Chicago Avenue Police station. Coinciding with the election of friend Dunne was the announcement from the Smith-Perry camp that a Lake Michigan cruise ship named the *City of Traverse* would set sail from the Illinois Central Slip at the 68th Street Crib.

The boat was a thirty-six-year-old steamer that White, Pat O'Malley, and Charles "Social" Smith purchased from the Hibernian Bank, following their foreclosure against the previous owners. The combine spent $40,000 to make the ship seaworthy. That meant redecorating the cabin and building a well-stocked bar where the infirmary once stood. Wireless telegraphic equipment ran to the masthead of the ship. Dr. Lee DeForest, who pioneered the radio, agreed to the installation of his new invention on board the *City of Traverse*. By doing so, DeForest invited a score of legal battles with the city. The question was whether he was aiding and abetting an illegal enterprise. He eventually obtained an injunction in the courts, claiming that what they did with the device was not his concern.

Sharp flashes of light and metallic clicks from the wires brought the race results to a single operator sitting inside the cabin. He telephoned the names of the horses in cipher code to the bookmaking stands in the lower deck. The transmissions were tested forty miles out into the lake by Bud White, who pronounced the ship ready.

The gambling boat set sail on June 29, 1905, with several hundred sports on board. Bud White commandeered the vessel twenty-two miles southeast of Chicago, and ten miles north of the Indiana shoreline. Detectives Breternitz and Schubert from Herman Schuettler's gambling squad were interested observers, but there was nothing they could legally do.

"Gentlemen, we are now outside the jurisdiction of Illinois. Start gambling," Bud White said, casting a glance toward the Chicago detectives. Pasteboards bearing the name of horses running in the first race at Buffalo were posted for the gamblers. A string orchestra played ragtime, while White chatted with the detectives. "And there are no U.S. laws prohibiting gambling. I think this here undertaking's going to be a big success." The ship returned at 6 P.M., after all the betting slips had been tossed into the boiler. The gamblers were left at the South Water Street pier. (When the city put the heat on the boat operators, the ship anchored offshore. A boat named the *Eagle* was used to ferry the gamblers to the *City of Traverse*.)

When pressed for an accounting of what the state's attorney's office planned to do, John Healy expressed the opinion that it was up to the Chicago police. There was a raid a few days later, but the boat continued to run till August, when it closed its first season.

The Illinois Central provided special race trains to the dock, and there wasn't a thing the police *wanted* to do about it. The boat ran two full seasons, and it employed twenty-one ex-constables that had been fired from municipal court employ. Dunne and Collins allowed the ship carte blanche, while the *Tribune* alleged that $2,000 a week in protection was paid by the Smith combine. The DeForest Wireless Company had an exclusive contract to provide racing results, but the betting patrons could never be sure whether the tellers or operators were legit.

Fourth of July, 1906, brought out larger crowds than expected. Gamblers lost over $10,000 when the board flashed a 7-1 longshot as the winner. The horse named Beau Brummel really had failed to show, so after the Beau Brummel ticket holders jammed the windows to redeem their stubs, the board corrected itself and listed Attention as the rightful winner. By this time, the winning gamblers destroyed their tickets or were so far back in line when the windows closed that they were unable to cash in.

That same week, Tennes got into the navigation business himself. "Why, there is good money in it," he explained from the deck of his *John R. Sterling*. "I might as well run a boat just like those people." It was a costly, disappointing venture for Tennes (nearly $75,000). The *City of Traverse* had to go, and Mont realized that direct competition was not the answer. The standard police raids also failed. When Herman Schuettler built a wireless station on the Indiana shoreline to intercept and spoil the boat's circuit, the Smith-Perry forces burned it down in the middle of the night. Attorney Ben Hyman represented the combine in court, effectively checking State's Attorney John Healy's probes.

Smith and Perry retaliated against Tennes when he opened the Dearborn Park Pavilion outside of Hammond, Indiana. Tennes advertised his place as a "safe and attractive place for the following of the ponies." It was understood that the local police chief, Joseph Martin,

... Of Bombs, Gamblers, and Racing Wires 187

would not interfere with the gamblers who gathered to bet on the Jacksonville races. Tennes and his partner Tom McGinnis constructed betting cages, boards, and rows of seats for Chicago gambling patrons. Wireless equipment was on order from New York so that police officials would be unable to cut any wires.

The grand opening was held January 1, 1910. Train loads of bettors arrived from Chicago, just in time to sample homemade pie provided by Tennes. Everyone settled down to do some serious wagering, when suddenly the wires went dead. Sheriff Thomas Grant appeared with his deputies to announce that the park was closed by order of Governor Thomas Marshall, who was perceived to be a liberal ally of Tennes. Something had gone wrong. Marshall vowed to send the militia in, if the gamblers showed up again. He also promised to destroy any wireless towers that Tennes tried to install. Harry Perry and Social Smith had somehow reached the governor's office. So Mont lost some of his customers to Jim O'Leary's Stockade in DuPage County, where twenty guard dogs patrolled a 150' x 120' building surrounded by a high fence. Western Union provided the telegraph results, and race trains from Chicago were provided by the Santa Fe. O'Leary was safe and sound in his fortress built on the Chicago Sanitary District. The Stockade lasted only as long as it took Attorney General William Stead to "convince" the Santa Fe and Western Union that it would be in the public interest if they discontinued the service. Tennes and O'Leary had both found the hinterland not to their liking.

The changing winds of Chicago politics brought an unexpected victory for Mont Tennes in 1907. Ex-saloon keeper and coal magnate Fred Busse ran for mayor on the Republican ticket against Dunne. He was supported by the big-money interests, who were anxious to see through a traction ordinance that would give the city 55 percent of the net operating profits of the line. Dunne was hostile to the bill because a closer examination of what was at stake showed that the 55 percent was actually 27 percent. The $90 million in revenue guaranteed the Chicago City Railway and the Chicago Railways Company a fixed 5 percent profit *before* the city could participate in the net. Of the $40 million new capital, the two companies were allowed to reap 15 percent and then a continuous 5 percent annually. What all this meant was that Chicago received 27 percent of the net profit and 10 percent of the gross. At this time the Chicago City Railway was still under the control of J.P. Morgan and John D. Rockefeller.

The *Tribune* accused Dunne of "Hearstism" (the worst possible

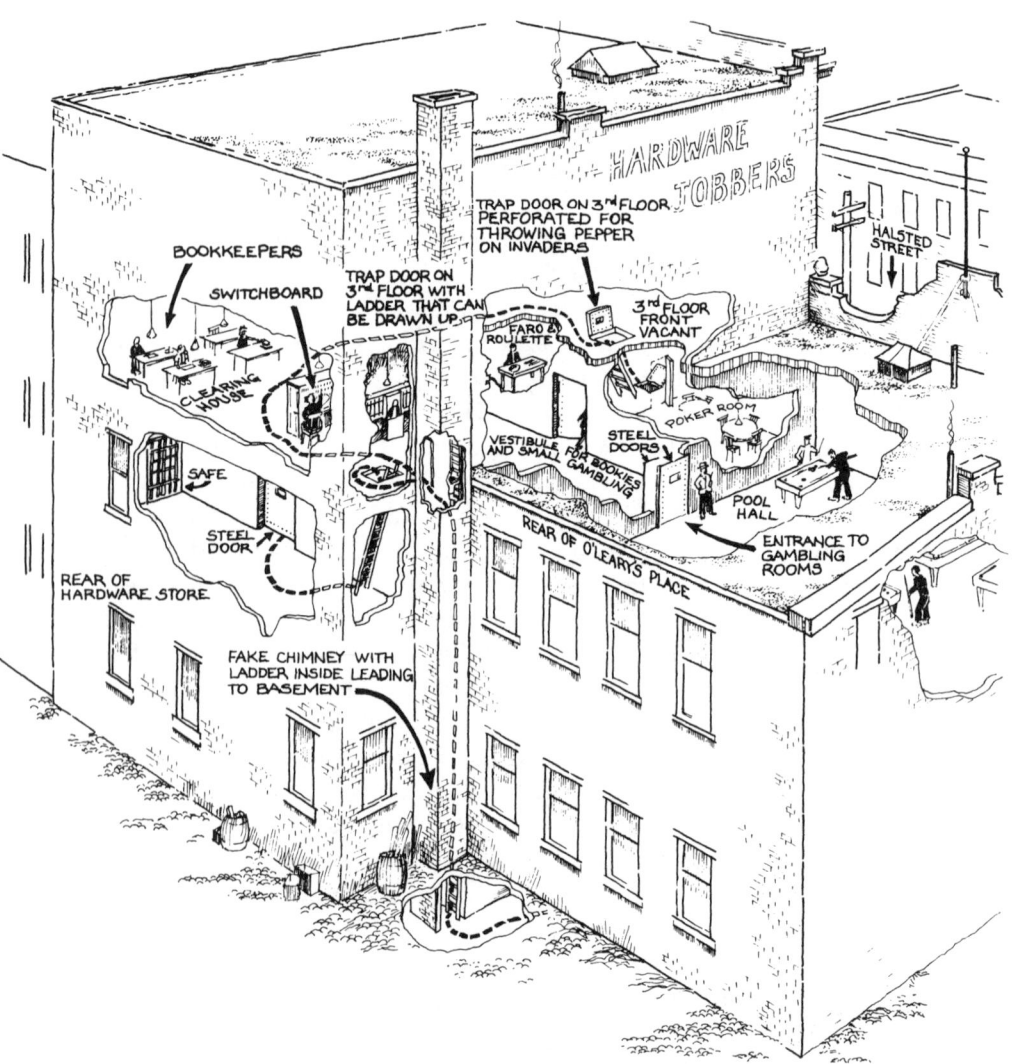

A cutaway drawing of Big Jim O'Leary's Halsted Street gambling fortress. On August 12, 1907, a bomb was placed in the second-floor poolroom. The explosion caused little damage because the doors were made of heavy-duty iron. O'Leary hired a gas-pipe repairman to tell the cops that a faulty pipe had blown out.

crime in their view) in one of the dirtiest of city elections. Dunne was charged with shaking down tavern owners to further his campaign. Police Chief John Collins and William O'Connor, commissioner of public works, were indicted in 1907 for a conspiracy to violate the civil

. . . Of Bombs, Gamblers, and Racing Wires 189

service law. They assessed a series of fines to city employees that were funneled directly into Dunne's campaign.

With the election hanging in the balance, a deal was struck between the traction people and the first ward. Kenna and Coughlin agreed to deliver 12,000 votes (of questionable origin) to Busse if four conditions were met. First, the wide-open city would continue unabated. Second, the Bath and the Dink would be given a free hand in their district. Third, the *City of Traverse* would be closed for good (Mont allied himself with the first-ward bosses in his war against Smith-Perry). And fourth, Inspector Patrick Lavin and Nicholas Hunt would both be reinstated to the police force that they had recently been suspended from.

Hunt owned $400,000 of Hyde Park real estate and had allowed the vice district to run wide open before his dismissal. Lavin accepted racing horses as a gift from call-house madams and was given $40,000 worth of Swift stock as a reward for brutally dispersing the 1904 stockyard strikers.

Busse was swept in. Lavin was reinstated, and the traction ordinances passed. Over $33 million was spent on new equipment for the railway lines, but there was an unforeseen problem. The new, wider cars that provided room for more standing patrons only allowed a nine-inch clearance when they passed each other on the street. Fifteen people were crushed to death in just one month after being sandwiched in between.

In May 1907, the first and only arrest of *City of Traverse* gamblers was made at South Chicago Water Street. Three cops in disguise sat on the wharf idly rolling a log, when the tugboat *Robert Burke* pulled to shore. While the tug deposited its passengers, Detective Shea fired three warning shots into the air. The gamblers ran pell-mell but were blocked by a uniformed squadron. The remaining 400 still on board were taken to the Indiana state line, far beyond police jurisdiction. Of the seventy-five arrested, six were released following a private conference on the beach. Syndicate bondsman Johnny Burns emerged from one of the nearby saloons with a fistful of bonds. The other gamblers were thus spared exposure and embarrassment in the morning papers.

The license of the *City of Traverse* was revoked on July 10. In September of that year, the Smith-Perry group abandoned their attempts to keep the ship operating. It was sold to the Graham & Morton line, which planned to use it to run excursions from Chicago to St. Joseph, Michigan. Later, the boat became a permanent fixture at the dock in Benton Harbor.

The very same day that the license was revoked the opening shot of the second Gambler's War was thrown at "Blind" John Condon's house at 2623 Michigan Avenue. Blind John was relaxing in the rear of his home at the time. Fortunately for him, the bomb was time-fused, causing only slight damage to the façade. The war of revenge and spoils was on. Other theories for the bombings were advanced, but no one could produce any hard evidence.

Before his death in 1915, "Blind John" Condon was one of the most powerful bosses of the gambling fraternity. An early partner of Mike McDonald in The Store, Condon bought up racetracks in Indiana before taking over the Harlem Racetrack in 1899. In his early days, he worked as a barber. This talent helped him out in later years, when he trimmed his rivals during the violent racetrack wars.

... Of Bombs, Gamblers, and Racing Wires

Bombs

The Gambler's War of 1907 illustrated how inept the Chicago police were in dealing with bombing outrages. And despite the *Tribune's* boast that gambling was closed down tighter at that time than it was ten years before, Mont and his associates assumed a business-as-usual attitude.

Twenty policemen scoured the south side for clues concerning the Condon bombing. Nothing turned up, of course, so Shippey made a token raid on Pat O'Malley's establishment at 421 Clark Street, where dope sheets, blackboards, and the keeper of the house were seized. "Arrests will be made as fast as I can find these places," Shippey bragged.

Two days later, on July 25 at 9 P.M., Mont Tennes's house at 404 Belden Avenue was bombed by person or persons unknown. It was a steel-cased bomb that landed in a paved alley directly in back of the house. Mont was enjoying a bath at the time, and luckily for him, the bomb just broke a few panes of glass. "It was just the work of some mischievous boys who set off a cannon cracker," Tennes told Sergeant Kilgore of the Halsted detail.

After this, the bombs began flying thick and fast, and the pattern was always the same. A deafening blast with little or no damage, followed by the arrival after the dynamiters were long gone of three helmeted police blowing whistles and toting nightsticks.

Jim O'Leary's saloon at 4183 Halsted was wrecked on August 12. O'Leary's poolhall was honey-combed with secret passages, trap doors, steel-walled rooms, and a fake chimney that contained a ladder inside for a fast getaway during a raid. Buildings a block away shook from the impact. People ran madly down the street, and all O'Leary had to say for himself was that a cap on his gas pipe blew out. To support his claim, Big Jim hired a phony gas inspector to tell the cops an outrageous lie.

There were more raids and more bombs. Mont's front yard was hit again on August 19 with only slight damage. "I know nothing about the *City of Traverse*," Tennes demurred. "I was as surprised as anyone when the government put it out of business." The bomb was later found to contain "safeblower's soup"—a combination of nitroglycerin and TNT used by "Paddy" Guerin, recent escapee from Devil's Island and a man well known to Pinkerton agents. Guerin operated a handbook out of the back of "Paddy" Grimes's saloon at 63rd and Cottage

Grove. But Guerin was just another fall guy, and the bombs continued after his arrest.

August 25. O'Malley's saloon at Clark and Kinzie was next. The owner gave the usual stock answer. "I don't mix with gamblers and I don't have no enemies." And the moon is made of green cheese. Ex-sheriff James Pease was himself a victim on September 1, after a group of men wearing straw boaters driving a touring car apparently mistook his house for that of Bud White who lived two blocks away on Magnolia. Pease, whose innocence in this affair remains suspect, also thought it was a firecracker.

Chief Shippey appointed a special task force again headed by Herman Schuettler to get to the bottom of it. It can be said of Schuettler that he was probably the best of a rotten bunch. He survived the scandals, numerous shakeups, and always seemed above board. When he died in 1918, he was Chicago's wealthiest cop.

Using the seldom-enforced vagrancy law, Schuettler's men made some arrests. He claimed to have traced the bombs to an inner circle of safe blowers and ex-*Traverse* employees. Revenge was the motive according to the inspector, so Chicagoans were understandably relieved when a pair of known dynamiters named Elihu Rosencranz and Ed Kelly were nabbed on September 7. The evidence was circumstantial, and the motive for arrest seemed to be revenge. Several months earlier, Kelly was arrested and taken to the Des Plaines station. While being led to his cell, he slipped a pistol out of a policeman's holster. He backed out of the station. But the second arrest lasted only as long as it took bondsman Charles Erbstein to arrive at the jail.

Schuettler had imagination and good intentions. He instructed his men to disguise themselves as train conductors, teamsters, peddlers, and cattlemen wearing bearskin gloves. They climbed telephone poles while posing as linemen, so they could watch the game in progress. Once, the gambling squad traced a crap game in progress to a bank

(Right) "The Gambling Crusade," was seen by *Tribune* cartoonist John T. McCutcheon. During the 1911 probe, Chief John McWeeney fell under heavy criticism for allowing the gambling parlors to flourish under the nose of city hall. The first panel identifies "Sherlock Holmes McWeeney on the job." The second illustration explains what happens when "Schuettler is on the job." Herman Scheuttler was one of the most honest cops of that era. Until the city hall hacks transferred him Scheuttler headed up the relentless "flying squadron." (Reproduction by Bob Deckert.)

... Of Bombs, Gamblers, and Racing Wires 193

vault. When the occupants locked the safe and refused to come out, Schuettler sprinkled red pepper under the crack of the door until the men emerged choking and gagging. When the bookies discovered Schuettler's men placing bets at the handbook parlors under cover,

they created a special cipher system for transmitting their race results to the betting parlors. The code was cracked by the gambling squad after many weeks.

The coding system involved alpha designations. The race the horse was entered in was coded by the name of a state (see chart). There were seven states selected to allow for a full card. The first and last letter of the horse's name were used. The track that the horse was entered was given last. The tracks were coded by use of a bird's name. If the horse's name was long, the gamblers used the first, second, and last letter of the name.

Name of Horse

A—Match
B—Market
C—Majority
D—Medal
E—Monologue
F—Medley
G—Mansion
H—Matinee
I—Mosaic
J—Morning
K—Molest
L—Moccasin
M—Music

N—Mate
O—Moderate
P—Magnet
Q—Master
R—Major
S—Minstrel
T—Mitten
U—Mimic
V—Mighty
W—Mountain
X—Military
Y—Mystery
Z—Maroon

Race Number Designation

First—Ohio
Second—Iowa
Third—Utah
Fourth—Idaho

Fifth—Texas
Sixth—Michigan
Seventh—Colorado

Track at which Horse Was Entered

Oakland—Crow
Juarez—Swallow

Jacksonville—Bantam
Tampa—Canary

. . . Of Bombs, Gamblers, and Racing Wires   195

Example: The horse Tipster, a 20-1 shot, wins the first race at Juarez. Ohio-Mitten-Major-Swallow-20-1-First.

Schuettler raided Mont's clearing house at 823 Larrabee Street a dozen times, but each time the gamblers were found playing checkers or conducting prayer meetings in an empty room. Finally, several men from the squad scaled a telephone pole next to the clearing house. They broke through the window, smashed the switchboard, and seized the valuable paintings that hung on the wall. Gambling "widows" read about these raids. They phoned Mrs. Herman Schuettler at Lakeview-1671 to plead for an end to the games that deprived their husbands of their earnings.

The ninth bomb was hurled at Mont's cash-register business at 123 Clark Street. Over the years Tennes disguised his activities with a variety of fronts, but his Western Cash Register Company was the best cover. It concealed a gambling annex in the back and a special ladies betting salon. The bomb thrown on September 26 was a combination of nitroglycerin and potash steel-cased in an old sock. The cops theorized that Tennes was running a protection racket for gamblers. Those outside the trust were visited by a nocturnal bomb thrower. "Why would anybody want to be put on the payroll of a little cash register store?" Tennes asked.

Why indeed? A grand jury was summoned. The Chicago Telephone Company, a long-time partner of the rival gambling factions, was called in to explain why dozens of phones used for illicit purposes refused to list their numbers in the directories. P.J. Pierce of the phone company said that his company could not act as a judge and jury against its clients. This was a well-worn path, told again in 1911 and 1916.

One hundred subpoenas were served to big gamblers. O'Malley, Tennes, White, Perry, Smith, Condon, Grimes all passed in review but could offer little except a smile and a decoy. When ex-alderman Johnny Rogers was summoned to tell what he knew, a bomb was directed at his Madison Street saloon. If it was a warning against squawking, it worked. The case collapsed, and the only pigeon was Horace Argo, Tennes's mousey, southern confident. Instead of reciting the "I was in it once, but now I'm out of the game" gambit, Argo's refusal to say anything invited a contempt citation. State's Attorney John Healy grilled Argo for hours while he just stared at the wall.

"Hinky Dink" Kenna (left) and Alderman John "Johnny DePow" Powers prepare to lead the famous Democratic Marching Club. Powers had deep ties to the gambling "trust." During the 1907 war, another alderman, Johnny Rogers, was the target of a bomb. When asked what he knew of the affair, Rogers said it was a "good-natured joke by the boys."

Q—Did you ever hear during the time of the *Traverse* that certain part of the money was being paid for [police] protection?

. . . Of Bombs, Gamblers, and Racing Wires

A—No comment.

Q—Do you know that certain poolrooms and gambling games are permitted to operate in Chicago with police protection?

A—No comment.

Q—Do you realize that you are likely to go to jail for this?

A—It's all a part of the game.

The grand jury reported no indictments after two weeks, but Argo was sentenced to six months in jail and a $500 fine. The case went through appeals, and Argo never did spend a night in jail. That winter there were several more bombs, but that soon ended, and Tennes was the victor. But against whom? And for what?

There is no sure explanation for the gambler's war. In 1911, a disgruntled associate of Tennes named Tim Murphy caused a sensation by bearing some secrets. Murphy provided the first and only inside look at the empire in a 1911 newspaper exposé. According to the gambler, a vicious blackmailing outfit was loose in the city in 1907, exacting protection money from the syndicates. They placed nightly telephone calls announcing that "Smith and Jones" were calling. Tennes himself was rumored to have spent $1,500 a week following the second attempt on his home. The fact that several Black Hand safeblowers were active in Chicago at this time lends credence to his theory. But more likely, this was a war of revenge and conquest started by O'Leary and the Smith combine but finished successfully by Mont Tennes.

The Racing Wire

The transmittal of racetrack information by telegraph had been a dangerous and lucrative business since the early 1890s. Until 1899, the Ditmus Company of New York had a monopoly of the distribution of racetrack results to bookies. But Western Union muscled in on Ditmus that year, offering larger percentages to racetrack officials for exclusive rights. In 1904, F. Norton Goddard of the New York City Club launched a civic crusade to smash the cozy relationship the company enjoyed with the underworld.

Western Union defended its right to choose its customers and won some major victories in court. The publicity besmirched the good names of Chauncey DePew, J. Pierpoint Morgan, and John Jacob Astor of the Fifth Avenue crowd, who were officers of the corporation.

At the urging of stockholder Helen Gould, Western Union withdrew from the field.

The pieces were picked up by the Metropolitan News Company of Louisville and a Cincinnati telegraph operator named John A. Payne. The Payne service stretched into fourteen states and Canada, while Metropolitan's income was estimated to be $800,000 to $1 million a year. At first, Tennes bought Payne's service, receiving telegraphed race returns at a switchboard located in the Forest Park train station. The switchboard was a trunk line that contained forty to forty-five wires distributing the information to several hundred Tennes handbooks and poolrooms. The phone numbers of the gambling dens were kept secret by the Chicago Telephone Company, frustrating any legitimate grand jury investigation.

A switchboard operator would then hand the results of races staged at Latonia, Saratoga, and Gravesend to a caller with a megaphone. These results were transmitted in cipher code. For the use of the Payne service, Tennes charged his bookies $25 to $50 a day. Protection was routinely paid to the police, and all income derived from the handbook operators went into a miscellaneous ledger named the "Caldwell Account."

The same Tim Murphy who betrayed the trust attempted to compete directly with Payne, but with little success. In November of 1909, Murphy went to Chicago to sell out to Tennes. As expected, Mont was willing to oblige—with a hard bargain. Horace Argo directed Murphy into Mont's office in the Monadnock Building on Dearborn Street. Tennes agreed to purchase one-third of Murphy's concern for $4,500, but only if the deal might be expanded to half interest for $5,000. Tennes later manipulated Murphy into surrendering all but 10 percent.

By nature Tennes was not prone to violence. He was a family man, devoted to his three sons, and had an easy-going, effusive personality. But he was very much a part of Chicago's criminal underworld of 1910, a collection of "Mustache Petes" who utilized the dynamite bomb as the closer in their dealings.

Murder was a desperate last measure but one that Tennes did not have to revert to in his struggle to establish control of the wire. It was the effective use of the bomb that brought Tennes to the forefront of organized crime during the winter months of 1909–10.

In December, Tennes's agents threw the first bomb at Jake Webber's poolroom in Columbus, Ohio, when he refused to abandon Payne. Bombings were later reported in Hanover, Indiana, St. Louis,

... Of Bombs, Gamblers, and Racing Wires 199

and there were shakedowns of Payne employees in Chicago. In May of 1910, H.I. Brown, manager of the Jacksonville, Florida, racetrack challenged the Tennes dynamiters "to do their worst." Before they were through, Brown's track was burned down *three* times. John Payne's spacious $12,000 house at Crystal Lake, Kentucky, was also destroyed. On May 1, 1910, Payne agreed to meet Tennes secretly in Hammond, Indiana. He sold out for just $300 and a meager 5 percent interest in the business, which was reorganized and renamed the General News Bureau.

Mont had at last succeeded in going nationwide. He blazed a trail of bombs and extortion until the following cities were paying a monthly tribute to the General News Bureau.

New York	$3,000	San Francisco	$1,800
Detroit	400	St. Louis	1,000
Louisville	750	Albany	1,000
West Baden	400	Pittsburgh	700
Buffalo	963	Oklahoma City	105
Cleveland	300	Salt Lake City	125
Baltimore	125	San Antonio	62
Toledo	100	Terre Haute	25
Norfolk	800	Muncie	193
New Orleans	100	Cincinnati	415
Indianapolis	400		

Tennes brought the tracks into line that still persisted in using Metropolitan. He sent agents into Canada, openly defying the Miller Law, which prohibited this kind of activity. One man would stand by the rail, while another would position himself in the clubhouse with a telescope. The man by the rail would flash hand signals to the other operative, but many times the results were inaccurate. Tennes would then sell this information as a part of his pari-mutuel service. When the Canadians heard of the scheme and tried to run Tennes out, the track was burned.

Big Jim O'Leary announced his first retirement from the gambling business on December 1, 1911. Real or imagined, it signaled the dominance of the Tennes forces, who had nothing left to fear from rival groups. Mont's battles continued with the stumbling police and various do-gooders like Harry Brolaski, a reformed gambler who realized that a safer fortune lay at the end of the lecture circuit. He spoke to ladies' clubs, civic federations, and religious groups about the ills of gambling. In 1911, Brolaski sued Tennes for $25,000 after Mont called him a grafter. But it was never clear who the grafter was. In circuit court it was revealed that Brolaski paid $400 to Nicholas Hunt of the police department for a private look at the "protected" lists of handbooks. When the gamblers threatened to stick a bomb under Brolaski's bed, he backed down.

The years before World War I were quiet times for the Tennes syndicate. The territory was neatly divided into three fiefdoms. Barney Grogan controlled the west side, Hinky Dink Kenna from Madison Avenue south to the river, and Mont's own alderman, James Aloysius "Hot Stove" Quinn, from the river north to Wilson. Schuettler continued his raids, but most of the big fish were tipped off well in advance. Tennes equipped his cars with calliope whistles that traveled about Chicago streets looking for police wagons. When a raid was imminent, the whistle would blow, and a lookout stationed outside would alert the occupants.

In April of 1911, Carter Harrison was returned to the mayor's chair after a seven-year hiatus. Tennes spent $20,000 to help put Harrison's liberal administration back in business. In 1914, he was rewarded for his efforts when Herman Schuettler was removed from the gambling detail for the second time. Chief James Gleason appointed William Schubert, a stumbling, portly, old veteran who was so out of shape that he could not pass his physicals. Through Kenna and Coughlin's intervention, Schubert was allowed to keep his position.

Gambling raids were directed against the Negro policy rings and the gamblers who supported Harrison's opponent in the election. There were no specific charges of graft made against Schubert, but it was understood that Mont's places were to be left alone. Whenever a small raid was conducted, Tennes's lawyers would demand a trial jury, and the case would be transferred to a north-side court, where the case was dropped. With his friend Schubert heading up the gambling detail, Tennes began to run baseball pools in his handbook operations. This was five years before the Black Sox Scandal.

The poolrooms and lotteries ran unmolested until the *Daily News* posed the question to the public on August 30, 1916: "Does Tennes control the police?" Mont had just secured the title of chief concessionaire at the Hawthorne Racetrack by paying $10,000 to the Jockey Club, whose notable members included William Wrigley, Jr., Jim Colosimo, and Captain Morgan Collins of the first precinct.

. . . Of Bombs, Gamblers, and Racing Wires 201

Judge Kenesaw Mountain Landis decided to "get" Tennes himself. Landis subpoenaed Willie Tennes, Horace Argo, Eph Harding, Mont, John Morelock (acting manager of General News), Bernard E. Sully, and F.W. Tracey of the Chicago Telephone and Tunnel Company on October 1.

The scowling Landis took his place under a painting of King John receiving the Magna Carta at Runnymede in the federal courtroom and the investigation was on. Landis, who was known to bend jurisprudence when the situation suited him, faced a worthy council in Clarence Darrow. Tennes hired Darrow, realizing that Landis was wily and unpredictable. The Indians at Burt Lake, Michigan, where the judge occasionally dropped a fishing pole, called him "Sago-Ye-Wat-Ha" (translation: *He who keeps them awake*).

Horace Argo was the first to the stand. He listed his ownership of the "Argo Eye Remedy" as his occupation. "Who is in this company?" Landis asked. "Mont Tennes and I have 37½ percent, and his brother has 25 percent." "Are you doing well?" Landis persisted. Argo paused. "There's a lot of competition."

Willie Tennes was arrested for refusing to give evidence, but this did not bother the sun-tanned Mont, who took the stand. He listed his principal occupation as real estate, with offices at 604 Straus Building.

Q—Don't you think Mr. Darrow might as well go back to his office?

A—I don't understand the law. I'd rather have him stay.

Q—Do you know what kind of real estate journal this is? [Hands Tennes a racing sheet]

A—I'd rather not answer that. I'd incriminate myself.

And so it went. Eph Harding took the stand. When the gambler frustrated Landis with evasive answers, the judge tried to jar his moral conscience.

"Wouldn't you like to get into some other business where you don't have to handle slimy money?" Landis wanted to know. "He [Tennes] goes to California in the winter to take it easy while you handle slimy money." Harding gulped and said nothing. Years later, when Harding was broke and ill, Tennes supported him with a monthly stipend. (Eph later committed suicide.)

Nothing new emerged from the Landis inquiry. Revelations of wrongdoing at Hawthorne and the story of protected gambling stores brought a change in police administration, but Tennes escaped again. The judge assailed the telephone company, and under some pressure Argo finally admitted that General News made $15,000 to $20,000 a month but that money was not listed in a ledger book anywhere. And there wasn't a thing Landis could do about it, and he knew it. Tired of the whole thing, Landis pulled up tent on October 4 to go to Indiana for a golfing holiday. His final pronouncement in the case was to Tennes concerning his legal debt to Clarence Darrow.

"Don't give Mr. Darrow money covered with dirt and slime, with the blood that has come from a lot of young fellows about the town who are made criminals. Better give Mr. Darrow money from your eye remedy funds."

Mont Tennes steered his ship around the iceberg again. He always avoided the pitfalls and traps that seem to catch up with the big-time hood. In 1920 the headlines revealed that the mighty Chicago White Sox had thrown the 1919 World Series. And where was Mont Tennes at this time?

He spent that summer gambling at Saratoga, New York, postwar playground of the nouveau riche. Over dice and cocktails, he advised his old friend and one-time owner of the Chicago Cubs Charles Weeghman on how to bet on the upcoming (1919) series. "He mentioned their names and said the tip was straight, but he didn't want it," Weeghman said. "He liked baseball but wouldn't get in on a crooked deal. I understand that in spite of the tip, Tennes bet $30,000 on the Sox." Mind you, this was several weeks *before* the fix was said to have taken place.

Yes, Mont probably knew about the fix before anyone else did. But it was too large and foolhardy a proposition to be pulled off. Tennes quickly divorced himself from all association with the Black Sox by issuing a terse statement to the press. The grand jury later passed him by in their examinations.

"I'm willing to tell them all I know about baseball and betting on baseball games, but I can't tell them nothing about fixed games. I never told Charley Weeghman about fixed games. Weeghman's intentions are good I'm sure, but he was misunderstood. Whether Weeghman and I met at Saratoga I can't say. I remember meeting him at the racetrack last summer. I bet on the Sox, I lost my bet, and I made no cry of fraud."

By 1925, many of Tennes's former rivals were retired from the business or dead. He stood atop his throne, but the era was disappear-

. . . Of Bombs, Gamblers, and Racing Wires   203

ing. Despite his dynamite bombs and the 1910 terror campaign, Tennes was the last of a breed of gentlemen gamblers glorified in literature by Damon Runyon. Jim O'Leary was mourned by newsmen and former rivals when he collapsed in his Garfield Boulevard home on January 22, 1925. He was retired from the gambling business for four years, working quietly in a brokerage business. Judge Kenesaw Mountain Landis closed his saloon in 1921, following a violation by O'Leary of the Volstead Act. In his usual fashion, O'Leary told the judge that the milkman accidentally left his flask while making a delivery.

Police Chief Michael Hughes went after the remaining gambler factions in 1920, using the Illinois Criminal Code rather than the municipal code because penalties were more drastic. The cleanup campaign seemed to be at odds with Mayor William Hale Thompson's cavalier wide-open approach to vice. With Thompson and Hughes calling the shots, the cost of protection rose. When Paul Jones galloped home a long-shot winner in the Kentucky Derby, favored politicians were given inside knowledge, courtesy of the General News Bureau, now located at 431 Dearborn Street.

Mont Tennes went on trial March 27, 1922, for conspiring to operate horse-race betting books. It was a petty charge, but it was only the second time Tennes had been formally indicted in his life. Clarence Darrow wasn't available, so Mont hired the deposed State's Attorney MacLay Hoyne to serve as his defense counsel. The case was *nolle prosequi* because the prosecution was unable to prove a conspiracy. It was a neat little piece of Chicago politics. Robert Crowe, a Republican, had succeeded Hoyne. Crowe announced a war on vice, much to Hoyne's dislike.

The lid got tighter in 1923 when William Dever was elected mayor. Chief Morgan Collins closed 200 Loop handbooks, forcing Mont into the suburbs.

Bandits broke into a Tennes poolroom at 120 S. Clark on August 21, 1925. Thirty gambling patrons were lined up against the wall and relieved of their valuables. A wild car chase down Clark Street ensued, while shotgun blasts punctuated the air. Thousands of midday Loop shoppers and businessmen witnessed the event, but it went unreported in the papers. A traffic cop was later censured for talking about the heist to a reporter. It can be surmised that several cops on Mont Tennes's payroll were asleep at the switch, and only his considerable clout succeeded in keeping it all quiet.

Tennes was not the big shot he used to be. His losses were reported at $500,000 in 1924 because the syndicate-controlled Empire News Service out of New York competed directly with General. For a time, Mont was able to tread a thin line between the warring gangster factions on the north and south sides. Tennes sold his racing information to both Al Capone on the south and Joe Aiello-Bugs Moran on the north. But the Capone interests realized that it was foolish to pay for something that could be taken for free. Jimmy Mondi, spokesman in Capone gambling affairs, demanded 25 percent of the earnings for "protection," after several Tennes handbooks were bombed. Realizing that every man has his day, Mont searched for someone to take over his affairs so that he might live another day.

Newspaper Wars, the Annenbergs, and a New Era

Let's digress a moment. The story of Mont Tennes and the alliance he ultimately formed with Moses Annenberg would not be complete without a look back at the early days of this publishing family. The Annenberg clan has deep ties to turn-of-the-century Chicago, no doubt a source of continuing embarrassment to Walter Annenberg, friend to Ronald Reagan and a respected publishing mogul. Walter is the son of Moses and the nephew of Max.

The brothers Annenberg were born street fighters. They grew up in the "Patch," that tough Irish neighborhood at 48th and Halsted. To be Jewish and to stay alive in the Patch during the 1890s required brains, brawn, and some street sense. The father, Tobias, escaped the pogroms of East Prussia only to face the fierce anti-Semitic attitudes of his Chicago neighbors. But his sons Moses and Max survived. People would later remember Moe as the quiet planner, the one under the thumb of his bellicose older brother. While Max would settle disputes with his fists and a snappy reply, Moe would think the situation through before embarking on a *thoughtful* revenge plan.

When Mont Tennes opened his first saloon on Center Street, Max and Moe were getting up each day at five to hawk *Tribunes* on the other side of town. The newspaper business of the 1890s was competitive but still friendly. The big dailies at this time supported the gospel of Republicanism—big business, high tariffs, and cautious imperialism. The Chicago *Inter-Ocean*'s slogan was "Republican in Everything, Independent in Nothing."

All that changed when press czar William Randolph Hearst was

. . . Of Bombs, Gamblers, and Racing Wires

elected president of the National Association of Democratic Clubs in 1900. William Jennings Bryan was on the ballot for president, and Hearst realized his candidate could not win without urban support. It was necessary for Bryan to show well in Chicago, so Hearst set aside six weeks to start a newspaper in Chicago to promote the cause. "The Madhouse at 216 Madison Street" got rolling in no time, turning out its first edition on July 2, 1900. The editorial content of the new *Chicago American* turned the *Tribune* and *Inter-Ocean* men white.

Hearst brought with him columnist Arthur Brisbane, a veteran of Joseph Pulitzer's *New York World* and an early role model for Moe Annenberg. Brisbane lent respect to a newspaper that defied all journalistic traditions. Most newspapers of this era were dull "tombstones," void of headlines and slow to move away from old-fashioned woodcuts to modern photography. In 1900, Hearst introduced Chicago to five-inch headlines reeking of society scandal, crime, orgy, and havoc. Within three months, afternoon commuters were titillated with such delightful headlines as: "Woman Shoots Her Prosecutor," "Sought to Slay Steel Kings," "Gangs of Ruffians Hired to Worry and Insult Bryan," "Dying Young Girl Tried to Sell the Secret of the Insurance Fraud Plotters," "Conspiracy by Means of Poison," "Beautiful Young Woman Victim of Poison Plot."

Scarcely a day went by without the word *poison* in a column heading. In order to sell his scandal sheet, Hearst required men like Max Annenberg to boost circulation. In 1902, "Long Green" Andy Lawrence hired Max to use whatever resources he had to sell *Americans*. Max sent Moe into the outer reaches of Cook County to sell subscriptions while he personally recruited a gang of toughs that included Red and Dan Connors, "Mossie" Enright, Joe Kane, Walter Stevens, Tom Looney, and James Ragen, leader of the south-side "social athletic" club known as Ragen's Colts. These men intimidated newsstand dealers into accepting larger quantities of *Americans*, a policy known as "bootjacking."

The circulation war did not start until several years later when Hearst introduced a morning edition known as the *Examiner*. This was too much competition for Victor Lawson of the *Daily News* and Robert McCormick and his cousin Joe Patterson of the *Tribune*. In 1910, McCormick and Patterson gave editor James Keeley a $1 million budget to take the circulation battle to the streets. Keeley watched Max Annenberg's progress with a favorable eye. He had to be impressed when Max led sixty delivery drivers and newsboys on a raid of Marshall

Field's, circling the store chanting "Field's Closed, Field's Closed!" while toting night sticks and chains. The next day, the department store quietly reinstated a canceled advertisement in the *American*. In 1910, Annenberg jumped his contract with Hearst to sign on with the *Tribune* for $20,000, taking Ragen and the boys with him. Meanwhile, Andy Lawrence dredged up a new gang of toughs worse than what Annenberg found. In this group could be found the little choir singer and future flower-shop owner Dion O'Bannion, Frankie McErlane, and the four Gentleman brothers, Peter, Mike, Gus, and Dutch.

Tribune circulation stood at 175,000 a day when, on October 3, 1910, they cut their price to one cent. "Now only a penny, and better than any," the paper extolled. The war was on, as Hearst armed his men with pistols and blackjacks. Max directed his troops with a pork pie hat slung low over his brow, and the sweater of a street thug. In July of 1912, Moe saved his older brother's life by sticking a gun in the head of Harold Whipple after Max had exchanged ten shots during the noon hour at State and Madison. Whipple was arrested; Annenberg was commended. By the time the last shot of the circulation war had been fired in 1913, twenty-seven newsdealers had been gunned down by Hearst-*Tribune-Daily News* armies.

The sluggers were men with little formal education and raised in the teeming ethnic ghettos of Chicago. They were hired guns, frequently clashing in labor-management disputes and union power struggles where the best solution was at the point of a gun.

The Briggs House was a popular Loop watering hole for gamblers, fences, labor officials, and hired sluggers. The bar was crowded with men the afternoon of March 23, 1911. Leaning against the bar was Vincent Altman, blackmailer of tradesmen and recent employee of the *Chicago American*. He was laughing and joking with "Mossie" Enright, a *Tribune* man who had an axe to grind. Moss was currently doing his slugging on behalf of the Steam Fitter's Union, but he greeted his former rival like a lost brother. Moss placed one hand on Altman's right shoulder, the one that controlled the trigger hand. Suddenly Enright jerked Altman downward. He fired two shots into his abdomen. Enright tucked the gun into his pocket and ran upstairs. A doctor attempted to remove Altman's coat, but the slugger told him to back away or die. He refused assistance again and passed away the next day maintaining the code of silence.

In May, William Gentleman was shot in Pat O'Malley's saloon after he burst in looking for Enright. He pulled a gun and said, "Did you say you wanted to see me?" Whereby Enright pumped ten slugs into Gentleman, who uttered a dying epitaph: "I had to get him before he got me."

Mossie went to trial that fall for the murder of Altman. John Wayman secured a life sentence for Enright based on a discarded gray coat found on the fifth floor of the Briggs House. The defense contended that the murder of Gentleman was an act of self-defesne, but it didn't matter to the jury. Enraged, Mossie attacked his lawyer Charles Erbstein. "You're a liar! You're a four flusher!!" Mrs. Enright fainted away. But this wasn't the end of it for Moss. On February 3, 1920, he was shotgunned to death by a passing auto while attempting to start his car in front of the family home at 1110 Garfield Boulevard. His nine-year-old son stood on the sidewalk, watching the whole thing.

The last of Papa Robert Gentleman's boys, young Peter, got his on September 1, 1919. Pete was first arrested in 1906. He was a gambler, a dip, and known slugger.

In February of 1919, Gentleman met a girl named Margaret Malley. She was an Irish lass who mistakenly thought she could reform him. Just three days before they were scheduled to get married, Pete was arrested with two other men for pickpocketing on board a 63rd Street trolley. In a tearful courtroom scene, Margaret told the judge that she tagged Gentleman during a Red Cross drive, and the two fell in love after that. She promised to reform him, and the jury showed leniency. After that, Gentleman saw the error of his ways—and dropped her.

"As they live, so shall they die," Chief of Detectives Mooney said when he heard the news. Pete Gentleman was dead. He lay face down in a pool of blood in a cigar store and poolroom at 2220 S. Wabash, not far from his favorite levee haunts. Gentleman was a "piker." He did not like to lose, and when he did, he made every attempt to recoup his losses. At 1:30 in the afternoon, Pete burst into Marty Guilfoyle's place on Wabash to demand satisfaction. He pushed Guilfoyle to the floor (interrupting a good poker hand), stuck a gun in his stomach, and said: "I'm going to kill you, you son-of-a-bitch . . . just because I don't like you!" Guilfoyle struggled with him, succeeding in chasing him out of the bar. The card game naturally resumed.

At 7:30 that evening, Gentleman showed up again, carrying a brick. He walked into the store and threw it at the cigar case. Terrified for his life, Guilfoyle stood up from the poker game and fired five shots into Gentleman's back. The girlfriend, Winnie Brooks, testified that she was with Gentleman all day and suggested that her boyfriend was framed. But as Chief Mooney admitted: "As hard as it may be to say, I confess I'm glad he's gone."

This was the world from which the Annenbergs came. Max was groomed by Hearst, but he betrayed him for *Tribune* riches. Only once was Max arrested, that being on July 4, 1913 when he slugged a gambler who questioned the right of a *Tribune* photographer to take his picture. The paper later paid a $25,000 bail.

While Max fought his newspaper wars in Chicago, Moe made his fortune in Wisconsin, quietly buying up newspaper distributorships. Moe met Randolph Hearst in 1917 and was placed in charge of all of his magazine concerns. Ambitious, intelligent, and less prone to histrionics than his brother, Moe wrapped up $400,000 in a roll of old newspapers in 1922. He walked through the deserted streets of Manhattan to meet a former *Tribune* sports editor named Frank Bruenell, who had founded a profitable little newspaper called the *Racing Form*. Bruenell lacked Annenberg's imagination. He was more than ready to sell out for what he considered a bonanza. With this latest acquisition, Annenberg was able to create a coast-to-coast empire. He created seven individual *Racing Forms* but soon realized that there was one more hurdle. Mont Tennes and his General News Bureau.

After seventeen years, Mont decided to sell out. Willie and Edward Tennes died a year apart in 1926-27, creating a vacuum in the syndicate management. Tennes looked around him and saw a changed world. Machine guns, the one-way ride, the beer hijacks, and the vicious character of the decade represented a way of life foreign to the old-line gambler factions who threw bombs at each other's establishments.

Late in 1927, Moses Annenberg bought 48 of the 100 shares of General News Stock from Tennes. Mont's various enterprises yielded an annual income of nearly $364,000. To insure that there was still a degree of family control in the operation, a nephew of Mont's (also named Mont) purchased a number of the shares with Lionel and Edward Lenz. The remaining 40 shares were sold to Jack Lynch for $500,000. He operated one of Chicago's largest handbooks from the rear of a barber shop at 3114 Madison Street.

The ink was barely dry on the contract when young Mont nearly got himself killed. His nineteen-year-old bride of just five months gored him with a kitchen knife in their apartment at 6320 Kenmore Avenue on February, 17, 1929. She penetrated his left lung and even the doc-

... Of Bombs, Gamblers, and Racing Wires 209

tors didn't give him much of a chance. "He sat in the living room and said he was going to stay up all night and read," Helen Tennes told the cops. She was freed on a $300 bond. Her husband lived, so the elder Mont did not have to come out of retirement.

For the first time in his life, Mont Tennes went legit. He invested in some big land deals in the Edgewater community, took over management of the Shafer Roller Bearing Company, and settled into that real or imagined Tennes and Sons Real Estate Company that he listed as his occupation during the gambling probes.

Things were not nearly as tranquil at the General News Bureau. Moe started a trade war against the Empire Service and the Greater New York News Service, owned by racketeers Frank Erickson and Waxey Gordon respectively. Four-thirty-one Dearborn was now called "Annenberg Alley," and the business was run by one-time slugger James Ragen.

A $150,000 slush fund was established to suborn politicians, but Annenberg underestimated the nature of the Chicago gangster. With his beer and alky industry fading in 1930, Capone looked again at the racing wire as a source of income. Capone's muscling in on the racing wire may have figured directly in the sensational murder of *Tribune* reporter Alfred "Jake" Lingle on June 9, 1930.

Jake was a high-living jazz baby, a thirty-eight-year-old crime reporter who didn't do much reporting. His talent was in the streets. He was an intimate of Al Capone and Police Commissioner William F. Russell. He was quick with a joke. He knew all the Chicago police, and it was said that he could fix the price of bootleg beer. Not bad for a $165-a-week reporter. One Christmas, Al Capone presented Lingle with a diamond-studded belt buckle. He wore it the afternoon of June 9, when he decided to get away for a day at Washington Park racetrack. Lingle was a gambler and closely in touch with the General News Bureau and all of its problems.

With a cigar hanging from his mouth, he walked east on Randolph Street to the Illinois Central depot on Michigan Avenue. Lingle paused to buy a *Racing Form* at the entrance when a roadster pulled up to the curb and the occupant said, "Play Hy Schneider in the third!" Lingle nodded and said "Got him!" Two men accompanied Lingle, but he seemed not to notice them. One had blonde hair and wore a straw boater, the other had a dark blue suit. The blonde man dropped behind Lingle in the station; he produced a .38 revolver and fired it into Lingle's neck. A concerned citizen attempted to block the blonde man's accomplice after the apparent killer had escaped down Randolph Street. A suspicious-looking priest blocked the man from tripping up the accomplice. Earlier Lingle had alerted a police sergeant that he was being tailed. The trap was cleverly laid. Lingle walked into it blind, or was he led into it? It's possible that he descended into the tunnel at the point of a gun and had no other choice.

Colonel Robert McCormick offered a $25,000 reward for the identity of Lingle's murderer. It was a nice gesture, until the details of Lingle's double life began to leak out. Secret bank accounts totaling $63,900 at the Lake Shore Trust and Savings were made public. Lingle carried with him $9,000 in cash at the time of his murder.

Many theories for the Lingle murder have surfaced over the years. The convicted killer, one Leo Vincent Brothers of St. Louis, served eight years of a fourteen-year sentence without divulging a hint. However, it is known that Lingle owed Jimmy Mondi $2,000. Mondi had once worked for Tennes before joining the Capone armies. Lingle may have owed some money to some very dangerous people, but it seems that his role as unofficial referee in the General News war with Empire and the Greater News Bureau may have had something to do with it.

In January, Lingle brought together the rival factions for a peace conference designed to merge the various racing wires into one syndicate. Lingle represented General News, which Capone was anxious to take over. An uneasy truce was signed, one that Al may not have been happy with. When asked who killed Lingle, Al Capone answered; "Jake was a dear friend of mine. The Chicago police know who killed him."

The truce, if there really was one, was short-lived. On August 20, 1931, Jack Lynch's car was forced off the road in Walworth County, Wisconsin, outside Lake Geneva. Three men dragged him from the car and took him to a nearby cottage where a ransom call was placed. The kidnappers wanted $125,000 for his safe return. The first call went to Marty Guilfoyle, the gambler who shot Pete Gentleman. A-quarter-of-a-million was the price, or Lynch would be sent home in a box. Guilfoyle said he wanted Lynch back, but there was no way he could raise the cash. The next call went to Anna Lynch, who said that the most she could raise was $50,000. When the kidnappers persisted in their demands, she asked them where she could turn. "Ask Mont Tennes," they said.

Mont was in retirement and was still waiting for some money that

... Of Bombs, Gamblers, and Racing Wires

Lynch owed him. Tennes said he couldn't help out with the ransom, but he told her to give the kidnappers his phone number and he would try to work something out.

It finally took the intervention of Al Capone to secure his release. Reportedly, Capone paid $50,000 to the kidnap gang that may have been led by George "Red" Barker. Pat Roche, an assistant to the state's attorney, swore out a warrant for Capone's arrest for going above their office. But Lynch was returned with two broken ribs and a damaged ego.

The wealthy gamblers were frequent targets of the kidnap gangs. It's likely that they were operating independently of the organization, though it was suggested that Capone engineered the whole thing to scare Lynch into selling his interests in General News. After this, the old-line gamblers formed a protective association to guard against abduction.

In December of 1934, Lynch and the Lenz brothers took Annenberg and James Ragen to court, seeking an accounting of aggregate profits dating back to 1929. They claimed that Moe owed them $250,000, and they were probably right. Attorney Weymouth Kirkland prepared an ingenious defense for Annenberg that proved that Lynch had come into court without clean hands. He cited an English judge who refused to help highwaymen in 1725 recover their lost profits. Despite appeals, the case was thrown out.

What Annenberg did was freeze his partners out of profits while establishing the new Nationwide News Service on August 27, 1934, which competed directly with General. In 1934, General News reported profits of $1.4 million, while Nationwide lost $3,788. A year later the profit/loss picture was reversed. General News lost $45,634, while Nationwide reported a $1.1 million profit. Moe succeeded in this newest venture by using deadened wires and by undercutting the prices charged by General. AT&T was now leasing their wires to Moe.

But the racing wire became a source of grief to Annenberg, as it did to everyone who became involved with it. It besmirched the family name of Annenberg at a time when Moe was grooming Walter to take his place as heir. The wire became an important cannon shot for the New Dealers who decided to "get" Annenberg on an income-tax rap following years of bitter denunciation of Roosevelt politics in Moe's paper, the *Philadelphia Inquirer*.

In May of 1937, Annenberg was charged with a monopoly on the horse-racing news by the *Turf Bulletin Record* Company of Chicago.

State Senator Dan Serritella was the president of Madison Publishing and was named as a co-defendent with James and Frank Ragen. When Annenberg's income-tax troubles became more pressing, he prudently divested himself of Nationwide. Moe sold the wire to James Ragen on November 15, 1939, who then renamed it the Continental Press.

But the racing wire was *still* an issue worth fighting for among the gangsters. Moe Annenberg paid his penalty by serving a jail sentence (for income tax evasion). Jim Ragen lost his life because of it.

Ragen reformed in his later years. He avoided smoking, drinking, and the gambling game that he himself provided. He also distanced himself from intrusions of a new generation of hoods that included Jake Guzik and Tony "Joe Batters" Accardo, who tried to purchase half of his 600 Continental shares. Ragen kept his race wire solvent by courting the favors of politicians, including first-ward committeeman, state senator, and erstwhile partner in the business, Dan Serritella.

Six-hundred thousand dollars was reportedly spent between 1934 and 1936 to politicans proving favorable to the Illinois racing cause. But when Ragen set up the *Green Scratch Sheet* in direct opposition to Serritella's *Blue Scratch Sheet*, a contract was put out.

Ragen was driving south on State Street on June 24, 1946, when a truck loaded with orange crates pulled up next to his sedan at Pershing Road and State. The car in front of Ragen stopped abruptly, thereby preventing any chance of escape. Shotgun blasts roared from the tarpaulin-covered truck, mangling Ragen's arms and legs. He lived until August 15, but before he died, he revealed the existence of an affidavit given to State's Attorney William Touhy claiming that Guzik, Accardo, and Murray "The Camel" Humphries and others were plotting to take control of his news service. As it turned out, the affidavit turned up missing.

Mont Tennes did not live to see these bloody events transpire. He died of a heart attack on August 6, 1941, following a year-long battle with heart disease. His last residence was listed at 2430 Lakeview Avenue, and he was survived by his wife of many years, Ida. Interment was at Calvary Cemetery in Evanston.

There is no record of his sons involving themselves in the racing and gambling world. One of his sons served on board the *Enterprise* at Pearl Harbor, just before the attack, while another was an automobile dealer.

There is very little left today that would help us render a judgment about the character of a man who forged a gambling trust that survived

... Of Bombs, Gamblers, and Racing Wires   213

in one form or another to the modern era. Tennes never served a day in jail. His picture rarely (if ever) appeared in a major newspaper.

But he did bequeath $10,000 a year to the establishment of a "character home" for wayward boys, to be called Camp Honor. This act of charity on Mont's part does not seem to be the last will of a dying millionaire instilled with St. Peter's guilt.

On February 8, 1927, Tennes was enjoying one of his winter retreats at Palm Beach, Florida. While swimming 100 yards off the Breakers Casino, a heavy surf with a strong outward tow began pulling him out to sea. A nineteen-year-old lifeguard named Wetherall Austin, who once raced Johnny Weismuller, swam out and dragged Tennes to shore.

For saving his life (and perhaps saving his deal with Annenberg, if one wants to be speculative about life-and-death matters), Tennes rewarded the young man with an all-expenses-paid college education at Peekskill Military Academy in preparation for Yale.

Family man, newspaper man, real-estate speculator, lover of children, gambler, and extortionist, Mont Tennes wore many masks in his time. But which one fits the best?

8.
A Summer of Lost Innocence, May to August 1919

IT WAS AN IDLE SPRING DAY, "THE DAY WHEN ANXIETIES AND TROUBLES were over, and the time of rejoicing began," a reporter scribbled on his notepad as he walked along the Michigan Avenue parade route. Small boys wearing knickers and floppy hats pushed themselves to the front of the police lines to get a look at the conquering heroes. Chicago loves a parade. Chicago politicians love a parade.

Mayor William Hale Thompson was a last-minute arrival. He hadn't counted on welcoming the 33rd Prairie Division in person, but it was an election year and to shun the heroes of the Meuse-Argonne would be political suicide. "William the Brash" ordered a reviewing stand built for himself directly across Michigan Avenue from that of Governor Frank Lowden, who headed up the official welcoming party. Lowden was an enemy but a smart one. He was popular. He was well thought of. He was a man counted on to make a run for the 1920 presidential nomination. He had also forgotten that Big Bill Thompson and Fred "The Poor Swede" Lundin had made him what he was this fine May afternoon. Kingmaking does not come without a price. Lowden had put his own men in key positions, not the ones endorsed by Thompson. The mayor would not forget that slight.

Flanked by General Leonard Wood and Major George Bell, Lowden smiled and waved to the first Chicago men returning home from the French battlefields. Trained at Camp Logan and decorated for bravery by King George V, the first troops arrived in the 14th Street yards at midnight, May 25, 1919. Anxious sweethearts slept all

A Summer of Lost Innocence

night in the train stations awaiting their doughboys. A private reception was held in Grant Park earlier in the day, but the afternoon of May 26 was for everybody. Thousands and thousands lined the parade route from 12th Street north to Randolph along Michigan, west to State Street, and then south to Adams.

Girls wearing their new spring finery with high hats carried baskets of flowers, strewing the path of the soldiers with poppies and roses. A flivver carrying Company L of the 132nd Machine Gun Division displayed a sign that read "NO BEER? NO WAR STORIES." It was a jibe at National Prohibition, scheduled to start July 1.

Overhead, a biplane circled the Loop. Aviation was the eighth wonder of the world, and just eleven days earlier the Navy Seaplane NC-4 had made it to the Azores from a starting point in St. Johns, Newfoundland.

With the strains of "Illinois" playing in the background, the Prairie Division marched smartly past Governor Lowden's reviewing stand. At the front of the column was Colonel Abel Davis, veteran of the Spanish-American War, the Mexican insurrections, and Europe. Davis was returning to his job at Chicago Title and Trust and what he hoped would be a budding political career. He ordered the customary "eyes right" command in respect to Lowden, but then Davis noticed the second reviewing stand across the street. The mayor hung a painted sign that said "THOMPSON" across the platform shortly before the parade began, but out of good taste it was taken down. The perplexed Davis ordered his men to look "eyes left," in what must have been a serious violation of protocol. So the men saluted the mayor with their *left hands*. The trenches, the Germans, and the whole war had not clouded Davis's perception of Chicago politics. He had done the right thing.

Chicago felt young again. The war had created its share of problems. Just about everything in Chicago had gone up in price since 1915, and the sad fact remained that many would not be coming home. But summer had arrived, had it not? So why couldn't the world go back to that wonderful time before the Great War? All the glittering society parties, a fine German meal at Vogelsang's on Madison Street, and a stroll down the midway at White City . . . it was all so grand.

But it would never be the same again. Theodore Roosevelt was no longer riding on horseback at Oyster Bay, commanding the forces of government while breathless reporters fought to keep up. Woodrow Wilson was a Democrat, a man of scholarly, but timorous ideals that were at that moment being dissected by the uncrowned heads of Europe at the Paris peace table.

Thousands of blacks had poured into Chicago since 1915, swallowing up jobs in the private sector that once belonged to the doughboys passing in review down Michigan Avenue. A new kind of hatred would soon flare up. Universal suffrage was being debated in the Illinois Senate, and the labor unions were gearing up for some tough demands after several years of war-time sacrifice.

Prohibition. Perhaps more than any other event that summer, the Volstead Act would change the character of American society. The dry law did exactly the opposite of what was intended, and nowhere else but in Chicago would this point be so sorely apparent. Prohibition would forever chase away the Victorian era and its charming but outmoded way of life. It can be said that Chicago and the rest of the country truly entered the twentieth century in 1919.

These were times of tragedy, moments of irony, shock over the disappearance of a little girl, the joy of a tainted, pennant-bound baseball team, and that day on the beach. This was Chicago in 1919, and the old guard really didn't know what to make of it.

Hinky Dink Kenna had some serious "evaluatin' " to do. The whole world was changing before his eyes. The Sunday school reformers like Arthur Barrage Farwell, with their limited views of what was good for man, were about to enjoy their day. So the Dink went off to Hot Springs, Arkansas, on May 17 for a long vacation. One afternoon Kenna was seen sneaking out the back door of the hotel wearing a phony beard and golfing attire. The boss of the first ward was going to try his hand at golf, but he didn't want the boys at Pat O'Malley's saloon to get wind of it. They did. "The country's goin' dry on July 1, and Hinky Dink is playing golf," moaned Baldy Sowers. "What's this world coming to?"

What indeed? Cheek-to-cheek dancing was reported at the South Shore Country Club, arousing the ire of the long-time members whose ranks once included John J. Glessner, Martin Ryerson, Victor Lawson, and Mrs. George Pullman. When a guilty offender was spotted, a page boy would approach the man and hand him a calling card served on a tray. His presence was requested in Room 101 for a discreet conference, where he was reminded about polite conduct in society. On Decoration Day 1919, rules against cheeky dancing and smoking in the clubhouse and public room were posted for all concerned.

A Summer of Lost Innocence

The first holiday of the summer found the White Sox in front of the American League by five games. Kid Gleason's boys had just won twenty-three of their first thirty games when they engaged the Cleveland Indians at Comiskey Park. This was the finest group of players Charles Comiskey had ever assembled, better than the champion 1886 St. Louis Browns that Comiskey had captained, and better than the 1906 Hitless Wonders. It had taken patience and a lot of money to build this team. They were not yet in the frame of mind to blow ball games. They wanted to win—and claw their opponents in the process.

Chick Gandil had been around the game for fourteen years. He played in the mean border towns of Mexico and had picked up money on the side by prize fighting. He was quick with his fists and wouldn't take anything, especially from a Texas college boy like Tris Speaker. Speaker was the famous "Grey Eagle" in 1919 and the leader of the contending Cleveland ballclub.

In the eighth inning of an apparent Sox victory on Decoration Day, Speaker chopped a grounder to Gandil at first. It was an ordinary play, but Speaker hot-dogged it by sliding into first, spikes flying. Gandil was cut on the shins, and he didn't appreciate it.

"What in hell are you doing?" he murmured as Speaker retreated to the bench after being called out. Gandil glared into the Cleveland dugout as the Indians called him a yellow crybaby.

The inning ended. Speaker trotted out of the dugout to take his place in center field. Gandil waited for him at second, and the scrap was on. The two men rolled in the Comiskey Park dust for a full three minutes before seven cops broke them up. At last they were separated. Gandil was bleeding from the face because Speaker had spiked him. The game resumed, but the fans were in an ugly frame of mind. Since they couldn't get to Speaker in center (Comiskey Park did not have a center field bleacher at the time), the fans threw pop bottles at Jack Grancy in left. Finally, Kid Gleason went out to left field with a policeman to ask the fans to stop before the game was forfeited and someone was injured. The crowd settled down, but small groups of men waited by the visitors exit for Speaker. The next day Ban Johnson suspended both players.

War of a different kind was being waged in Mount Clemens, Michigan, a small town outside Detroit previously known for its health spas. In May the sleepy town was invaded by the press corps because the

Chicago Tribune was being sued by inventor, industrialist, and peace pacifist Henry Ford. At issue was whether *Tribune* editorial writer Clifford Raymond had damaged Ford's reputation after writing a June 23, 1916, editorial that labeled him an anarchist. Colonel McCormick approved the publication of the editorial, but as he admitted on the stand, "[His] mind was on other things, like the First Illinois Cavalry," when he gave the go-ahead. But neither would he retract it when asked to do so by Ford attorneys. It was the fourth libel suit against the *Tribune* in three years. Mayor Thompson had sued the paper three times for libel because he claimed that they gave his administration unfavorable coverage.

McCormick engaged his old law firm, now under the direction of Weymouth Kirkland, to represent him in court. When the Colonel refused to retract his editorial, Ford filed a $1-million lawsuit against the paper. Irony of ironies. The Ford Company was one of the largest sources of advertising revenue for the newspaper. This was going to become one of the decade's greatest sideshows.

Ford the "flivver baron" had only been in the public eye for a dozen years when the libel trial began. In October of 1908, the first Model-T rolled off the assembly line at the River Rouge Plant in Dearborn, Michigan. With it came a new way of life for everyone.

The Model-T drew rural communities closer to the city while changing America's work habits. By 1914, Ford was a folk hero to his workers after he shortened their hours and doubled their pay. Henry Ford, the rustic, shared everyman's common suspicion about professors and book learning. "Now I say history is bunk—bunk—double bunk. Why it isn't even true. They wrote what they wanted us to believe, glorifying some conquerer or leader or something like that," he said.

Ford was instilled with native puritanism and some checkered political views. He took a personal interest in the military adventures of nations, particularly the United States involvement in Mexico's border agitation against U.S. citizens. Raids into Columbus, New Mexico, by Pancho Villa's outlaw band left sixteen Americans dead. President Wilson called up 150,000 National Guardsmen to secure the border. Colonel Robert McCormick accepted a lower rank so that he could lead his First Illinois Cavalry to the front lines. His politically liberal cousin, Joe Patterson, joined the artillery division as a private. By the time the *Tribune* men arrived on the scene, there was very little going on. So McCormick drilled his men, took some time out to play polo, and even won a pistol competition.

Back in Detroit, the *Tribune* secured an interview with Ford vice-president F.L. Klinginsmith, who revealed a company plan to withhold wages and benefits of the employees volunteering for service on the Mexican border.

In December of 1915, the Ford "peace ship" *Oscar-Two* set sail from Hoboken, New Jersey, to try to stop World War I. Cynics called it the "good ship nutty" with good reason. Ford was convinced that the Hungarian pacifist Rosika Schwimmer was correct when she predicted that a delegation of leading citizens could succeed where the statesmen failed. The invitees included Thomas Edison, William Jennings Bryan, and Luther Burbank. They declined. Only Jane Addams gave the mission her support. Eighty-three delegates, fifty-four reporters, and Henry Ford set sail on December 5, 1915. The reporters and pacifists sipped cocktails from the promenade deck, while the ship negotiated through submarine-infested waters. Shuffleboard was the distraction. Ford took ill, choosing to spend most of his time in his cabin. When the party reached Oslo, he decided he had enough of Madame Schwimmer's dictates and his associates' festivities. After spending nearly a half-million dollars on the peace crusade, Ford returned to America. The peace activists continued on through Sweden, Denmark, and finally to the Hague. But they were met with more derision before ending the mission in mid-January 1916.

Ford intended to take his fight with the *Tribune* right to the American people. A special news service was installed across the street from the courthouse with telephone and telegraph lines. Despite Ford's hayseed sentiments, no one understood or appreciated the value of the printed word more. The Mount Clemens News Service supplied 15,000 free dispatches to the newspapers who requested it. Ford's staff people stuck colored pins into a national map to indicate which newspapers were favorable or negative to their man. "Send out the uncolored truth," Ford told them. What was the truth of the matter? The *Chicago Tribune* was careful to print only the editorials of other newspapers critical of Ford.

Jury selection in the Ford-*Tribune* case was completed on May 16, 1919. Presiding Judge James G. Tucker of the Circuit Court of Macomb County described it as best as any, after hearing the opening arguments. "This is an endless chain that is leading us God knows where." A jury of eleven farmers and one road builder listened to the objectionable editorial read to them forwards, backwards, and sideways. And in the end, they probably never did find out what an anarchist was.

Ford is an Anarchist

> Inquiry at the Henry Ford offices in Detroit discloses the fact that employees of Ford who are members of, or recruits in the National Guard will lose their places. No provision will be made for anyone dependent on them. Their wages will stop, their families may get along in any fashion possible, and when and if they apply for their jobs again, they will be on the same footing as any other applicants. This is the rule for Ford employees everywhere.

The editorial went on to criticize Ford's attitudes toward the Mexican problem. They posed the question to their readers: What would Ford do if the Villa band attacked his Detroit factory? But there was one strong paragraph that really made Ford bristle.

> If Ford allows this rule of his shops to stand, he will reveal himself not as merely an ignorant idealist, but as an anarchistic enemy of the nation which protects him in his wealth.

Attorney Alfred Lucking accused the *Tribune* of pro-Germanism and war profiteering by agitating for war with Mexico. He recited old editorials that showed the McCormick family connections to International Harvester and Standard Oil represented a vested interest. International Harvester bought $14 million a year in sisal fiber from the Mexicans, and 665 shares of company stock were held jointly by Katherine McCormick and her son, Colonel Robert. Edith Rockefeller McCormick held 1,200 shares of Standard stock. The company also purchased one-fifth of all its crude oil from the Mexicans.

The paper struck back at Ford by mentioning Robert McCormick's and Joe Patterson's heroic war records. Colonel Henry Reilly, commander of the 149th Field Artillery, was called as a character witness. He attested to their bravery, citing Joe Patterson's battlefield promotion to captain. *Tribune* attorney Elliot Stevenson inferred that Edsel Ford was a slacker by comparison. Henry Ford secured a draft exemption for him. Judge Tucker later threw the entire issue out, saying it was unwarranted and irrelevant.

Henry Ford's spokesman in the trial was Theodore Delavigne. In somber tones, he told the court that "Henry Ford, curse him as you will, is the Lincoln of today. A Lincoln with hands clean of blood."

Elliot Stevenson did not share this noble view. On July 14, Ford became the 101st witness to take the stand. Before squaring off against

Stevenson, Ford remarked that it was either going to be a "dogfight or a picnic."

The ignorant idealist versus the city-lawyer image gained Ford a lot of support among the farmers and city people. His confused answers to Stevenson's questions played into the defense's hands but really worked to his advantage. Stevenson recited a Ford editorial that said: "The men of the world, the ones in the ranks who would have us rush to the machine guns if war came, are beginning to take these preachers of war at their true worth and to see in all of them, including the Detroit brief holder for murder, only ballyhoos of their own wares of death."

Q—Do you know what *ballyhoo* means?

A —No, I do not believe I do.

Q—What did you expect the people who read it were going to understand it meant?

A— Ballyhoo was a blackguard.

Q—What?

A— Ballyhoo is possibly a blackguard. I don't know what it really means.

On the subject of treason, Ford had this to say:

Q—Do you know what treason is, Mr. Ford?

A— Treason is unlawful, I know that.

Q—Did you ever hear of Benedict Arnold?

A— I have heard the name.

Q—Who was he?

A— I have forgotten just who he was. He was a writer, I think.

Q—What subjects do you recall he wrote on?

A— I don't remember.

Q—Did you ever read anything he wrote?

A— Possibly I have. I don't know.

Q—Would you be surprised to be informed that Benedict Arnold was a general in the American Army who was a traitor and betrayed his country?

A— I don't know much about him.

Attorney Lucking objected to this line of questioning. "This is another illustration of what I have said. Mr. Ford is willing to confess anything against himself."

Stevenson then grilled him at length about an interview he granted the socialist writer John Reed in 1916 for the *Metropolitan Magazine*. Ford described nations and flags as being "silly." Captivated by Ford's liberal thinking, Reed entitled his article "Industry's Miracle Worker."

Q—That is quite a story, Mr. Ford, isn't it?

A—Yes sir, quite a story.

Q—Does it help refresh your memory?

A—I remember a little about it.

Q—"I don't believe in boundaries." Did you say that to Mr. Reed?

A—I don't think I talked to Mr. Reed about boundaries at all.

Q—Did you say, "I think nations are silly and flags silly too"?

A—I don't know of ever using the word *silly* anywhere, to him or anybody else.

Q—Did you say, "I am going to keep the American flag flying on my plant until the war is over, and then I am going to pull it down and hoist in its place the flag of all nations which is being designed in my office right now?

A—I noticed he had been reading Mr. Wood's article. I don't remember talking to him about it at all.

Q—How did Mr. Reed know that you were designing a flag?

A—I guess he saw it in Mr. Wood's article.

Q—There is nothing about it in Mr. Wood's article, Mr. Ford.

A—I don't know where he found out anything about it.

Wearing a light gray suit, Ford sat on the stand looking nervous and uncomfortable. He wrung his hands and fidgeted but remained polite and cooperative. The issue of Ford's patriotism did not make any sense, since the Dearborn factories produced millions of dollars worth of trucks and equipment for the government.

The real issue was anarchism, or what the term really meant. The *Tribune* took the word in its broadest sense. Ford considered it a smear. He believed the paper was attempting to portray him as a shifty-eyed bomb thrower.

Stevenson cited three interpretations of anarchism from the Century Dictionary. Professor Reeves of the University of Michigan was brought in to support the contention that Ford was an anarchist because the Supreme Court had defined it as an *absence* of government. Ford attorneys called Professor William A. Dunning of Columbia to the stand, who said that the prosecution would have an easier time of it if they tried to prove that George Washington and Ford were the same person.

After fourteen weeks of verbal sparring, the defense rested its case, and the jury retired on August 14. Nine ballots were cast by the jurymen during the hectic ten-hour session. The first tally resulted in a 7-5 decision in favor of the plaintiff, but this was later changed to 8-4. Finally, at 8 A.M. on August 14, foreman Orvy Hulett announced that a verdict had been reached. The *Tribune* was guilty as charged, but Ford was not present to savor his brief moment of vindication. It was just as well. The color that must have drained from Joe Patterson's face was restored when the foreman said that the newspaper would have to pay just 12¢ to the plaintiff for damages. Ford attorney Alfred Murphy was pleased. "He has been vindicated. Money damages were entirely subordinate and were not sought by Mr. Ford." Satisfied, the *Tribune* officials returned to Chicago. They had won their battle in Ford's backyard.

It is hard to determine what effect the trial had on Henry Ford. His liberal attitudes began to erode by 1920. Ford disbanded the Mount Clemens News Bureau in 1919 so that he could purchase the *Dearborn Independent*. He began a virulent anti-Semitic campaign with such articles as the "Jewish Exploitation of Farmer's Organizations" and "The International Jew: The World's Problem." He later reversed his views and apologized to his readers. In later years, Ford abandoned politics, preferring to rule his factories with an iron fist. By doing this, he failed to establish a logical system of executive succession.

One positive benefit of the trial was the formation of the Greenfield Village Schools and the Henry Ford Museum during the 1920s. It was said that the negative reaction to his "history is bunk" statement compelled Ford to create a place of learning for young persons and a museum devoted to American industry. This was the only worthwhile aspect to the months of litigation. The Ford-*Tribune* trial was much ado about nothing. The newspaper still labored under the stigma of Joseph Medill conservatism in 1919. They would not have printed an editorial like this, say forty years later. The tone of the article reflected the spirit of the time. The print media routinely called blacks "darkies" and to call a man of Henry Ford's reputation an anarchist was not unusual. Respect toward the dignity of man would come only after many painful years of racial and labor struggles that uplifted the quality of life and helped close some of the divisions between rich and poor.

May lapsed into June. The Women's Suffrage Bill cleared the Illinois House and then the Senate on June 10. Illinois became the first state in the union to ratify national suffrage, but two of the three dissenting votes came out of Chicago wards, where women were still considered the gentle sex.

The *Chicago Crime Report* listed a murder every third day. The last of the Fighting 33rd returning from France on June 4, at the same time the Gish sisters caught the filmgoers' fancy. Dorothy appeared in *I'll Get Him Yet* at the Castle Theatre, while Lillian arrived in Chicago on June 4 to promote her two newest films, *Broken Blossoms* and *True Heart Susie*, showing at the Illinois Theatre.

Lillian was a reigning beauty queen, capturing the innocence of girlhood with a steel fortitude that helped her survive the rigorous demands of David Wark Griffith—foremost director of the silents. It had only been seven years since the Gish sisters were dragged into the Biograph Studios in New York by their ambitious stage mother. The girls were mere striplings, but the mother believed that they would follow in the footsteps of Mary Pickford if they were given the chance. So she hauled them into the studio, one on each hand, to see Griffith, a man in motion.

He walked over to them and for some strange reason burst into a song. "She'll never bring them in! She'll never bring them in!" he crooned, shortly before offering them a role in one of his sister pictures. D.W. Griffith did not know their names, and he couldn't even tell them apart. He handed Dorothy a red ribbon and Lillian a blue one so that he knew who was who. And for the longest time, he called them Red and Blue.

A Summer of Lost Innocence

Accompanied by a muscular bodyguard and her overbearing mother, Lillian met the press. *Tribune* film critic Mae Tinee gushed over her charms. "Lovely as a piece of Dresden china!" Tinee had panned several of Lillian's earlier efforts, but *Broken Blossoms* won her approval. It was a little morality play concerning a brutalized waif who is treated kindly by a Chinaman shortly before the little blossom is beaten to death by her father. "I'm awfully glad you liked me . . . for once!" she said before leaving to meet her public at the Illinois Theatre. A packed house paid 25¢ to $2 apiece for a first-hand look at the movie queen. The Hollywood dream factory had its second star.

The battle of the Wets and the Drys commenced in June. But in Chicago everyone seemed to be all wet, as the fearful July 1 approached. "Chicago may be dry for two months, but not any longer," declared Alderman Anton Cermak. "It will be sort of a recess." By the time "Push Cart Tony" took his place as mayor in 1931, school was still out.

Prohibition meant the loss of hotel revenues, jobs, and a source of entertainment for thousands. The Hotel Sherman announced plans on June 7 to raise room rates from 50¢ to a dollar a night to cover losses. The dining room manager promised to make recipes, shakers, and nonalcoholic-ingredients available to patrons desiring to brew their own.

Wholesale prices of whiskey dropped as the deadline got closer. Surplus whiskey filled government warehouses in Chicago. A gallon of hooch sold for just 60¢, but carried with it a stiff $6.40 tax assessment. Still, there were many who believed that a scheme like prohibition wouldn't last two weeks. "We'll reopen after July 2," a sign over one Chicago saloon read.

On June 30, the same saloon displayed another sign. "Eat, drink, and be merry, for tomorrow we dry up." United States District Attorney Charles Clyne vowed to support the Volstead Act, a law that called for search and seizure of all beverages containing one-half of one percent alcohol.

A grim, but curious fatalism seemed to permeate Chicago saloons as the last hours dwindled away. "Where's your liberty?" a bughouse orator at Washington and Wells Street wanted to know minutes before midnight, June 30. "The foundation of our liberties is being knocked from under us. The . . ." (wooden crate was kicked from under him at that very moment). The police arrived just in time.

Cars raced down Madison Street pell-mell, while sottish revelers gleefully punched holes in straw boaters. This was a time-honored Labor Day custom, but, after all, June 30 *was* New Year's Eve, wasn't it?

State Street was a gloomy trail of broken bottles the next day. And at Hinky Dink's Workingman's Exchange, a trail of broken dreams. Groups of dry-eyed men gathered around the old place the next day, mourning the passing of the "world's biggest schooner," sold in better days for a nickel. "Naw, we ain't got no real beer, just this sissy near beer," said one of the white-aproned bartenders who would soon be looking for work at the U.S. Employment Service at 116 N. Dearborn. Sensing the plight of these men, the state of Kansas put out a call for Chicago barkeeps who would work the harvest season for 60¢ an hour.

But most bars did not close. They just changed the bill of fare. The LaSalle Hotel served a "buttermilk frappe," while other bars introduced for the first time "loganberry highballs," phosphates, and ice cream sundaes. But as though prohibition wasn't enough trouble, there was a critical shortage of ice in Chicago that summer. Seventy-five thousand gallons of ice cream were consumed during a typical heatwave, but it took 60–75 pounds of ice to freeze just one gallon of cream. A small harvest of natural ice during the previous winter left warehouses empty.

"The night of June 30 won't be a comparison with the night they shut off the ice cream," sighed "Carnation" Dan O'Leary. "I can see them right now sitting on high stools at drugstores, bawling and fighting for that one more little sundae."

Chicago saloons opened for business for the first Sunday in many years on July 6. The favored drink of the ladies who sallied forth into this previously unknown territory? Sundaes, naturally.

In the month of June, two Britishers named John Alcock and Arthur Brown flew a Vickers-Vimy bi-plane across the Atlantic to Clifton, Ireland, from St. Johns, Newfoundland. They predated Lucky Lindy by eight years, claiming the $50,000 prize offered by the *London Daily Mail* for the first successful nonstop flight across the Atlantic. The 1,960 mile flight took sixteen hours and twelve minutes. The plane crashed into a sandbog, but Alcock emerged smiling. "Our flight has shown that the Atlantic flight is practicable," he said. "But I think it should be done not with airplane or seaplane, but with flying boat."

A Summer of Lost Innocence

Aviation history on a smaller scale was made in Chicago on May 15, 1919, when Trent Fry inaugurated the Chicago–New York air-mail service, after several earlier attempts. The planes got as far as Cleveland, where the mail was transferred to steady, reliable, trains for the overnight portion of the ride. On June 17, the first air-mail plane arrived from St. Louis, carrying a letter from Mayor Henry Kiel to William Hale Thompson. The copilot, one Omar Locklear, put on quite a show for Loop office workers by climbing a connecting rope ladder into another bi-plane flying several hundred feet above.

Air shows over Grant Park dated back to August 12, 1911, when the Chicago Aero club sponsored the International Aviation Meet. Prize money for daring aviators was supplied by Harold McCormick (who would later dump his poor wife, Edith Rockefeller, for a Polish diva with limited talent named Ganna Walska). The show was an artistic but not a financial success. Two deaths marred the show. *Tribune* cartoonist John T. McCutcheon witnessed the crash of William Badger, who attempted a 300-foot dive but failed to pull out of it when the plane was just twenty feet above Grant Park. Orville Wright had offered the *Tribune* man a ride in one of his airplanes, when he witnessed Badger's fiery crash. There was a public outcry against the show, but it continued to play in front of thousands of people who lined Michigan Avenue and rented hotel space above it. An estimated crowd of 400,000 witnessed the day's events on August 13 alone. The world became closer, thanks to those daring young men in their flying machines. The risks seemed small because most people viewed the stunts of Locklear, Badger, and others as just pranks. For Chicago had yet to experience a major air calamity.

Monday, July 21, was one of those typical muggy mid-summer days. The heat was a concern, but there were more serious problems. The International Executive Board of the Street Car Employees Union (a group of cigar-smoking, back-room types) demanded a 17 percent raise for Chicago's surface line and elevated employees. Before World War I, transit men earned 30¢ to 41¢ an hour depending on whether they drove on the overhead rails or on the streets. Governor Lowden's "compromise" (which was no compromise to an angry Thompson, who pledged no new fare increases) called for an hourly rate of 65¢ to 67¢ an hour. If accepted by the brotherhood, that meant fares would rise to 7¢ on the surface lines and 8¢ a ride on the elevated. Would Chicagoans stand for it?

At Comiskey Park that day, a fine crowd of 14,000 turned out to see the White Sox capture their third in a row from the second-place New York Yankees. Just a day earlier, Shoeless Joe Jackson strode to the plate in the tenth inning of a deadlocked game. Swinging his "Black Betsy," he was encouraged by the fans who chanted "into the bleachers this time!" On a one-and-nothing count, Joe obliged. As he crossed the plate, his happy teammates and a group of Sox fans jumped out of the stands and lifted him to their shoulders. Joe was carried to the dugout amid a police guard. He was a rural southerner who once refused to report to Connie Mack because of rookie stage fright. But in 1919 he was in the middle of a career renaissance, just before his banishment from the game.

The World Series was on everyone's mind. Baseball attendance surged that year, and no one realized this more than the owners. There was some consideration given to expanding the series to nine games. This was an idea that gained momentum as the season dragged on. To a man, the White Sox players supported the idea. It meant extra cash in the pocket.

Baseball's governing body, the bloated and complacent National Commission, supported the resolution. That meant that only Charles Comiskey was opposed. In 1919, the White Sox owner stood alone against the baseball powers. His friendship with American League President Ban Johnson had withered on the vine for twenty years, and now the two men were barely civil to each other. Open warfare between the clubs threatened to break out after Johnson suspended a Boston pitcher named Carl Mays after he jumped his team. When the Red Sox owner traded him to New York, Johnson refused to lift the suspension.

Comiskey lined up with the Boston and New York owners against Johnson. This power struggle put baseball in a tenuous position just as it was about to enter its darkest hour. In September the owners overturned the National Commission and adopted the nine-game World Series format. Comiskey was not pleased at this attempt to shatter old traditions. The Sox were at the crest of their popularity, confident that each game would bring a new victory and sure that their team was going to become a dynasty.

The Sox players were united against Comiskey—at least Jackson and his pals were. Their mistrust of the "Clean Sox" (Schalk, Faber, and Kerr) and their owner made them strong. On July 20, their internal struggle was disguised to the public. What happened in the Loop the next day was not.

A Summer of Lost Innocence

At 4:52 P.M. July 21 the game was stopped. Just two minutes before, fans in the left-field pavilion watched in fascination as a 153-foot-long blimp circled lazily above the Loop. Now, in a frozen moment that they would remember the rest of their lives, the fans saw a jet of flame shoot out from the belly of the giant gasbag.

The great dirigible was called the Wing Foot. In that instant, it quivered, buckled, and then plunged an estimated 1,200 feet toward the central business district near LaSalle Street. Five men were seen parachuting from the craft, but fire consumed the chute of one of the men. He crashed through the roof skylight of the Illinois Trust and Savings at Jackson and LaSalle Streets, seconds ahead of the great bulk of the Wing Foot.

Inside the bank, it was the close of another business day. The bank had been closed to customers for an hour, but clerks and tellers were busy balancing their cash drawers and preparing to go home. A shadow passed over the bank, and that was all the warning they had. The next few seconds were described by those who survived as a "raining hell" and a "blast furnace."

First the mangled parachutist, and then the blimp itself fell through the skylight. Two LaRhone engines measuring fifty feet fell to the floor of the bank, exploding its two gasoline tanks instantly. Glass fragments fell from the ceiling as the fuel splashed the clerks, igniting them instantly.

The marble rotunda was surrounded by wire-enclosed teller cages. There were only two exits from inside, so many helpless clerks were compelled to jump to the street from second-floor windows. People trapped in the rotunda crawled away, many ablaze from gasoline. Most of these unfortunate clerks were girls—stenographers and telegraph operators.

Rose A. Meyer was sorting mail when she saw a momentary flash of light overhead. "It did not startle us," she said. "We thought it was just another picture being taken for the little magazine." (*Bank Magazine* was a house publication that frequently took pictures of employees during the work day.)

Eleven people were killed instantly, of which six were burned beyond recognition. Streams of blood ran across the marble floor, and blood was splashed against the walls. Within two minutes, firemen appeared on the scene, answering a 01-11 call. There was little they could do. Singular acts of heroism were displayed by several of the male employees who were only slightly injured by the crash. They carried

A Summer of Lost Innocence

women to the two available exits before manning the emergency fire hoses along the walls.

Outside the bank, 20,000 spectators filled the streets while ambulances carried a number of the injured to the Iroquois Hospital at Market and Madison Streets. But the facilities were poor, and many of the interns had left for the day.

Bank president John N. Mitchell was on his suburban train bound for home when he first heard of the disaster. Four hours after the flames had been put out, Mitchell personally supervised a team of carpenters to build benches and desks and a crew of scrub women to wash away the blood. Six policemen guarded $100 million locked safely in the vault. Incredibly, a number of injured employees returned to the bank to assist in the cleanup effort and salvage operation.

C.E. Smithman's hair was burned off the top of his head, but he went back. This stoic effort says something of the high regard toward the work ethic in America during 1919. Chicago, the city of breakneck speed, paused to mourn its dead, but business had to go on. John Mitchell took out an ad in the morning papers to reassure the bank customers that the setback was only momentary. The doors opened for business on time, a scant fifteen hours after the last of the dead had been carried out by soldiers assisting the rescue effort.

SPECIAL NOTICE

The Illinois Trust & Savings Bank regrets to announce that a dirigible balloon, while passing over our bank building late Monday afternoon, took fire and fell through the skylight, setting fire to the desks and furniture in the center of the bank, injuring and killing several of our employees. The teller's cages and other facilities were not affected.

The physical damage will be repaired so that the bank will be able to transact business today, Tuesday, July 22nd, and thereafter as usual.

Illinois Trust & Savings Bank
by John Mitchell, President

News of the calamity reached the families in different ways. Carl Otto's wife was sitting on the porch rocking her infant when a news-

(Left) The blimp falls, July 21, 1919. Goodyear spent a half-million to build a hangar for the blimp at Wingfoot Lake, near Akron. However, the crowded conditions at the field forced the owners to move the blimp to White City for its ill-fated flight.

paper reporter informed her of her husband's death. He had been crushed to death under the wreckage of the motors on this, his first day back on the job after several weeks of illness. His wife begged him not to go back. But he did.

Coincidence and fate frequently accompany a story like this. The fatal flight of the Wing Foot was almost canceled because mechanics discovered that the fuel mixture was not correct for the flight. Repairs were made with haste because the blimp was owned and operated by the Goodyear Company of Akron, Ohio. The firm was eager to sell the craft to Adams Aerial Transportation Company of New York. This was a test and demonstration flight designed to show the potential for a commercial dirigible business in the United States. Goodyear invested over a half-million dollars to construct a hangar and field at Wing Foot Lake, outside Akron. But the company had to look elsewhere in July to conduct the test flight, since the government was testing army and navy aviators. The only other suitable hangar in the Midwest was located at the White City Amusement Park at 63rd and South Park avenues on the south side. During World War I Goodyear had utilized the Chicago facility to construct navy blimps.

It was 9 A.M. when Captain Jack Boettner, a commercial pilot and veteran of forty-two dirigible flights, began steering the craft toward Grant Park. Nothing of consequence happened, and the flight landed routinely at Grant Park to permit spectators to view it first-hand. At noon, Boettner took off again for a short trip over Diversey Avenue and back over the Loop. Those on board included Earl Davenport, White City publicist Milton Norton, a photographer for the *Herald-Examiner*, mechanic Harry Wacker, Carl "Buck" Weaver (a mechanic nicknamed after the White Sox star third baseman). Boettner's quick reactions saved his own life, but Davenport and Weaver hesitated, costing them their lives. Weaver's chute was consumed in flames, and he fell through the bank skylight. Davenport was later found on the roof, and Wacker broke his back.

Boettner was taken in for questioning by the police. He testified that he had been flying at 1,200 feet and that he believed that static electricity had caused the accident, but he later changed his mind. At that time, he explained that the LaRhone motors may have been at fault. He theorized that a rush of air from the propellers fanned the exhaust flames against the bag.

All the experts were summoned, but nobody could provide a workable solution. William C. Young, aeronautical expert and owner of the

A Summer of Lost Innocence

Jack Boettner, pilot of the Wingfoot.

Wing Foot, appeared with a delegation of Goodyear people. Young offered very little, disclaiming any personal responsibility. He told the hearing that he begged Davenport not to fly in the craft just yet. The blimp was not considered safe until it had been thoroughly tested (but the test flight just *happened* to be over the Loop during a business day).

White City owner Herbert Byfield admitted no liability either. The blimp was merely assembled at his hangar, that was all. "This building is historic as being the only available hangar in the United States when the war broke out," he said. "In it, the Goodyear Company built the first two airships used by Uncle Sam for the war. This building lying idle was still the only airship hangar in Chicago and was so used by the Goodyear Company in its ill fated, but earnest effort to stimulate and promote the airship industry in America."

Unless there was strong evidence that the craft was improperly built or there was gross negligence, the hearing ruled that no blame could be affixed to any one individual. Many theories were advanced in the following weeks, while Boettner continued to contradict his stories. Sparks from the motor exhaust igniting the bag was the accepted theory, but the only problem with that was that the LaRhone motor *did not throw sparks*. Static electricity could not have caused it because all the wires on board were grounded internally. The Wing Foot did contain silk diaphragms that rubbed against each other, causing friction. Sabotage was one possible explanation not considered by the committee. More likely, the blame can be laid at the foot of Goodyear for sacrificing safety in favor of dollars. The bag was filled with 95,000 cubic feet of hydrogen, standard in blimps at the time. Had they used the safer, but more expensive helium, the tragedy would have been avoided.

Thirteen people died in the Wing Foot calamity. Families of the victims received upwards of $1,000 from insurance policies provided by the bank. The Goodyear Company agreed to settle all claims arbitrated by an impartial three-man committee that included future Illinois governor Henry Horner, John H. Wigmore of the Northwestern Law School, and bank president Mitchell.

The city council, about to engage in one of the most hectic summer sessions in Chicago history, introduced a panic resolution to ban all flying over the city. The wing walking exploits over Grant Park no longer seemed funny to Anton Cermak, who sponsored the measure. "This accident shows we must stop flying over this city sooner or later, and we had better do it sooner." A saner, more realistic view was offered by Alderman Guy Guernsey of the seventh ward who said, "Some regulation is necessary, but don't forget that aviation is here to stay. I think flying over Chicago should not be prohibited, and I am an interested party, inasmuch as had it not been for this council meeting, I would have been in that blimp that fell today."

A watered-down resolution later passed the council, which allowed the public works commissioner to review petitions for flying over the Loop. The furor soon died. Jack Boettner went on to log 10,000 miles before his death in 1961. The White City hangar was made into a roller rink, but sadly, what happened that day would be forgotten. Stories of the *Lady Elgin* sinking, the 1871 Fire, the Iroquois Theatre Fire, and the *Eastland* capsizing would be told to generations of Chicago school children. But the Wing Foot is never mentioned. It is only recalled by the very few still alive who chanced to be in the Loop that July afternoon.

Nobody seemed discouraged by the Wing Foot flight, certainly not the Goodyear Company, which pressed ahead with their plans to wholesale dirigibles for commercial use. Goodyear secured contracts

A Summer of Lost Innocence

with the U.S. government and the German-based Zeppelin Company during the 1920s. But the United States bowed out of the arrangement after the first two ships, the *Akron* and the *Macon*, were wrecked in storms in the 1930s. The deathknell for lighter-than-air craft came when the *Hindenburg* was consumed in fire at Lakehurst, New Jersey, in 1937.

Newsreels of the Wing Foot crash first played in the Metropolitan and Oakland Square Theatres two days after the tragedy. By that time it was just a page-four story. There were other, more sensational stories crowding it out of the public eye. Events were moving swiftly in Chicago. Late July. No rain for a month. There were labor tensions in the stockyard districts; the building trades and even the stage players went after the almighty dollar. And just six days before the most grisly race riot in the city's history began, a little girl named Janet Wilkinson disappeared from a public playground at the foot of Chicago Avenue and the lake, on the near north side.

This was a new kind of crime in Chicago—a city used to the gun play of William and Peter Gentleman. The victim and the killer could have blended well into the urban life of the 1970s and 1980s. If the crime had been committed in modern times, Thomas R. Fitzgerald would have been caught, tried, judged insane, and probably released in five years.

But on July 22, 1919, news of the crime stirred the community to a frenzy. Six-year-old Janet lived with her parents and sister in a three-story double-stone building at 114 East Superior. She was the youngest daughter of Scottish immigrants who owned a grocery store. She was their pride and joy, their "Dolly." That's what they called her. On July 22, she was given the privilege of walking to the playground by herself. It was the first time she had undertaken the trip. In the company of two friends, Janet left for the playlot at nine o'clock. At twelve o'clock Janet left her companions at Rush and Superior so that she could go home to her sister Berniece, who was making lunch. One of the girls, Marjorie Burke, later told police that she saw Janet stop to talk to an older man. But they thought nothing of it. The man was known in the neighborhood.

His name was Thomas Richard Fitzgerald, a thirty-eight-year-old night watchman, who lived on the second floor of Janet's building. He was a thin, taciturn man with a receding chin and hairline. Except for the gold spectacles he wore, he was otherwise average looking in appearance. He lived with his wife Muriel and a boarder named Edward Watson one floor below the Wilkinsons. Soft-spoken in his ways, Fitzgerald suffered from typhoid fever and rheumatism since he was fifteen. For a time he worked as a chauffeur but later became the night watchman at the Virginia Hotel from 7:30 P.M. to 7:30 A.M. In all respects, Fitzgerald was the model husband. But, in reality, he was a troubled, deranged man who once served time for grand larceny and had been questioned about molesting a child several years earlier. He was, as the newspapers later explained to readers, an erotic pedophile. Chicagoans knew little about the word or what he meant. It had been only ten years since Dr. Freud made his first trip to the United States to

This was little Janet, aged six in 1919, when she met her death at the hands of Fitzgerald. Sadly, her parents were aware of Fitzgerald's past misdeeds involving other children but neglected to tell the police until it was too late.

lecture about psychoanalysis and abnormal sexual desires. Most people just reacted naturally to a story like this—organize the lynch party.

Hours after Janet disappeared, a massive manhunt was underway. The lake was dragged in the vicinity of Chicago Avenue, and the high reeds that grew along the water's edge were cut. (Michigan Avenue was about to undergo major transformations. Until 1920, much of the area was a soggy marsh.)

Fitzgerald was arrested on Wednesday, July 23, after police received the tip from the Burke girl about his conversation with Janet. The man was taken to the basement of the Chicago Avenue Police station where he began 104 straight hours of interrogation by a host of policemen and reporters who drifted in and out of the building. Fitzgerald told the police that he returned to his flat at 9 A.M. and went to bed for the day. His wife Muriel was summoned from Bangor, Michigan, where she was on a holiday. After surrendering to the desk sergeant, she asked to speak to Fitzgerald. "When I received that telegram, I knew what was the matter," she said to her husband. "Stick to your story, Tom, and you'll be all right." A reporter recorded the mysterious conversation from the next room. He told police that Fitzgerald told the woman to go back to the Virginia Hotel to retrieve a package from the desk. The package turned out to be a revolver wrapped in a chamois.

Muriel Fitzgerald was detained, but no definite connection between Janet's disappearance and the gun could be established. Police believed that the girl was kidnapped by the pair, but still there were no leads and no body. The usual crank letters poured in saying Janet was alive somewhere in Indiana. The apartment building and the Virginia Hotel were ransacked, but no leads turned up.

Believing that Fitzgerald was guilty by circumstance, the police began a remarkable fourth degree "sweat" that lasted four days. It was the kind of grilling that Ben Hecht and Charles MacArthur borrowed from in their reminiscences of Chicago newspaper days, a time when the reporters were cozy with both the cops and the crooks. The crime was horrible, but the press sensationalized it. Walter Howey, the energetic force behind the *Herald-Examiner*, joined James Doherty and George Bryant of the *Tribune* in the questioning of the suspect.

The final eight hours before the confession were marked by a series of ploys, ruses, and plots to extract an admission of guilt. Fitzgerald showed nervousness when he took off his glasses, so they removed them altogether. They told him they knew where the body was, and how he

A Summer of Lost Innocence

did it. The truth was, the cops were baffled. A box of stale chocolates were thought to be the missing link. But the box had not been touched by Fitzgerald, and the boarder Watson could not remember anyone buying them. Where did Fitzgerald put the body? He could not have left the building carrying a child without being detected, and the roof and boiler had been searched. There were no traces of human remains in the boiler, so the only hope was a confession.

At 1 A.M. the next morning, the suspect said he wanted to sleep. A physician was brought in to conduct an examination. The doctor diagnosed advanced syphilis—all without a test. Fitzgerald was then brought into the matron's quarters of the jail where his captors spread plaster of Paris figurines before him on a table. Included were portions of dolls' arms and legs. Fitzgerald stared at them in wonder, shifting uncomfortably. After several minutes alone with the doll parts, Detective Frank Smith entered the room disguised as a priest. "As a priest of the church, it is my duty to visit my brethren in distress," he told him. Fitzgerald bowed and kissed the priest's hand. Smith promised that his secret would be held in strictest confidence, but Fitzgerald continued to deny his guilt.

At 3 A.M. Fitzgerald was brought upstairs where he was confronted by a reporter posing as a relative of the grieved mother. "Before noon you will be a double murderer, Tom," the man whispered. "Mrs. Wilkinson will surely die of grief. You have seen her around the building. Think of her cold body in the morgue beside that of the girl. Man, have you no feelings?"

The reporter was brushed off. By 5 A.M. Fitzgerald was begging for sleep, but was slapped in the face by the policeman standing guard. A confession in exchange for several hours of sleep was the deal.

Fitzgerald maintained bleary-eyed composure in the face of angry threats by the police in the small hours of the morning. "Tell us the truth!" Finally, the newsmen phoned their city editors that he wouldn't talk. Most of them went out for breakfast. Meanwhile, the cops resumed the tough-guy role. "You'll kill me if you hit me! I have a weak heart!" Fitzgerald cried.

At 8 A.M. the distant sound of church bells could be heard. The sun

(Left) The murderer, Thomas R. Fitzgerald. His wife Muriel tearfully described her nonmarriage to him. He was almost childlike in his ways and a man to be pitied. The courts didn't see it that way. He was executed several months after confessing to the crime.

did not filter into the airless, close little room. It was a Sunday, July 27 —Fitzgerald's thirty-ninth birthday.

"Send down Mr. Howe," Fitzgerald told a reporter. Lieutenant William Howe had assumed the nice-cop role during the interrogation. "I'm afraid you'll think I'm a horrible man," Fitzgerald told the officer, who assured him he would think no such thing.

Finally he confessed. This was Chicago's hottest scoop in a summer that was about to get even hotter. It was a real front-page extra that in a few hours would have all the newsies on the corner yelling "Extree! Extree!"

He admitted that he first saw Janet at nine o'clock when he returned home from his job. He went to bed but awoke at noon. Fate had intervened unfavorably. Janet was walking slowly down Superior toward the flat. Fitzgerald went to the door and asked the girl if she wanted some of the stale candy that had been sitting on the vanity table. She hesitated, and in that instant, Fitzgerald reached for her and picked her up. The girl struggled and screamed. Fitzgerald panicked, and began choking her. He rendered her unconscious, but dropped her on the sofa. He thought she was dead, when in fact the girl still lived. Fitzgerald changed his clothes and carried her to the basement without being detected. Over 120 tons of coal were piled in the basement, and there Fitzgerald buried the still-living girl between the chimney and furnace. He then returned home and went to bed.

"They won't string me up if I'm crazy, will they, Mr. Howe?" Fitzgerald signed the formal confession and returned with the police to the scene of the crime.

Three men from the street department were brought in to move coal from the spot Fitzgerald pointed out. Search crews had spent the entire week sifting through the coal without results. Now it only took several minutes to expose the body. A coroner's inquest showed that little Janet had died as a result of strangulation caused by an object thrust into her mouth. There were no marks of violence on the body and no evidence that Fitzgerald had sexually abused the girl. Janet's father, an immigrant from Glasgow who had offered a $1500 reward, identified the body. He told the police that Fitzgerald made one other improper move toward the girl, but his wife had talked him out of any action. Now it was too late.

An angry mob appeared at the Chicago Avenue police station to lynch Fitzgerald, but he was removed to the Criminal Courts Building where "Red Necktie" Jimmy O'Brien was waiting. He was the assis-

A Summer of Lost Innocence

The building at 114 E. Superior Street, where the Wilkinsons and the Fitzgeralds lived. Over fifty tons of coal were ransacked by the police in their search for Janet. When Fitzgerald confessed, the cops were brought back to the basement. The killer pointed to the exact spot, and in less than two minutes the body was uncovered.

tant state's attorney and a man known for his success in securing convictions for killers.

Roused to action by the "moron problem" (so described by the press), the aldermen debated the differences between "idiots," "imbeciles," "degenerates," and what a "low grade" and "high grade" moron was. Should these people be removed from society, and at what age was a person legally responsible? This was something new and ghastly, and, frankly, no one knew what to do. The *Tribune* called for speedy justice in an editorial appropriately entitled, "The Noose and the Moron." The machinations of justice went to work, and on September 22, Fitzgerald went on trial for murder.

Attorney John E. Northrup was court appointed to defend Fitzgerald, a task he tried to get out of. No other lawyer would have a part of it with public opinion against the defendant so strong. So Northrup entered a plea of guilty, calling in various specialists to determine whether an insanity plea could be supported in court. "Necktie" O'Brien predicted the case would be over in two days.

He was wrong. It only took one day. Fitzgerald sat motionless in court while Judge Robert Crowe instructed him that a guilty verdict would mean the death penalty. The next day the expected verdict was handed down. Fitzgerald was asked whether he had anything to say. "I'm sorry; I ask forgiveness." Janet's mother wept. Fitzgerald collapsed in his chair after the decision was announced—death by hanging on Monday, October 27, in the county jail.

At 9:23 on that gray morning, Fitzgerald took his place on the gallows of the jail wearing a purple shirt and a brown suit. The night before he had written six letters to his wife, but five were torn up. He expressed remorse but admitted to a guard that "there's this thing which makes me go wrong." A petition for a stay of execution had been denied by Kenesaw Mountain Landis on the basis that Fitzgerald had entered court as a mature, competent person and had declared his guilt of his own free will. At 9:25, the rope dropped him into eternity.

Little Janet was at last vindicated. The Wilkinsons picked up the pieces of their lives, and Chicago breathed easier now that the moron was dead. But there was a sense of loss afterwards. Parents that once had confidence in allowing their children to walk the downtown streets in the summertime now had reservations. In 1919, children held jobs, traveled the streetcars, and visited amusement parks. Now it was a changing time. Yes, something changed significantly after Janet. The air tragedy, the Wilkinson case, and finally, on the day that T.R. Fitzgerald signed the confession, the race riot.

Chicagoans of all ages had flocked to the Lake Michigan beaches to seek solace from the deadly heat waves that swept the city during the century's early years. Oh the joy of divesting oneself of hoop skirts, starched collars, and black high-button shoes for an afternoon in the cooling water! Good taste dictated that the frolicking be restrained and that the young people show proper decorum. In 1919 the old ideas were being challenged by the free-thinking postwar generation.

On July 4, while Jack Dempsey battled Jess Willard in Toledo for God and money, Chicagoans dived, splashed, and roasted hot dogs over driftwood fires long into the night. At Clarendon Beach, the censors put a rope out into the water to segregate the ladies from the men. A few did cross the picket line, however.

Louise Osborne Rowe of the city welfare department was one who noticed. She initiated a campaign that month to outlaw the indecent exposure of girl's legs on a public bathing beach. On the 13th, she personally inspected the south side, finding deplorable conditions. "I feel they must be morally degrading, these suits which permit the exposure

A Summer of Lost Innocence

of female flesh." From 51st Street on the south, up to Wilson, and on to Clarendon, similar conditions were found. "Trunks should extend to the knee," Miss Rowe explained. "A dainty skirt should rebuke the too interested male stare. Girls should keep their hair neatly done under a cap because if it flows about the neck it gives a September morn look."

Police Chief John J. Garrity himself inspected conditions at the Ziegfeld Theatre at 624 Michigan Avenue on the tip that female ushers were wearing bathing suits in respect to a showing of "Mack Sennet's Bathing Beauties." "You know, they just might catch cold wearing those things," he said. When shown an 1869-style bathing suit, Garrity said *that* was sensible.

Louise Rowe filed her report to the city council as she promised, but Alderman Edward Armitage of the 27th Ward chided his associates for their prudery. "Things have changed, boys. We are living in the twentieth century now." (We can imagine that the council was so moved by this refusal to bow to stilted Victorian morality that they introduced a resolution to rename a major north-side street after the alderman.)

But it was amid this tranquil scene of relaxation that Chicago's festering race problem came to a head. Chicago's blacks and whites had waged a cold war since the Negro migration to Chicago began sometime around 1915. Thousands of jobs in munitions plants and packing houses were up for grabs after the whites left for France. Depressed conditions and the Jim Crow laws of the South led blacks to the promise of a better life on Chicago's south side. In 1910, just 2 percent of the city population was black. By 1915, the "Black Belt" had expanded from Cottage Grove Avenue to include Garfield Boulevard and portions of Washington Park between 51st and 61st Streets. Frightened whites abandoned the neighborhoods during and after World War I, while the remaining unafraid faithful saw their property values sink through the floor. This uprooting created civil tensions that would continue to exist in one form or another until the modern day.

The racial war began on September 23, 1918, when the first of six bombs were hurled at black residences. In June of 1919, white attorney William Austin's home at 103 Bellevue Place was the target of an unidentified bomb thrower. Earlier, Austin rented a building to a black family at 4807 Grand Avenue. Hostile whites threw two bombs at the house in May. The Harrison family, who occupied the building, refused to move out. Armed guards positioned themselves on their roof, and no further incidents were reported.

Racial tensions extended all the way to the police department where three black patrolmen were suspended on July 10, from the South Wabash Station. The three men, led by officer William McCall, dared to sleep in the segregated white dormitory. When they were asked to leave, McCall brandished a pistol.

So what happened on the beach Sunday, July 27, was no surprise, though accounts of the incident vary. A boy at play, with no quarrel against anyone, became the first victim of the riot and the catalyst of black-white warfare. Fourteen-year-old Eugene Williams joined his companions at the 25th Street beach for a day of rafting in Lake Michigan. The five boys steered their raft into fifteen feet of water, forgetting about the invisible boundary between the 29th Street beach, which was white, and the black 25th Street bathing area. The day was hot, and everyone was having a good time. The boys were unaware of several rock-throwing incidents on the shore between blacks and whites.

From the beach, a man later identified as George Stauber of 2904 Cottage Grove Avenue began throwing rocks at Eugene and his friends. They thought nothing of it because during better days it was a common thing to duck rocks while in the water. It was a dangerous game that whites would play with blacks.

Eugene Williams's attention was diverted for one fatal second. A rock struck him on the head, and he slipped under the raft. He grabbed the leg of his friend John Harris as he went down. But the Harris youth panicked and swam away. There was blood in the water. Eugene did not appear. The boys returned to the beach and reported the incident to bathers at 25th Street. A black policeman called upon officer Dan Callahan of the Cottage Grove Police station to arrest Stauber, after a dozen witnesses pointed him out. Callahan looked at him but said nothing. He was eventually suspended by Chief Garrity, but it was already too late. He had ripped the lid off a simmering pot.

Minus shoes and socks, the Harris boy and his companions ran home, afraid of what their parents would say about the discarded items of clothing. Their friend Eugene Williams was pulled out of the water fifteen minutes later, dead.

When Callahan refused to act, the black men attacked Stauber. Indignant whites rushed to his defense, and the battle was on. More black men arrived from the 25th Street beach, and their presence temporarily drove the offending whites back into the water. With this accomplished, the Negroes chased Callahan down 29th Street. The policeman ran into a drug store to call the Cottage Grove Avenue station for reinforcements. Two wagon loads of armed cops appeared minutes later, exchanging the first shots of the race riot. Policeman John O'Brien was the first to fall, sustaining a gun-shot wound in the left arm.

Maclay Hoyne later claimed to have uncovered evidence that a crap game between blacks and whites staged a block away may have sparked the riot. Hoyne accused a black social organization known as the Ink Well Club of harboring weapons to start a riot with some of the notorious "Black and Tan" resorts along State Street. Still others maintained that a baseball game between a black and white gathering erupted into the beach riot. Nobody can say for sure; certainly all of these things inspired the terror that the next few days would hold.

The riot quickly spread to the "black belt," where gangs of whites stopped cars and pulled the black occupants outside, beating them with night sticks and rocks. In the next four days incidents of riot were reported in the stockyards district, genteel Hyde Park, and the changing Washington Park. In the stockyards, armed companies of black men sniped at passersby.

By midnight of the third day, 26 were dead and 300 more were injured. Sections of the black belt along Wentworth Avenue and on toward 58th Street were randomly torched by whites, while Mayor Thompson still did not call up the Illinois National Guard. The mayor still harbored an old grudge toward the governor and was reluctant to make himself look bad by admitting that things were beyond his control. Maclay Hoyne made political hay out of Thompson's dilemma by laying the blame at the doorstep of Alderman Louis Jackson of the second ward, the heir to Oscar DePriest's empire. Jackson was an important ally of the mayor. "I am investigating a case in which it is charged that a certain white politician has gone about distributing revolvers and cartridges among vicious colored persons who would likely engage in rioting," Hoyne said, referring to a cache of guns found at the Ranier Club, Mexican Frank's, the Pekin, and Pioneer Club at 3512 S. State. Billy Lewis ran the Pioneer Club. A capper stood outside asking the passersby to "try their wrist today." Organized graft, sanctioned in silence for black votes, allowed the gambling clubs to remain open. Each of the dives employed two patrol cars driven by men with sawed-off shotguns and pistols.

Chief Garrity finally requested mobilization from Governor Lowden and Adjutant General Frank Dickson, who prepared 4,000 guardsmen for combat readiness. Meanwhile, the rioting reached the fringe of the Loop, just as the transit workers made good on their threat to walk off the job. Downtown Chicago was in chaos, as commuters fought each other for space in the few available jitneys that rescued stranded workers. The first rain drops in over a month fell on July 31, just as businessmen left their offices wearing Palm Beach suits. Umbrellas were sold on street corners for a dollar to help prevent the natty-looking suits from wilting.

Was there ever a time such as this? During the strike, innocent blacks fled to the police stations and were personally escorted home in patrol wagons. Others were not so lucky. The Hotel Sherman and the Palmer House were raided by gangs of rampaging whites numbering five hundred. They were looking for black porters and maids. They found one man at Wabash and Adams. He was thrown to the ground, kicked, trampled, and then shot in the chest.

Finally Thompson called up the guard after he learned that plans were afoot to torch the entire black belt. The ramshackle wooden tenements were an inviting target during the bone-dry heat wave. Six thousand guardsmen representing seven reserve units were stationed on State Street, south to 51st, and up and down Cottage Grove Avenue. Guardsmen mounted guns on top of sandbags, and the city suddenly took on the character of war-time France. Blacks did not feel secure, for most of the guard were white. Separate blocks were quarantined, while the police department assisted the guard. Special details of motorcycle cops and the horse patrol toured Halsted, State, 35th, and Ashland to keep a lid on things. The south side was a virtual no-man's land before it finally quieted down on August 1. The elevated cars were not running. Telephone wires were cut, and the hospitals were crowded to overflowing. A touring car containing First Police Deputy John Alcock, R.R. Ronayne of the U.S. Army, and Thompson's secretary Charles Fitzmorris was fired on at 36th and Vincennes. They reported back to the mayor that things were under control.

Finally, the guard restored order to the stricken city. Passions were spent. An uneasy calm hung over the troubled south side. Then on August 2, the riot threatened to start anew. The homes of a number of Poles and Lithuanians in the Back-of-the-Yards neighborhood were set afire by persons unknown. It was later speculated that the arsonists were white gang members who applied shoe polish to their faces. They

A Summer of Lost Innocence

were reacting out of vengence to a plan to escort Negroes back to the stockyards under armed guard.

But there were no further outbreaks. The first of the guardsmen were released from further duty on August 8. They were given a downtown parade, just like the Prairie Division several months earlier. The excitement and the *joie de vivre* were missing.

Grand-jury selection for the riot trial began on August 4. Inquiry into the probable cause began. Maclay Hoyne presented seventeen cases to the jury, all involving black men. Hoyne was called a racist by the all-white jury, which walked out in disgust. They were reprimanded by Judge Robert Crowe, who became a hero after sentencing Fitzgerald. The riot that claimed the lives of fourteen whites and twenty blacks became another political football after Hoyne persisted in his charge that Thompson used the second-ward politicians to his advantage.

At the root of the black-white conflict were the south-side "social athletic" clubs. They stoked the fires of racial hate, upholding the long-standing traditions first established in Bridgeport during the railroad strikes of 1877. Organized gangs of various social strata combined their talents to fight a common enemy—if not a railroad, then a black man would do. The tenements of the south side created a strange symbiosis. The children were thrown together in the streets to survive and be tough or to perish. Within the childhood play groups, friendships and identity were first established. Acceptance in the club meant performing acts of valor, most often illegal. Petty acts of larceny caught the attention of the cops and the local ward organization. Later, the committeeman or alderman would isolate the leader of the gang and persuade him to run various "errands" on behalf of the party. Chicago park attachés would then organize the gang into a social-athletic club, where hostility could be vented during baseball games with rival clubs. Charters would be given to the clubs from a nebulous body called the South Side Clubs Association. In return for paying the rent for the gang's meeting hall, the club would perform their political errands. They included falsifying election returns, perhaps tearing down an opponent's campaign poster, or, in some cases, direct intimidation of the candidate. Political immunity allowed the larger gangs to dictate terms to the neighborhood cops, store owners, or anyone else challenging their rule.

Fredric Thrasher identified 1,313 organized gangs in Chicago during the 1920s. An average gang had six to ten members, but real political clout belonged to only one. The biggest and meanest of the south-side clubs was Frank Ragen's Colts ("Hit Me and You Hit 2,000"), whose clubhouse was in a store at 5528 S. Halsted Street. A professionally lettered sign that said "RAGEN A.C." hung over the entrance. Smaller boys, envious of the tough-guy Colts, lingered outside the door. They organized themselves as the Morgan Athletic Club in 1902, but Frank Ragen succeeded to the presidency in 1908, and through use of brute force, changed the name. Ragen advanced himself from a street-smart organizer to member of the Cook County board. As a commissioner, his favorite debating tactic was to call his opponent a liar. During one board session, a *Tribune* reporter recorded eight variations of the same accusation by Ragen. "The president is lying." "His reason is a lie." "He has lied to me." "He has lied to a thousand." (The commissioner always viewed things in the thousands.) "He has lied to every man around here." "He went after the assistant state's attorney last week for calling him a liar." "I can call him a liar." And the classic "You're a liar." When Ragen failed to convince the other commissioners of his wisdom, he occasionally relied on other methods. In 1914, he punched Joseph Mendel in the eye and clouted Commissioner Cooney over the head with a book.

The noted Colt alumni included a prize fighter named "Yiddles" Miller, the murderer William "Gunner" McPadden, and Harry Madigan, owner of the Pony Inn of Cicero, a favored gangster rendezvous.

The Colts were an Irish gang, one of seventy-five operating in the city at the time. There were 99 Italian gangs and 148 of Polish origin. Most of the time, the Jewish gangs from the near-west-side fought the Italians from "Little Hell" or the north, who battled the Poles from "Pojay Town." The favored weapons were bricks, glass, and stones. Sometimes they used pistols. There were other clubs, smaller in size, all equally effective with a brick and a shiv.

The Aylward Club, Gerdon's, Lorraine, Our Flag Club, and the infamous Dirty Dozen from Hyde Park were gangs active during the riots. "Shaggy" Martin, a member of the dozen, pulled a trolley off a streetcar. While his associates boarded the bus to shake down the black riders, a woman seated in the last seat pulled out a razor. She slashed him in the chest, and he fell to the street dying. To his companions he asked: "What will mother say?" These clubs had their licenses temporarily revoked by Bill Thompson during the riots. "Big Bill" had many shady supporters in his time, but the clubs were not among them. Not only was he a Republican, but his clout came from the black belt. After some pressure from Ragen's city-hall connections, the charters were restored.

The Hamburg was a neighborhood that extended from 31st Street to 40th, cut off from Canaryville by the streetcar tracks. Gang members from both sides of the tracks were Irish, but their Saturday night "wars" were fierce vendettas. The early power of the eleventh ward was nurtured here when a serious-minded law student named Richard Daley ascended to the presidency of the Hamburg Athletic Club. We will never know what young Daley was up to during the thick of the rioting, but we can be sure that the "Hamburgers" were not out promoting good will among men.

Curbing the power of the political clubs was one of the grand jury's first recommendations, one that the black newspaper the *Chicago Defender* called for as early as July 12, 1919.

> Gangs of young hoodlums from the district west of Wentworth Avenue have been making it a practice of attacking our people under the cover of darkness, and so far have been able to elude the police. Most of these young men come from the so-called "athletic clubs" that are so numerous in the territory aforementioned. These clubs are nothing more than hangouts for gangs and young toughs. The records of the police department show that much of the banditry now prevalent in this city is due to the activity of this class of men.

They first met in the streets as little boys. They sold newspapers, (maybe did a little slugging on the side), helped put the local alderman in office, went after the blacks, finally drifting to other pursuits during the 1920s and 1930s. Some of them became saloon owners in Cicero. Others worked for the city and raised their kids the same way they were brought up. A few, like Richard Daley, went into politics. And then there were those who never outgrew gang activities. Dion O'Bannion, who fought the Italians in "Little Hell" as a lad, died at their hands when he was an adult. The circle was complete.

Of course, organized thuggery was not confined to the white areas alone. The cabarets along State Street were used as storerooms for pistols, rifles, and razors. Raids by Maclay Hoyne after the rioting quieted down bore this out.

But the marauding tactics of Ragen's Colts, the Dirty Dozen, and others failed to stem the Negro quest for a better life in Chicago. White flight from neighborhoods such as Washington Park accelerated. In 1920, only 15 percent of the community was black. By 1930, that figure had swelled to almost 92 percent. James T. Farrell was a Washington Parker by birth. He captured in his writing the spirit of the time and the plight of the south side Irish, seen through the eyes of Studs Lonigan. Life was good in 1916, not so in 1931 when the novel closes with Studs's death at an early age and the father's boozy disillusionment with life.

For the blacks, Governor Lowden promised better housing. It never came, and the old wounds were slow to heal. But the race problems of Chicago were not so unique and certainly not isolated. There were race riots in Washington, D.C., long before the first rock was thrown on 29th Street. And in Omaha, the mayor orderd the theatres to remove D.W. Griffith's *Birth of a Nation* from the screen for fear of a Chicago-style riot.

Something died in Chicago in 1919. Perhaps the notion of Chicago becoming the garden city of the Midwest ended the day the riots began. But the erosion of the creative spirit began several years earlier when Theodore Dreiser became the first literary rebel to flee the city. In July of 1919, Dreiser was vacationing at Asbury Park, New Jersey, with Estelle Kubitz, his live-in mistress.

Asbury Park was a wide-open town of amusement parks, gin mills, cabarets, and other nighttime gaiety, shunned by the neighbors of Ocean Grove. The adjoining town had a strict dry law that had been in the books since 1869 and was governed by the Methodist Camp Meeting Association. In his diary, Dreiser notes with joy the girls in their daring bathing costumes at Asbury Park. Here was Dreiser, America's foremost crusader against the traditional value system, vacationing in an area that presented a stark contrast between where the nation had been and where it was now going.

The erosion of the creative spirit continued when Floyd Dell, Margaret Anderson, Edna Ferber, and Sherwood Anderson left the city to discover these contrasts for themselves. They had all written of Chicago and had roamed its streets and known its people.

And now in 1919, Ringold Lardner, beat writer for the White Sox, author of *You Know Me, Al,* and the proprietor of the *Tribune*'s "Wake of the News" column for six years, was about to join the exodus. Lardner's journalistic career in Chicago began in 1907 when he worked for

A Summer of Lost Innocence

the *Inter-Ocean* for $18.50 a week. Now, with his *Tribune* contract about to expire, he was preparing to go to New York to write syndicated features for John Wheeler of Bell and to take a shot at playwriting.

His was the world of sport. Lardner drank with the hustlers, the pugs, and the card players on board the all-night Pullmans that raced through midwestern flatlands toward the Dearborn Station. His was not the grim realism of Dreiser but the wonderment of a rookie's first day in training camp. In June, he began work on his last major story for the *Tribune*, the Jess Willard–Jack Dempsey bout in Toledo. But Ring was sidetracked on June 17, just three days before his last scheduled column. He was hauled into speeder's court for driving thirty-eight miles an hour through Lincoln Park. "Twenty days in jail!" thundered Judge Stelk. "Don't you think that's pretty severe?" a reporter asked Lardner. "Well, it's 50-50. If I don't go to jail, I'll have to go to Toledo. Which is worse?" Lardner chose Toledo and settled for a $50 fine. But his luck did not improve. He put his money on Willard, who staggered through four rounds before collapsing on the mat.

But to each man comes a tribute, and on August 13, his friends roasted and saluted him at Comiskey Park, courtesy of the Woodland Bards (that group of camp followers and Sox fans who had the time and money to accompany Lardner to various American League cities). Judge Henry Horner presented him with a gold, engraved lifetime pass to Comiskey Park. It was a gesture of magnitude on Charles Comiskey's part, for he was known to be tight with a dime. The only other men so honored were John L. Sullivan, George M. Cohan, and Sir Thomas Lipton. Lardner took his bows and headed to New York because Chicago had ceased to be a creative outlet and because America's literary elite were searching for new vistas.

Lardner never wrote that great novel. He found disillusionment instead. He covered the 1919 World Series for the Bell Syndicate, but suddenly the joy of baseball disappeared. In a roadhouse in Bellevue, Kentucky, Lardner wrote a terse, cynical poem with Jim Crusinberry of the *Tribune*, following the second game of the World Series.

> I'm forever blowing ballgames,
>   Pretty ballgames in the air,
> I come from Chi,
>   I hardly try
> Just go to bat, and fade and die,
>   Fortunes coming my way,

> That's why I don't care
> I'm forever blowing ballgames,
> For the gamblers treat me fair.

Lardner did not write baseball fiction for the next six years. Nor did he find the literary gold that he thought he would find in New York. Perhaps if he searched within himself, he would have understood that his casual midwestern style could never blend into the Broadway scene. But then, if the Black Sox had not shaken his faith in life, perhaps things may have been different. Lardner moved into a spacious house at Great Neck, Long Island. His neighbors included George M. Cohan, Flo Ziegfeld, Moe Annenberg, and F. Scott Fitzgerald. Here he was, a pilgrim in the land of plenty. Lardner was quiet, polite, and somewhat of a wit at the Great Neck parties. But his dreary view of the Long Island social set was carefully disguised to all but Fitzgerald, who met with him each night. Comforted by a bottle of champagne, their midwestern bonds, and a shared contempt of the era's frippery, the conversations lasted till dawn.

The novel that lurked inside of Lardner was written by Fitzgerald. It was *The Great Gatsby*, and it included all the old themes—idealism, ambition, betrayal. It was a brilliant, sad commentary about a changed America in the 1920s.

Meanwhile, the "Wake of the News" column continued on under the stewardship of Jack Lait, the man who brought winsome Dale Winter to Big Jim Colosimo.

If the film and arts community saw horizons outside Chicago, there were those who didn't. In August, Bill Haywood stopped over in Chicago just before he left for Russia to see through his dreams of living in a socialist utopia. Haywood, head of the IWW (the Wobblies), was saved from the gallows in 1907 by Clarence Darrow, after being implicated in the assassination of Idaho Governor Frank Steunenberg. IWW agitators poured into Chicago in August of 1919, to inspire the steel and iron workers, the stockyards men, and a new group flexing some labor muscle, the lunchroom workers.

Before McDonalds, before Burger King, Chicago had fast-food franchises. "Lucky Charlie" Weeghman was the king of the one-armed dairy lunch. At the pinnacle of his fortune, he owned ten Weeghman's restaurants in the Loop, which served 35,000 diners a day. Patrons

A Summer of Lost Innocence

were served while seated in a small chair with a counter in front of them, much like the old-fashioned school desk. Young, affluent, and good looking, Weeghman was a self-made man. He came to Chicago in 1892 and worked as a busboy at King's restaurant in the heart of the Loop theatre district. With pluck, determination, and boyish charm, he saved his nickels and opened his own little diner.

But Charlie Weeghman lusted after the public favor. He was not content to devote his resources to his booming restaurant chain. Rather, he preferred the company of sportsmen and politicians. In 1914, he sunk a goodly portion of his restaurant profits into the purchase of the Chicago entry in the newly organized Federal League. While the team won a championship in the second year of its brief two-year history, the experience drained him financially. Later, Weeghman sold the Chicago Cubs to a group of Chicago sports led by William Wrigley, Sr.

In 1919, with his baseball days behind him, Weeghman faced stiff challenges from the Thompson and Messenger chains, all of which were targets of IWW agitation. A pitched battle between cops and IWW representatives took place on August 17, after leaflets were handed out to the waiters, cooks, and cashiers. Bill Haywood, out on bail from Leavenworth, was present at the meeting of restaurant workers seeking higher pay and the eight-hour day. The Chicago Federation of Labor refused them a hearing, and Thompson recruited scabs to work the counters. Hired guns boarded the trucks to intimidate and bully the scabs, while diners fled from the restaurant.

Police wagons pursued the sluggers through the Loop, firing bullets over their heads. The next day, reporters found Haywood at the IWW Hall at 119 Throop Street. He sat at a desk cluttered with files and memoranda in a large room at the top of a long, narrow stairway. His clothing was modest. He wore a dirty white shirt with a tie hung loosely around his neck. Haywood's suit was an ill-fitting pin-stripe. "We are peaceable folks," he explained. "But you take them capitalists now, the ones that's trying to starve our boys in jail down in Kansas. Someday somebody's goin' to give them their desserts. There'll be an industrial upheaval in America some day. See if there ain't!"

Haywood smiled and turned away. He knew that he was putting them on. Fourteen years had passed since June 27, 1905. Fourteen years of hard struggle since the founding of the IWW at Brand's Hotel at Erie and Clark. The idealism of the labor movement was reflected in the speeches of Mother Jones, Lucy Parsons, and Eugene Debs that afternoon. The spirit of the working class, echoed by Debs. "I am in accord with the movement and it seems to be absolutely necessary that we have an industrial form of government for labor founded on the class struggle." Haywood was elected the temporary chairman, and two days later the labor congress named itself the Industrial Workers of the World. The IWW repudiated the AF of L and Samuel Gompers, whom Debs called a "misleader of the working class." It was to be a union "for all the people." But when the goals were not so easily achieved—violent overthrow of the system was considered.

There would be no revolution in America, not in 1877, 1886, or 1919. Haywood and Weeghman were born to modest nineteenth-century rural backgrounds. One was thrifty and followed the prescribed path toward success. The other saw clearly the starvation and wealth. Rather than become a part of it, he first tried to change it, but then fought it to the death. Weeghman squandered his fortune. His restaurant chain was thrown into a receivership on August 13, 1920, because he wanted to be a high-living sportsman who saw his name in the papers. Weeghman ended up managing two short order cooks in his bar and grill on Fifth Avenue in New York. Haywood chose to become an expatriate in Russia, dying in a land about to be swallowed by Stalin hegemony. Who's to say which man understood the right and true path through life?

Finally there was time for the important things in life. Baseball and the pennant-bound White Sox. Babe Ruth poled a mighty home run off Sox pitcher Erskine Mayer on August 16 that sailed over the right-field bleachers and into an adjoining soccer field. There was some talk in the dugout about home runs. Everybody recalled the big one that they had seen. Buck Weaver, who was around in 1913, recalled that a second-line rook named John Beall once drove one down the right-field line, but that was a whistling liner that barely got higher than the fence. Babe Ruth's home run seemed to gain momentum as it sailed.

Who was this Babe Ruth? More than any idea or political happening that summer, the spindly legged youngster playing his last year in Boston would come to symbolize a new era. The veteran White Sox were still clean, but they would soon pass into an age that ended too quickly.

The Chicago White Sox shrugged off the home run as one of those freak things. In the ninth inning of a tie game, Hap Felsch and Chick

Gandil singled. Swede Risberg walked, and Ray Schalk won the game with a perfectly laid squeeze bunt. Handshakes all around for a job well done. Ahead now by four games.

The fans streamed out of the ballpark and home to dinner. The trains and streetcars were running again. All was quiet along Cottage Grove Avenue, and the beefy gambler Joseph "Sport" Sullivan was still thirty-three days away from making his rendezvous with Chick Gandil in Boston's Buckminster Hotel to discuss a "little business proposition."

The skies were a smoky haze of pollution, but that could only mean that things were back to normal again. The boys were working. But that old order was gone . . . long gone. Nobody paid attention. The streetcar was pulling away from the curb.

Sources and Notes

There are several ways to write a book about Chicago. I happen to think the best approach is to select *aspects* of city history. To begin the story with the death of John Kinzie and continue it through the "council wars" is a lengthy, risky undertaking. Somewhere along the line, an important theme will be sacrificed. Emmett Dedmon surveyed the scope of Chicago history as well as any in his book *Fabulous Chicago*. Finis Farr duplicated the effort in 1973 with his book *Chicago: A Personal History of America's Most American City*.

I don't believe that a subject like the levee can be dismissed in two paragraphs or two pages. During my research, I must have read the same story about Mike McDonald and the Everleigh Club at least six times. Unfortunately, the tendency is to copy information from the last author to write about the subject and hope it is correct. This was especially true concerning William McGarigle. Aspects of the case were distorted, but nobody seemed to want to verify the facts from the primary source—the newspapers. (Without a reliable index to the Chicago papers, this sometimes proved to be a hopeless task.)

The following books proved to be the most helpful tools during my research; *Organized Crime in Chicago, Part Three of the Illinois Crime Survey*, by John Landesco; *Torture Doctor*, by David Franke; *The Gang*, by Fredric Thrasher; *History of Chicago, vol. 3*, by the A.T. Andreas Company, and *The History of the Haymarket Affair*, by Henry David.

Population of Chicago, 1871–1920

They came from all corners of the globe—Italians, Poles, Swedes, Irish, Jews, Germans, Chinese—all in search of the better life that they had heard about. Chicago in all its wicked, corrupt elegance welcomed them. This chart reflects the phenomenal growth of a city in that time.

Year	Population	Year	Population
1871	334,270	1897	1,490,937
1872	367,396	1898	1,557,164
1873	380,000	1899	1,626,333
1874	395,408	1900	1,698,575
1875	400,500	1901	1,747,236
1876	407,661	1902	1,795,897
1877	430,000	1903	1,834,558
1878	436,731	1904	1,893,219
1879	491,516	1905	1,941,880
1880	503,185	1906	1,990,541
1881	540,000	1907	2,039,202
1882	560,693	1908	2,087,862
1883	580,000	1909	2,136,525
1884	629,885	1910	2,196,238
1885	665,000	1911	2,249,363
1886	703,715	1912	2,301,946
1887	760,000	1913	2,354,529
1888	802,651	1914	2,410,806
1889	935,000	1915	2,464,189
1890	1,099,850	1916	2,517,172
1891	1,148,795	1917	1,569,755
1892	1,199,730	1918	2,622,338
1893	1,253,022	1919	2,675,921
1894	1,308,682	1920	2,766,815
1895	1,377,813	1920	2,766,815
1896	1,427,527		

Source: *Daily News* Almanac, 1946

Sources and Notes

Bon-Ton Directory,
Giving the names in Alphabetical Order of Addresses and Hours of Reception of the Most Prominent and Fashionable Ladies Residing in Chicago, 1879–1880
(An Excerpt and Partial Listing)

"Notes of invitation to a large party can be printed in any style you wish, but always worded in the third person. Invitations should be written or printed upon a whole sheet of small note paper, and should be issued at least a week before the time appointed for the party, so that if necessary, a suitable dress may be obtained. For a costume ball or masquerade, two weeks is the usual time allowed for preparation.

"The letters R.S.V.P. are sometimes put at the end of a note. They stand for the French phrase Réspondez s'il vous plait: an answer if you please. It is better, however, when an answer is particularly desired to say, an answer will oblige. It is courtesy to reply promptly to a note of invitation requesting an answer. If no reply is requested, and you send no regrets, it is understood that you accept the invitation.

"Send invitations to persons in your own city or neighborhood by your own messenger. It is regarded as a violation of etiquette to send them by mail."

Armour, Mrs. P.D. 987 Prairie Avenue.
Friends always welcome.

Baker, Mrs. O.P. 48 St. Johns Place.
Friends received Tuesdays and Thursdays after October 1.

Barbe, Mrs. Martin 1677 Wabash Avenue.
A most hearty welcome accorded friends at all hours, day and evening.

Bonfield, Mrs. J.F. 1476 Wabash Avenue.

Comiskey, Mrs. R. 142 Lytle Street.
Friends most cordially received at all times.

Dent, Mrs. Thomas 43 S. Sheldon St.
A welcome always awaits my friends.

Dexter, Mrs. Wirt 869 Prairie Avenue.

Field, Mrs. Marshall 923 Prairie Avenue.
Fridays.

Leiter, Mrs. L.Z. 60 Calumet Avenue.
At home after September.

Onsley, Mrs. J.O. 245 Ashland Avenue.
No reception days.

Palmer, Mrs. P.B. 844 W. Adams St.
To friends always.

Pullman, Mrs. George   879 Prairie Avenue.
At home Fridays.

Rumery, Mrs. M.A.   11 S. Sheldon.
Our friends know that we are always glad to see them.

Spalding, Mrs. Albert G.   212 Vincennes Ave.

VanPelt, Mrs. John   41 Honore St.
Friends always welcome.

Sources and Notes
Cook County Government and Law Enforcement, 1871–1920

Year	Mayor	Chief of Police	State's Attorney	Sheriff
1871	Joseph Medill	W.W. Kennedy	Charles Reed	Henry Cleaves
1872	Joseph Medill	Elmer Washburne	Charles Reed	Timothy Bradley
1873	Harvey D. Colvin	Washburne-Rehm	Charles Reed	Timothy Bradley
1874	Harvey D. Colvin	Jacob Rehm	Charles Reed	Francis Agnew
1875	Harvey D. Colvin	Rehm-Hickey	Charles Reed	Francis Agnew
1876	Monroe Heath	Michael Hickey	Luther L. Mills	Charles Kern
1877	Monroe Heath	Michael Hickey	Luther L. Mills	Charles Kern
1878	Monroe Heath	Hickey-Seavey	Luther L. Mills	John Hoffman
1879	Carter Harrison	Seavey-O'Donnell	Luther L. Mills	John Hoffman
1880	Carter Harrison	O'Donnell-McGarigle	Luther L. Mills	Orrin Mann
1881	Carter Harrison	William McGarigle	Luther L. Mills	Orrin Mann
1882	Carter Harrison	McGarigle-Doyle	Luther L. Mills	Mann-Hanchett
1883	Carter Harrison	Austin Doyle	Luther L. Mills	Seth Hanchett
1884	Carter Harrison	Austin Doyle	Julius Grinnell	Seth Hanchett
1885	Carter Harrison	Doyle-Ebersold	Julius Grinnell	Seth Hanchett
1886	Carter Harrison	Fredrick Ebersol	Julius Grinnell	Canute Matson
1887	John A. Roche	Fredrick Ebersold	Julius Grinnell	Canute Matson
1888	John A. Roche	Ebersold-Hubbard	Joel Longnecker	Canute Matson
1889	Dewitt Cregier	George Hubbard	Joel Longnecker	Canute Matson
1890	Dewitt Cregier	Fredrick Marsh	Joel Longnecker	James Gilbert
1891	Hempstead Washburn	Robert McLaughery	Joel Longnecker	James Gilbert
1892	Hempstead Washburn	Robert McLaughery	Jacob Kern	James Gilbert
1893	Carter Harrison	Michael Brennan	Jacob Kern	James Gilbert
1894	John Hopkins	Michael Brennan	Jacob Kern	James Pease
1895	George Swift	John Badenoch	Jacob Kern	James Pease
1896	George Swift	John Badenoch	Charles Deneen	James Pease
1897	Carter Harrison, Jr.	Joseph Kipley	Charles Deneen	James Pease
1898	Carter Harrison, Jr.	Joseph Kipley	Charles Deneen	Ernest Magerstadt
1899	Carter Harrison, Jr.	Joseph Kipley	Charles Deneen	Ernest Magerstadt
1900	Carter Harrison, Jr.	Joseph Kipley	Charles Deneen	Ernest Magerstadt
1901	Carter Harrison, Jr.	Francis O'Neill	Charles Deneen	Ernest Magerstadt
1902	Carter Harrison, Jr.	Francis O'Neill	Charles Deneen	Thomas Barrett
1903	Carter Harrison, Jr.	Francis O'Neill	Charles Deneen	Thomas Barrett
1904	Carter Harrison, Jr.	Francis O'Neill	John Healy	Thomas Barrett
1905	Edward Dunne	O'Neill-Collins	John Healey	Thomas Barrett
1906	Edward Dunne	John M. Collins	John Healey	Pease-Strasssheim
1907	Fred Busse	George Shippey	John Healey	Chris Strassheim
1908	Fred Busse	Shippey-Steward	John Wayman	Chris Strassheim
1909	Fred Busse	Leroy Steward	John Wayman	Chris Strassheim
1910	Fred Busse	Leroy Steward	John Wayman	Michael Zimmer
1911	Carter Harrison, Jr.	John McWeeney	John Wayman	Michael Zimmer
1912	Carter Harrison, Jr.	John McWeeney	Wayman-Hoyne	Michael Zimmer
1913	Carter Harrison, Jr.	McWeeney-Gleason	Maclay Hoyne	Michael Zimmer
1914	Carter Harrison, Jr.	James Gleason	Maclay Hoyne	John Traeger
1915	Wm. Hale Thompson	Charles Healey	Maclay Hoyne	John Traeger
1916	Wm. Hale Thompson	Charles Healey	Maclay Hoyne	John Traeger
1917	Wm. Hale Thompson	Healey-Schuettler	Maclay Hoyne	John Traeger
1918	Wm. Hale Thompson	John J. Garrity	Maclay Hoyne	Charles Peters
1919	Wm. Hale Thompson	John J. Garrity	Maclay Hoyne	Charles Peters
1920	Wm. Hale Thompson	Charles Fitzmorris	Hoyne-Crowe	Charles Peters

BIBLIOGRAPHY

NEWSPAPERS (1880–1920)

CHICAGO AMERICAN	CHICAGO RECORD-HERALD
CHICAGO DAILY NEWS	CHICAGO TIMES
CHICAGO DEFENDER	CHICAGO TIMES-HERALD
CHICAGO HERALD-EXAMINER	CHICAGO TRIBUNE
CHICAGO INTER-OCEAN	NEW YORK TIMES
CHICAGO JOURNAL	NEW YORK TIMES INDEX
CHICAGO POST	NEW YORK TIMES OBITUARY INDEX

BOOKS

1. Clark, Herma, *The Elegant Eighties*, A.C. McClurg & Co., 1941. An overview of the decade with special emphasis on society and customs.
2. Dedmon, Emmett, *Fabulous Chicago, A Great City's History and People*, 1953, by Emmett Dedmon. Enlarged edition, Atheneum, 1981. It's a quick guide through Chicago history, considered by many, to be the best survey of major Chicago events.
3. Dreiser, Theodore, *Newspaper Days*, Horace Liveright, 1922.
4. Ginger, Ray, *Altgeld's America: The Lincoln Ideal Versus the Changing Realities*, Funk Publishers, 1958. A political and social review of Altgeld's era.
5. Harrison, Mrs. Carter, *Strange to Say: Recollections of Persons & Events in New

Sources and Notes

Orleans & Chicago, A. Kroch & Sons Publishers, 1949. A charming, graceful book with no attempt at analysis. Her intention was to write a gentle book that would be pleasing to her friends and relatives still alive in the 1940s.

6. *History Of Chicago, Volume Three*, 1884, A.T. Andreas & Co., Chicago. An excellent source of biographical information on prominent Chicagoans of the period.
7. Lait, Jack, & Mortimer, Lee., *Chicago Confidential: The Lowdown on the Big Town*, Crown Publishers, 1950. No mistake. Jack Lait was right off the "front page."
8. Longstreet, Stephen, *Chicago: 1860–1919*, New York, David McKay & Co., 1973.
9. Lowe, David, *Lost Chicago*, Houghton-Mifflin Company, 1975.
10. Mayer, Harold, & Wade, Richard, *Chicago: Growth Of a Metropolis*, University of Chicago Press, 1969.
11. Nash, Jay Robert, *People to See*, New Century Publishers, Inc., 1981.
12. Smith, Page, *The Rise of Industrial America: A People's History of the Post-Reconstruction Era*, McGraw-Hill Book Company, 1984.
13. *This Fabulous Century, 1870–1900*, Time Inc., 1970.
14. Wendt, Lloyd, *Chicago Tribune: The Rise of a Great American Newspaper*, Rand McNally & Co., 1979. A vast undertaking, but it does not discuss the Ford libel trial.
15. Winslow, Charles, *Historical Events of Chicago*, Soderlund Printing Service, 1937. In absence of a reliable index to Chicago history, this thin little volume is as good as any in listing the yearly events of Chicago.
16. Winslow, Charles, *Biographical Sketches of Famous Chicagoans*, no publisher listed, 1948.

Miscellaneous

1. Kenosha Historical Society, City Directory for 1907.
2. St. Elizabeth Hospital Medical Records, Mrs. Spicknell, Director.
3. Potter Palmer papers, Chicago Historical Society. The financial ledgers and transactions were donated to the Society in 1967, but there are no personal references to the family in this collection.

NOTES

Chapter One: Chicago's Labor Pains

1. Adelman, William, *Haymarket Revisited*, The Illinois Labor History Society, 1976. This interesting "tour" of the Haymarket sights loses its credibility when the author loses his objectivity and continuously introduces his prolabor sen-

timents. What, for example, does the Marina City complex have to do with a tour of Haymarket? Answer: the offices of the Chicago Federation of Labor are located there.

2. *The Anarchist Cases in the Supreme Court*, Abstract of the Record, Vol. 2, 1887.
3. Ashbaugh, Carolyn, *Lucy Parsons: American Revolutionary*, Charles A. Kerr, Publishing, 1975.
4. David, Henry, *The History of the Haymarket Affair*, Russell & Russell, 1936. The most definitive study of the Haymarket Riot to date.
5. Ebersold, Frederick, *Annual Report to the City Council for 1886*, B. Kenney, printer.
6. Flinn, John, *The Chicago Police*, W.B. Conkey, 1887. Written for the Chicago Policeman's Benevolent Association, Flinn's book is an attack on the labor movement, as most accounts of that era were.
7. Foner, Philip, ed., *Autobiographies of the Haymarket Martyrs*, Charles A. Kerr Publishing, 1976.
8. *Charles Harpel Scrapbook, Volume Seven; 1887-1903*. Various newspaper clippings collected by Harpel are in the collection of the Chicago Historical Society.
9. Kebabian, John S., *The Haymarket Affair*, H.P. Kraus, 1970.
10. Lum, Dyer, *The Trial of the Haymarket Anarchists*, Arno Press, 1969.
11. Kogan, Bernard R., *Chicago Haymarket Riot; Anarchy On Trial*, D.C. Heath & Co., 1959.
12. Schaak, Michael J, *Anarchy and Anarchists*, F.J. Schulte & Co., 1889. A lavish, preposterous book that Schaak hoped would expand his own inflated image.
13. Edward Steele Papers; Chicago Historical Society, including letters from Bonfield to Ward and from the station commanders to Ebersold detailing their accounts of the riot.
14. Wish, Harvey, "Governor Altgeld Pardons the Anarchists," *Illinois State Historical Society Journal* 1, no. 4 (December 1938).

Chapter Two: The Boodler's Bathroom Escape

Several of the other books in this listing mention the McGarigle escape, but too often have presented erroneous information that was copied by future authors who never checked the dates. Herbert Asbury states in *Gem of the Prairie* that McGarigle remained away from Chicago for twenty-two years. This mistake was repeated by Stephen Longstreet, and again by Norman Mark in his book, *Mayors, Madams, and Madmen*. It's hard to understand why the "boodle case" has been disregarded by local historians, but the following books helped steer me on the right track.

1. Kinsley, Philip, *The Chicago Tribune*, Volume Three: 1880-1900, The Chicago Tribune Company, 1946.
2. McPhaul, John, *Deadlines and Monkeyshines*, Prentice-Hall, 1962.
3. Canute Matson papers, Chicago Historical Society. Letters to Matson from Spies asking for permission to visit with his wife, and a letter from boodler Mike Leyden are included in this collection that was donated by Isabel Hofmann of Ottumwa, Iowa.

Sources and Notes

CHAPTER THREE:
A SUMMER OF GOLD: CHICAGO FROM MAY TO AUGUST, 1896

1. Bryan, William, *The First Battle*, W.B. Conkey, 1896. The candidate and his wife coauthored this readable review of the 1896 election.
2. Bushnell, George D. "When Chicago Was Wheel Crazy," *Chicago History* (Fall 1975): 167-75.
3. Casey, Robert J. *Chicago Medium Rare, Chicago Herald-American*, Publishers, 1949. While in his sixties, Casey wrote this breezy reminiscence about his Chicago boyhood of the 1890s.
4. Coletta, Paola, *Williams Jennings Bryan: Political Evangelist, 1860-1908*, University of Nebraska Press, 1964.
5. Corbitt, Robert L. *The Holmes Castle*, Corbitt & Morrison, 1895. (Microfilm) The author was an acquaintance of Holmes. He wrote this pamphlet before all the evidence was in. Based on his own personal search of the castle, Corbitt concludes that Minnie Williams was alive in England, which was, of course, bosh.
6. Franke, David, *Torture Doctor*, Hawthorne Press, 1975. The author borrowed heavily from Geyer's book, but this is the only accurate contemporary telling of the Holmes case.
7. Geyer, Franklin, *The Holmes-Pitezel Case: History of the Greatest Crime of the Century*, Publisher's Union of Philadelphia, 1896. The book is concise and avoids much of the self-praise that characterized Michael Schaak's book.
8. Golden, Harry, *A Little Girl Is Dead*, Avon paperbacks, 1965. The story of the Leo Frank lynching and a review of Thomas Watson's career.

CHAPTER FIVE: LEVEE LOW LIFE

1. *Chicago Police Reports*, 1905, 1906, 1907
2. Clayton, John, "The Scourge of Sinners: Arthur Barrage Farwell," *Chicago History* (Fall 1974): 68-77.
3. Harrison, Carter, *Growing Up With Chicago*, Bobbs-Merrill, 1944.
4. Harrison, Carter, *The Stormy Years*, Bobbs-Merrill, 1935. The first part of a two-volume autobiography of the mayor.
5. Kelly, John personal letters on file at the Chicago Historical Society.
6. McPhaul, Jack, *Johnny Torrio: First of the Ganglords*, Arlington House, 1970.
7. Pruter, Robert, "The Prairie Avenue Section of Chigago: The History and Examination of Its Decline," Unpublished graduate thesis, Roosevelt University, 1976.
8. Reckless, Walter, *Vice in Chicago*, University of Chicago Press, 1933.
9. Sharpe, May Churchill, *Chicago May: A Human Document by the Queen of Crooks*, Sampson, Low, & Marston, no date listed.
10. *The Social Evil in Chicago*, Gunthrop & Warren Publishers, 1910. This is the controversial report of the vice commission, considered too hot to handle by the U.S. Postal System in 1910.

11. Stead, William, *If Christ Came to Chicago*, Laird & Lee, 1894. A landmark book in its time, *If Christ Came to Chicago* was recently serialized in derisive fashion by the *Chicago Reader*.
12. Steffens, Lincoln, "Chicago: Half-Free, and Fighting On," *McClure's Magazine*, (21 October 1903): 563-577.
13. Washburn, Charles, *Come into My Parlor*, National Library Press, 1934. The story of the Everleigh sisters and their times.
14. Wendt, Lloyd, and Kogan, Herman, *Lords of the Levee*, Bobbs-Merrill, 1943. The only levee "source book" at this late date.
15. Wilson, Samuel Paynter, *Chicago by Gaslight*, No publisher listed, 1909. More religious dogma by the author.
16. Wilson, Samuel Paynter, *Chicago and its Cesspool of Infamy*, No publisher listed, January 1909. A moralizing, pedantic, little volume.

Chapter Seven: Of Bombs, Gamblers, Racing Wires, Newspaper Wars, & Mont Tennes

1. Asbury, Herbert, *Gem of the Prairie*, Alfred Knopf, 1940
2. *The Chicago Crime Book*, Albert Halper, ed. World Publishing, 1967.
3. *City Directory*, 1897, 1898, 1899.
4. Cooney, John, *The Annenbergs: The Salvaging of a Tainted Dynasty*, Simon & Schuster, 1982. Not enough material regarding the sale of General News by Tennes, a common problem for anyone trying to research his life.
5. Duis, Perry, & Holt, Glen, "Playing the Ponies on Lake Michigan," *Chicago Magazine* (August 1981): 108-12.
6. Erbstein, Charles, *The Show Up: Stories before the Bar*, Pascal Govici, 1926. In his time, Erbstein defended murderers, sluggers, gamblers, and blackmailers. Someone had to do it.
7. Flynn, John T., "Smart Money," *Collier's Magazine*, serialized September 13-27, 1940. Nothing new about Tennes in these articles either.
8. Griffin, Richard, "Big Jim O'Leary: Gambler Boss 'iv th' Yards," *Chicago History* (Winter 1976-77): 213-22. Good background material but nothing about O'Leary's role in the gambler wars of the early 1900s.
9. Kobler, John, *Capone: The Life and World of Al Capone*, G.P. Putnam's Sons, 1971. The best biography of Capone published to date.
10. Landesco, John, *Organized Crime: Part 3 of the Illinois Crime Survey*, University of Chicago Press, 1929. A thoughtful study of the organized crime problem that has plagued Chicago. The review of Mont Tennes' early career, was the only one I could find that went into any detail.
11. Murray, George, *The Madhouse on Madison Street*, Follett Publishing, 1965. The story of William Randolph Hearst and his newspaper.
12. Peterson, Virgil, *Barbarians in Our Midst*, Little, Brown, 1952.
13. Russell, Charles Edward, "Chaos and Bomb Throwing in Chicago," *Hampton's Magazine* (March 1910): 307-20.
14. Sasuly, Richard, *Bookies & Bettors: Two Hundred Years of Gambling*, Holt, Rinehart & Winston, 1982.

Sources and Notes

Chapter Eight: A Summer of Lost Innocence

1. Allen, Frederick, *Only Yesterday, An Informal History of the 1920s*, Harper and Row, 1931, Paperback edition, 1964.
2. Asinof, Eliot, *Eight Men Out*, Ace Books, 1963. A classic of American sports publishing.
3. Dreiser, Theodore, *American Diaries: 1902-1926*, Thomas P. Riggio, ed., University of Pennsylvania Press, 1983. A revealing look at the author's life and infidelities.
4. Fanning, Charles, and Skerritt, Ellen, "James T. Farrell and Washington Park: The Novel as Social History," *Chicago History* (Summer 1979): 80-91.
5. Gies, Joseph, *The Colonel of Chicago: A Biography of the Chicago Tribune's Legendary Publisher, Colonel Robert McCormick*. E.P. Dutton, 1979.
6. Gosnell, Harold F., *Negro Politicians*, University of Chicago Press, 1935.
7. LeVot, Andre, *F. Scott Fitzgerald, A Biography*, Doubleday & Co., 1982.
8. Lindberg, Richard, "The Chicago Whales & the Federal League of American Baseball," *Chicago History* (Spring 1981): 2-12. Also accompanying notes on Charles Weeghman's life.
9. *This Fabulous Century: 1910-1920*, Time-Life Inc., 1969.
10. Thrasher, Frederic, *The Gang*, University of Chicago Press, 1927. A sociological study of gangdom in Chicago.
11. Tuttle, William, *Race Riot: Chicago in the Red Summer of 1919*, Atheneum, 1978.
12. Wallechinsky, David and Wallace, Irving, *The People's Almanac*, Doubleday, 1975.
13. Wendt, Lloyd, and Kogan, Herman, *Big Bill of Chicago*, Bobbs-Merrill, 1953.
14. Wik, Reynold M., *Henry Ford and Grass Roots America*, University of Michigan Press, 1973. A disappointing, patronizing account of Ford.
15. Yardley, Jonathan, *Ring: A Biography*. Random House, 1977.

INDEX

Abbot, Willis J., 112
Abbott, Charles, 59
Abbott, Cora, 153
Abrahams, "Ike," 42
Ackerman, J.E., 184
Accardo, Tony "Joe Batters," 212
Adams, Francis, 70
Adams, Kate, 153
Adams, Phyllis, 152
Ade, George, 134
Adler, Jakie, 163
Aeillo, Joe, 203
Aeolus Cyclinc Club, 76
Alcock, John, 226, 246
Altgeld, John Peter, 35; frees Haymarket men, 39-40; quoted, 57; Chairman of the State Convention, 104; opposition to 1894 troop intervention, 106
Altman, Vincent, 206-7
Amart, Detective Fred, 156-57
Ames, Miner T., 57
Anderson, Margaret, 250
Anderson, Sherwood, 250
Andrews, Aaron, 158
Andrews, Deputy Coroner, 173
Annenberg brothers, 204-5
Annenberg, Max: heads gang of sluggers, 206; arrested, 208

Annenberg, Moses: buys Racing Form, 208; court proceedings, 211-12; sells to Ragen, 212; mentioned, 213, 252
Annenberg, Tobias, 204
Annenberg, Walter, 204
Anson, Adrian "Cap," 78
Anthony, Judge Elliot, 55
Argo, Horace, 195, 197-98, 201-2
Arimondi, Victor, 164
Arlington, Billy, 71
Armitage, Alderman Edward, 243
Armour, J. Ogden, 1, 13, 137
Arnold, Adolph, 76
Arnold, Benedict, 221
Arnold, C.W., 89
Arnold, Judge Michael, 96
Arvey, Jake, 167
Astor, John Jacob, 197
Atwell, Lyman, 141-42
Austin, Frederick, 13
Austin & Rosenbecker's First Regimental Band, 3
Austin, Wetherall, 213
Austin, William, 243
Aylward Athletic Club, 248

Badger, William, 227
Baker, George, 78

Index

Barber, Adam, 24
Barker, George "Red," 211
Barkley, Sam, 71
Barrett, Charles, 150
Barrett, John, 25
Barrett, Thomas, 181–82
Bartels, George, 30
Barton, Clara, 116
Barton, Fred, 98
Bartram, Sergeant, 13
Batchelder, Frank, 44
Bauler, Mathias, "Paddy," 168
Baxter, James, 67–68
Bayard, Thomas, 67
Beall, John, 254
Beaubien, Alexander: first white child born in Chicago, 81
Beaubien, Mark: pioneer days, 3
Behan, Louis J., 123, 125
Belknap, Jonathan, 84–85
Belknap, Myrtle Z. (Mrs. H.H. Holmes): marries Holmes, 84; mentioned, 94, 97
Bell, Major George, 214
Bellbunce, Oliver, 2
Beman, Solan, 3
Berkeley Light Guards, 7
Bernhardt, Sarah: visit to Chicago, 74–75
Bipper, Fred, 54
Birmingham, Thomas, 44
Birns, Stanley, 156–57
Black, C.W., 91
Black, Williams Perkins: accompanies Parsons to court, 29; defends Haymarket men, 33; appeal to Supreme Court, 34
Blackburn, Joseph, 104
Blair, Chauncey, 1
Blaine, James G., 52
Bland, Richard Parks: authorship of Bland-Allison Act, 104; portrait hung, 105; delegate count, 105
Bloom, "Ike" (Isaac Gitelson): appears in court, 123; intimidates witnesses, 125; opens Freiberg's, 134; First Ward Ball, 139; payoffs, 145; mentioned, 150, 153; quoted, 153; meets Nootbar, 161; license restored, 161; death of, 165
Bluemenberg, Robert, 30
Boettner, Captain Jack, 232–34
Boies, Governor Horace, 104–5, 110
Bond, L.L., 16
Bonfield, James, 14, 30
Bonfield, John: commands 22nd Street Detail, 14; mentioned, 15, 18, 40, 41; assures press, 21; dispatches police to Haymarket, 25; attitude toward anarchists, 26; sends police to meeting, 29; witnesses execution, 39; confronts *Times* editor, 42; quote about, 43; suspended, 43; death of, 43; conducts McGarigle investigation, 65
Bonfield, John Jr., 148
Booth, General William, 176
Boyington, William, 5, 13
Brainerd, E.R., 52
Brennan, Ed, 178
Brennan, John, 42
Bressi, Caterina, 129–30
Breternitz, Detective, 185
Brewster, John, 4
Brisbane, Arthur, 205
Brixey, John, 34
Brolaski, Harry, 199–200
Brooks, Virginia, 151
Brooks, Winnie, 207
Brothers, Leo Vincent, 210
Brown, Arthur, 226
Brown, Dan, 179
Brown, H.I., 199
Bruenell, Frank, 208
Bruisard, Carlos, 137
Bryan, William Jennings: agrarian ideal, 103; at convention, 106; quoted, 107; early life, 107–8; Cross of Gold speech, 109; speech to supporters, 111; begins campaign, 112; unsuccessful bid, 113;

delegate totals, 110; Chicago press support, 205; declines Ford invitation, 219
Bryant, George, 237
Buckley, Captain William, 38, 41, 51
Burbank, Luther, 219
Burke, Marjorie, 235
Burns, John, 189
Busse, Mayor Fred, 128, 141–42, 145, 187, 189
Butterly, Peter, 24
Buxbaum, Ferdinand, 139
Byfield, Herbert, 233
Byrnes, Inspector Thomas, 26

Callahan, Dan, 244–45
Callahan, Lieutenant, 10
Calumet Club, 3
Cameron, Lucille, 147
Capone, Al, 123, 164, 167, 177, 179, 204, 209, 211
Carey, J.A., 154
Carlyle, Thomas, 109
Carnegie, Andrew, 111
Caruso, Enrico, 133–34
Caruth, Thomas, 15
Casselman, Christian, 60
Caton, Arthur, 1, 4, 6
Cermak, Alderman Anton, 225
Chandler, Senator William Eaton, 103
Chapin, Charles, 67, 69
Chase, Mary, 144
Chicago American: quoted, 114
Chicago Daily News: quoted, 180
Chicago Defender: quoted, 249
Chicago Federation of Labor, 253
Chicago Inter-Ocean: quoted, 3
Chicago Presbyterian Seminary, 18
Chicago Times: quoted, 43
Chicago Tribune: quoted, 10, 35, 47–48, 77, 85, 220
Chrisman, Robert, 129
Chrisman, Thelma, 129
Cigrand, Emmeline, 92, 98
Ciago, Dominick, 141

City of Traverse, 185–86, 189, 191
Clafin, Dora, 119
Clan-Na-Gaels, 182
Clemenz, Theodore, 53
Cleveland, President Grover, 19, 52, 67, 104–5, 108, 113
Clyne, Charles, 225
Cobb, Henry Ives, 117
Cody, William, "Buffalo Bill," 108–9
Cohan, George M., 251
Cole, George "King," 122
Collins, Chief John: closes Whiskey Row, 126; replaced, 148; career discussed, 182; mentioned, 183; quoted, 184; allows *Traverse* to run, 186; indicted, 188
Collins, Captain Morgan, 200, 203
Colosimo, "Big" Jim: early life, 133; opens cafe, 134; at First Ward Ball, 139; at cafe, 153; calls Levee conference, 154; at Birns shooting, 156; arrested, 158; remains in Levee, 162; purchases Arrowhead, 163; marriage to Dale Winter, 163–64; death of, 164; mentioned, 165, 252; member of Jockey Club, 200
Colvin, Mayor Harvey: administration of, 8; influence of McDonald, 16; mentioned, 50
Comiskey, Charles, 217, 228, 251
Commercial Club, 3
Condon, "Blind" John: owns Roby Racetrack, 178; mentioned, 180; house bombed, 190; illustrated, 190; Grand Jury Probe, 195
Connelley's Patch, 121
Connolly, Arthur, 24
Connor, Icilius "Ned," 89
Connor, Julia: works for Holmes, 89; death explained, 90; mentioned, 91, 94, 98
Connor, Pearl, 89
Cook, John, 154
Cooney, Dennis "the Duke," 122–23

Index

Corbitt, Robert, 98
Corrigan, Edward: ownership of West Side Grounds, 4, 5
Corrozzo, "Dago" Mike, 133
Couglin, "Bathhouse" John: mentioned, 45, 128, 133, 153, 160, 168; on behalf of cyclists, 76; early life, 121; quoted, 122; commands Levee, 134; First Ward Ball, 139-42; nominates Wayman as "handsomest man," 151; death of, 167; election deal, 189
Coxey, Colonel Jacob, 111
Craig, Andy, 126, 139, 184
Cramer, Daniel, 24
Crane, Richard T., 44, 117
Cronin, Dr. Patrick, 28, 182
Crowe, Robert, 203, 241, 247
Cruisinberry, Jim, 251
Cudmore, Captain William, 138, 149-50
Cullett, "Chicken" Larry, 154
Cusick, Harry, 148, 150, 158

Daley, Richard J., 168, 249
Daniel, Senator John, 105-6
Dannenberg, William C.: heads Morals Squad, 154; Birns shooting, 156; illustrated, 159; later years, 166
Darrow, Clarence: quoted, 110; Scopes Trial, 113; mentioned, 134, 252; defends Tennes, 201-2
Davenport, Earl, 232-33
David, Henry, 20
Davies, Professor Henry, 115
Davis, Colonel Abel, 215
Davis, Mrs. Charles, 174
Dean, Dickie, 180-81
Debs, Eugene, 112-13, 253-54
Dee, Daniel, 178
DeForrest, Lee, 185-86
DeFrere, Desire, 164
Degan, Mathias, 25
Delavigne, Theodore, 220
Dell, Floyd, 250
Dell, Levi, 63

Dempsey, Jack, 242, 251
Deneen, Charles, 182
DePew, Chauncey, 197
DePriest, Alderman Oscar, 162-63, 245
DeSousa, May, 167
Dever, Mayor William, 203
Dickson, General Frank, 246
Dineen, John, 139
Dirty Dozen Athletic Club, 248-49
Dixon, Joseph, 49, 55
Doepp, Edward, 63-64
Doherty, James, 237
Dolan, Judge, 152
Donoghue, Cliff, 50
Donohue, Jerry, 30
Dorr, Jeannette, 147
Dorset, Pearl, 138
Dougherty, Edward, 63
Doyle, Chief Austin J.: interviews Bonfield, 15; replaces McGarigle, 17
Doyle, John, 24
Dowling, John, 51
Drake, Marion, 153
Dreiser, Theodore: *Sister Carrie* mentioned, 126; at Ocean Grove, 150; mentioned, 151
Drury, Horace, 84
Dunlop, Joseph, 42
Dua, Octave, 164
Dunn, Alderman, 123
Dunne, Mayor Edward, 149, 182, 185, 187, 189
Dunning, William, 223
Durkee, Kate, 89

Eastland sinking, 234
Ebersold, Chief Fredrick: appointed chief, 18; deploys police, 19; calls revenge circular unimportant, 22; mentioned, 26; attitude toward radicals, 26; appoints Schaak to case, 28; assures Governor, 29; orders Schnaubelt released, 30; tactics of, 31; attends executions, 38-39; death of, 43

Edison, Thomas, 219
Egan, J.J., 20
Egan, James J., 115
Elmer Gantry, 143
Engel, George: case against, 21–22; attends Monday Night Conspiracy, 33; will not ask clemency, 35; executed, 39
English, Nellie: early life, 78; shoots Hawkins, 79; quoted, 81; illustrated, 80
English, Joseph: quoted, 78, 81; arrested, 79; illustrated, 80
Enright, Lieutenant, 144
Enright, Morris "Mossie," 151, 157, 166, 205–7
Erbstein, Charles, 155, 192, 207
Erickson, Frank, 209
Esposito, "Diamond Joe," 165
Essig, Charles, 162
Everleigh, Minna & Ada: victim of Shaw scheme, 138; at First Ward Ball, 140, 142; quoted, 144, 146; bars Jack Johnson from club, 147; mentioned, 161; deaths, 165

Faber, Frederick, 58
Faber, Urban "Red," 228
Fabri, Arturo, 163–64
Falconet, Mrs. Cameron, 147
Farrell, James T., 250
Farwell, Arthur Barrage, 141, 150, 152
Feldman, Flora (Mrs. Mike McDonald), 71–73
Felsch, Oscar "Happy," 254
Ferber, Edna, 250
Fidelity Mutual Insurance Company, 93–98
Field, Marshall, 35, 206
Field, Marshall Jr., 137
Fielden, Reverend Samuel,: addresses rally, 12; *Times* description of, 20; confronts William Ward, 23; mentioned, 26, 33; arrested, 30; sentence reduced, 35; fate of, 39

Fields, Vina, 120
Fink, Charles, 24
Fischer, Adolph: to meet with Parsons, 23–24; prints Revenge Circular, 33; mentioned, 34; will not ask clemency, 35; executed, 39
Fisher, Tony, 142
Fiske, David, 84
Fitzgerald, F. Scott, 252
Fitzgerald, Frank, 138
Fitzgerald, Muriel, 236–37
Fitzgerald, Thomas R.: Wilkinson murder, 235–42; illustrated, 238
Fitzmorris, Charles, 246
Fitzpatrick, Mac, 156–57
Flavian, Timothy, 25
Flinn, John: quoted, 6, 14
Flynn, Elizabeth Gurley, 41
Ford, Edsel, 220
Ford, Henry: political and social views, 218; peace ship launched, 219; news service of, 219; *Tribune* editorial quoted, 220; interviewed, 221–22; later years, 223–24
Forrester, William, 61
Foster, William Z., 33, 41
Franche, Cyril, 155
Franche, James, "Duffy the Goat," 155, 161
Frank, Julius, 148–49
Frank, Leo, 113
Frank, Louis, 148–49
Franke, David, 84
Franks, Charles, 30
Frazer, Albert, 142
Freedman's Bill, 108
Freer, Captain John, 66–67
Friedman, Sollie, 134, 139–40, 157
French-Potter-Crockery Firm, 86
Freud, Sigmund, 236
Fry, Trent, 227
Funkhouser, Metellius, 154, 159, 162

Gallin, Frank, 50
Gandil, Arnold, "Chick," 217, 255

Index

Garfinkle, David, 132
Garrity, Chief John, 243-44, 246
Garrity, William P., 105
Gary, Judge Joseph: believes Schnaubelt guilty, 30; conducts Haymarket trial, 33; instructs jury, 34; accused of prejudice, 40; mentioned, 41; convicts gamblers, 51; frees George Silver, 128; quoted, 128
Gaston, Lucy Page, 152
Gelert, John, 44
Genker, "Monkey Face" Charley, 134
Gentleman, Dutch, 206
Gentleman, Gus, 206
Gentleman, Peter, 208, 210, 235
Gentleman, William, 206, 235, 157
George, Henry, 35
George, King, 214
Gerdon Athletic Club, 248
Geyer, Detective Franklin, 95-96
Gibson, Charles Dana, 170
Giels, Christian, 60, 69-70
Gillespie, Joseph, 171-73, 176
Gilmer, Harry, 34
Gish, Dorothy, 34
Gish, Lillian: visit to Chicago, 224-25
Gleason, Chief James, 159, 162, 200
Gleason, William J., "Kid," 217
Glessner, John J., 216
Goddard, F. Norton, 197
Goldman, Emma, 19
Gompers, Samuel, 18, 254
Gordon, "Waxey," 209
Gore, James, 51
Gould, Helen, 198
Gove, C.H., 85-86
Grabiner, "Jew Kid," 163
Grant, Sheriff Thomas, 187
Gray, "Blubber Bob," 135
Gray, Mrs. Griswold, 117
Gray, Senator, 105
Griffith, David Wark, 224, 250
Grimes, "Paddy," 191, 195

Grinnell, Julius: believes Schnaubelt guilty, 30; Haymarket prosecutor, 34; mentioned, 41; begins "Boodle" investigation, 54; criticized, 55; illustrated, 57; mentioned, 58; proves conspiracy, 60; refuses deal, 61; persues McGarigle, 67; mentioned, 68, 70; meets with Klehm, 69; now a judge, 70
Grogan, Barney, 200
Guerin, "Paddy," 16, 179, 191-92
Guerin, Webster, 72-73
Guernsey, Alderman Guy, 234
Guilfoyle, Marty, 207-10
Gunther, Alderman Charles, 139
Guzik, Jake "Greasy Thumb," 212

Haas, Louis, 25, 33
Haines, Professor Walter, 52
Halpin, John, 150
Hamburg Athletic Club, 249
Hand, Johnny, 118
Hanes, J.M., 20
Hankins, Effie, 146
Hankins, Jeff, 50-51
Hanna, Marcus Alonzo, 103, 110-11, 113
Hansen, Nels, 25
Harding, "Eph," 201
Harding, George, 162
Harding, Patrick, 148, 150
Hare, Sam, 162
Harrigan, Major Lawrence, 94
Harris, Al, 150
Harris, Hattie, 138
Harris, John, 244
Harrison, Carter: elected mayor, 12; breaks up street disturbance, 14; appoints McGarigle, 17; quoted, 18, 47, 51; issues Haymarket permit, 21; visits Bonfield, 25; testifies, 34; buys newspaper, 42; warns McGarigle about election, 45; mentioned, 50, 108; upholds saloon closing on New Year's Eve, 116; re-

elected, 123; closes Silver's saloon, 128; asked to close Levee, 129; orders vice crackdown, 145; mentioned, 152; opinions of segregated vice, 160; closes Freiberg's, 161; re-elected, 200
Harrison, Mrs. Carter, (Edith Ogden), 5
Hart, Mike, 130–31
Hart, Mollie, 130–31
Hartford, Patrick, 24
Harvey, William, 108
Hassett family, 11
Hatch, Sam, 150
Haverly, Colonel Jack, 49
Hawkins, Frank, 81
Hawkins, William: confronts English, 78; shot, 79; illustrated, 80; recovers, 81
Hay, John, 111
Hayes, President Rutherford B., 11
Haywood, William: burial site, 41; visit to Chicago, 252; quoted, 253; I.W.W. involvement, 254
Healy, John J., 123, 151, 186, 195
Hearst, William Randolph, 204–6
Heath, Mayor Monroe, 8, 14, 16
Hecht, Ben, 237
Hedgepath, Marian, 93–94
Heissler & Jung, 53
Heitler, Mike "de Pike": mentioned, 132; McCann scandal, 148; white slaver, 150
Henagow, Isaac, 155, 157, 159
Henrotin, Ellen, 145
Hickey, John, 11
Hickey, Chief Michael: warns Parsons, 8; career of, 9; appointed chief, 16; voted out of office, 9; connection with McGarigle, 67
Hill, Senator David: contender for nomination, 104; enters convention hall, 105; quoted, 106; to debate, 107
Hill, Harold, 143
Hill, Joe, 41
Hoffman, Michael, 28

Hoffman, Coroner Peter, 176
Holden, Mrs. E.S., 85
Holland, Harry, 52, 61, 179
Holt, Charlotte, 77
Honore, Adrian, 116
Hopkins, Harry, 163
Horan, Michael, 24
Horner, Henry, 234, 251
Howard, James, 75
Howe, Colonel Jeptha, 75
Howe, John, 154
Howe, Lieutenant William, 240
Howey, Walter, 240
Howells, William Dean, 35
Hoyne, MacLay: probes Levee shooting, 158–59; runs for State's Attorney, 162; defends Tennes, 203; riot investigation, 245; called a racist, 247; raids of, 249
Hubbard, George, 30, 41
Hughes, Chief Michael, 203
Hullett, Orvy, 223
Humphries, Murray "the Camel," 212
Hunt, Inspector Nicholas, 146, 180, 189, 200
Huret, Jules, 122
Hyman, Attorney Ben, 186

Ingram, Zella, 155
Iroquois Club, 3
Iroquois Theatre Fire, 234
Irving, Captain John, 62, 65, 69

Jackson, "Shoeless" Joe, 228
Jackson, Alderman Louis, 245
Jameson, Alexander, 24
Jamieson, Judge Egbert, 60, 69
Jansen, Ed, 101
Jefferson, Thomas, 103, 108
Johnson, Anna, 166
Johnson, Byron Bancroft, 217, 228
Johnson, Jack, 125, 146–47
Jones, Harry "Teenan," 162
Jones, Senator James K., 106
Jones, J. Russell, 14–15
Jones, Mother, 253

Index

Jones, Roy: arrives in Levee, 125; conspires to disguise Moore death, 138; Franche shooting, 155; Cadillac Saloon, 160
Joplin, Scott, 135
Joseph, Sarah, 131-32

Kadish, R.D., 14
Kane, Joseph, 205
Kavanaugh, Harry, 178
Kee, James W., 60
Keeley, James, 205
Keeley, Michael, 55
Kelleher, Lieutenant, 138
Keller, August, 24
Kelly, Ed, 192
Kelly, John, 167
Kenna, Michael, "Hinky-Dink": mentioned, 45, 133, 150, 153, 158, 160, 168; quoted, 119, 122, 128, 159; First Ward Ball, 139-42; death of, 167; gambling influence, 179, 200; election deal, 189; illustrated, 196; visits Hot Springs, 216; saloon closed, 226
Kerr, Dickie, 228
Kiel, Mayor Henry, 227
Kilgore, Sergeant, 191
King, John, 24
King, John A., 55
King, Wyncie, 141-42
Kinzie, John, 3
Kipley, Chief Joseph, 116, 182
Kirkland, Weymouth, 211, 218
Kledzic, Anna, 27-28
Klehm, George, 69
Klinginsmith, F.L., 219
Klokke, E.F., 16
Kohlsaat, Herman, 117
Komens, Chris, 30
Ku Klux Klan, 112

Lady Elgin sinking, 234
Lait, Jack, 163, 252
Lakeview Cycling Club, 76
Lame Jimmy, 139
Landis, Judge Kenesaw Mountain: conducts Tennes probe, 201; quoted, 177, 202; closes O'Leary saloon, 203; denies Fitzgerald appeal, 242
Lardner, Ringold: covers graft trial, 163; leaves Chicago, 250-51; disillusionment of, 252
Lavin, Patrick, 182, 189
Lawrence, "Long Green" Andy, 205-6
Lawrence, Harry, 50
Lawson, Victor, 181, 205, 216
LeGallicare, Richard, 114
Lehmann, E.J.: partnership with McGarigle, 48; purchases house for McGarigle, 62; mentioned, 64, 70; leaves town, 65
Lehr und Wehr Verein, (Study and Resistance Group), 12, 29, 34
Leiter, Levi Z., 1
Leiter, Mary, (Lady Curzon), 1
Lenz, Ed., 208, 211
Lenz, Lionel, 208, 211
Leonard, "Kid," 51
Leslie, Richard, 75
Leutgart, Adolph, 27
Levee, map of, 124
Lewis, Billy, 245
Lewis, "Dago" Frank, 147-48, 150, 163
Lewis, Judge Henry, 110
Leyden, Mike, 58, 60
Liebman, Adolph, 152
de Ligne, Prince Henri, 75
Lincoln, Abraham, 35
Lincoln Cycling Club, 76
Lincoln, Robert Todd, 117
Lindbergh, Charles A., 226
Lingg, Louis: accused of making bombs, 21; mentioned, 30; commits suicide, 31; illustrated, 32; will of, 42
Lingle, Alfred "Jake": murder of, 209-10
Lipton, Sir Thomas, 251
Little, Ed, 146
Little Egypt, 126

Little, George, 125, 139
Lobstein, J.G., 53
Locklear, Omar, 227
Lodge, Henry Cabot, 103
Loewenstein, Jake, 28, 42
Loewenstein, Mabel, 42-43
Longnecker, Joel, 70-71
Lonigan, Studs, 250
Looney, Tom, 205
Lorraine Athletic Club, 248
Louis, Frank, 25
Lovering, Clara (Mrs. H.W. Mudgett), 83-84, 94, 97
Lowden, Governor Frank: attends Palmer reception, 117; reviews troops, 214-15; streetcar compromise, 227; promises to blacks, 250
Lucking, Alfred, 220, 222
Lundin, Fred "the Poor Swede," 214
Luthardt, William, 162
Lynch, Anna, 210
Lynch, Detective, 152
Lynch, Jack: buys Tennes stock, 208; kidnapped, 210-11
Lynn, Charles, 60, 69

MacArthur, Charles, 237
Maciavelli, Niccolo, 82
Mack, Connie, 228
Mack, Judge, 123, 125
Mackin, "Oyster Joe," 52, 61, 69
MacMillan, Alexander, 176
Madigan, Harry, 248
Mahan, Alfred Thayer, 103
Malato, Stephen, 38
Malley, Margaret, 207
Mann, James, 133
Marsh, George, 66-67
Martin, Joseph, 39
Martin, Joseph, 186
Martin, Morris, 50
Martin, "Shaggy," 248
Mason, Mayor Roswell, 7
Masters, Edgar Lee, 107
Matthews, Governor Claude, 104

Matson, Sheriff Canute: will not permit Spies wedding, 35; letter to, 36; quoted, 39, 63-64; illustrated, 57; takes McGarigle home, 61-62; mentioned, 66
Matteson, Delos, 85-86
Mattocks, John, 47
Maubaum, Charles, 147
Maubaum, Julius, 147
Mayer, Erskine, 254
Mayer, Levi, 181
Mays, Carl, 228
McAvoy, John, 47
McCafey, Therese, 135
McCall, William, 244
McCann, Inspector Edward: scandal of, 148-49; mentioned, 150, 166-67
McCarthy, James "Buck," 58, 60-61, 69-70
McCormick, Cyrus Hall, 13
McCormick, Cyrus Hall Jr., 18-19, 23, 40, 105
McCormick, Mrs. Cyrus Hall, 116
McCormick, Edith, 220, 227
McCormick, Harold, 227
McCormick, Katherine, 220
McCormick, Colonel Robert: circulation wars, 205; offers reward, 210; sued by Ford, 218; war record, 220
McCutcheon, John T., 227
McDermott, Elizabeth, 174
McDonald, Edward: engineer at hospital, 53; mentioned, 54, 61; arrested, 55, 57; visits Normal School, 58; son killed, 60; released, 70; visits Mike's deathbed, 73
McDonald, Guy, 72
McDonald, Michael Cassius: mentioned, 8, 12, 41; political influence, 16; gambling connections, 17, 39; supports McGarigle, 46; *Tribune* quote about, 47; mentioned, 48, 52-53; early career, 49-50; as bondsman, 50-51; col-

Index

lects on courthouse job, 52; quoted, 57; as McGarigle bondsman, 61; private life, second marriage, 71-72; heads Illinois delegation, 104; gambling interests, 179; mentioned, 190
McDonald, Mrs. Michael (Mary Noonan), 71, 73
McDowell, Joseph, 51
McErlane, Frankie, 206
McFadden, Michael, 154
McGarigle, Anna, 63-66
McGarigle, Bessie, 63
McGarigle, Eddie, 66
McGarigle, 63, 66-67
McGarigle, William: implements patrol box system, 17; early career, 45-46; runs for Sheriff, 46-47; loses election, 48; Warden of County Hospital, 48; as commissioner, 49; collects boodle, 53; interviewed, 54; mentioned, 54, 69, 73; quoted, 55, 62; arrested, 55; enters into conspiracy, 58; controls commission pool, 59; formulates plans, 60; case against, 60; escape, 61-65; home of, (illustrated), 64; arrives in Canada, 66; movements in Canada, 67-68; returns to Chicago, 70; later years, 71
McGinnis, Tom, 178-79, 181, 187
McKenna, C.M., 138
McKinley, President William, 103, 111, 113, 116, 140
McLaughlin, P.F., 118
McLaughery, Richard, 60, 69
McLean, John, 105
McPadden, William "Gunner," 248
McVeagh, Franklin, 117
McWeeney, Chief John: mentioned, 129, 152, 159; reluctant to close resorts, 145; replaced, 146; illustrated cartoon, 193
McWhorter, Frank, 179-80
Medill, Joseph: administration, 8; fires board members, 16; quoted, 19; attends Palmer tea, 105; mentioned, 224
Meeker, George, 117
Mendel, Joe, 248
Merlo, Mike, 165
Merrill, Joseph, 156
Meyer, Rose, 229
Meyerbeer, Giacomo, 13
Middleton, Thomas, 59
Millard, Zoe, 146, 161
Miller, George, 25
Miller, Harry, 162
Miller, Polk, 75
Miller, "Yiddles," 248
Mills, Luther-Laflin, 61
Mitchell, John, 231, 234
Moissant, Father Joseph, 71
Mondi, Jimmy, 204, 210
Mooney Boland Detective Agency, 65
Mooney, Detective, 207-8
Moore, Helen Fargo, 137-38
Moore, James Hobart, 138
Moore, Nathaniel Ford, 137-38, 155
Moran, George "Bugs," 204
Morelock, John, 201
Moresco, Joseph, 158
Moresco, Victoria, 133-34, 164
Morgan, J.P., 187, 197
Moressey, Lieutenant, 159
Morton, "Jelly Roll," 136
Most, Johann, 8
Mudgett, Herman Webster (H.H. Holmes): quoted, 81, 97; illustrated, 82; early life, 83; marriage, 84; insurance swindle, 85; castle of, illustrated, 85; castle described, 84; furniture fraud, 86; business swindles, 87-88; murders Emily Van Tassel, 88; dealings with Williams sisters, 89-91; marries Georgie Yoke, 92; plans Pitezel swindle, 93; alibi of, 95; trial, 96; executed, 97; mentioned, 98

Muellenbach, Ollie, 159
Mulkowsky (Brunofsky), 28
Murphy, Alfred, 223
Murphy, Ed, 154
Murphy, Isaac, 4-5
Murphy, Lawrence, 24
Murphy, Tim, 197-98

Neebe, Oscar, 13, 33, 34, 39
Neilson, Nicholas, 174-76
Nind, Frederick, 87
Nixon, William Penn, 116
Nootbar, Captain Max, 120
Normoyle, Anna, 170
Norris, Frank, 13
Northrup, John, 241
Norton, Milton, 232
Norwood, Helen, 166
Noyes, George, 50

Oakley, electrician, 63-64
O'Bannion, Dion, 206, 249
O'Brien, "Red Necktie" Jimmy, 240-41
O'Brien, John, 245
O'Brien, Captain William P., 127, 162
Ochs, Adam, 55, 60, 69
O'Connor, William, 188
O'Donnell, Captain Simon: early career, 16; replaces Seavey, 17; opposition to radicals, 20; mentioned, 22, 182
Offenbach, Jacques, 3
Oglesby, Governor Richard, 35
O'Grady, Ed, 157
O'Hara, Barrett, 134
O'Leary, "Carnation" Dan, 226
O'Leary, Jim: opposition to Tennes, 178; saloon described, 178; mentioned, 179; accused, 180; raids McGinnis saloon, 181; the Stockade, 187; sketch of gambling parlor, 188; saloon bombed, 191; war ended, 197; retirement, 199; death, 203
Oliver, Richard, 55, 60, 69

Olmstead, Frederick Law, 78
O'Malley, Patrick, 133, 139, 185, 191-92, 195, 216
O'Neill, Francis, 182; illustrated, 183
Otis, Philo, 153
Otto, Carl, 231
Our Flag Athletic Club, 248

Palmer, Honore, 116
Palmer, Secretary John, 113
Palmer, Potter: indicted for gambling, 51; castle of, 116; builds Gold Coast, 117; remodels castle, 117-18
Palmer, Mrs. Potter (Bertha Honore): attends Derby Day, 4; mentioned, 6; hosts tea, 105; hosts New Year reception, 116-17
Paris Commune, 8
Parsons, Albert: early life and career, 7-9; addresses meeting, 6, 8, 10, 12; stages rally, 11, 13; editor of newspaper, 11; rhetoric of, 19; *Tribune* quote about, 20; arrives at Haymarket, 23; mentioned, 24, 33, 44; flees Chicago, 29; sentenced, 35; executed, 39
Parsons, Lucy: mentioned, 6, 23, 253; leads rally, 13; description, 19; attends execution, 38; mail tampered with, 38
Parsons, Samuel, 7
Patterson, Joseph, 205, 218, 220, 223
Patton, John, 163
Payne, John A., 198-99
Pease, Sheriff James, 192
Peterson, William, 159
Perry, Harry, 179, 187, 195
Pfennig, Ernest, 78
Phillips, Wiley J., 133
Pickford, Mary, 224
Pierce, P.J., 195
Pietrowsky the Junkman, 141
Pinkerton, Allan, 67
Pitezel, Ben, (Benton Lyman): meets Holmes, 83; receives deed, 91; body exhumed, 94; mentioned, 97

Index 279

Pitezel, Carrie, 93-95
Pitezel, Nellie, 94, 96
Pizzi, Baptista, 129-30
Pizzi, Santina, 129
Plummer, Wharton, 86
Powers, Alderman John "de Pow," illustrated, 196
Proudhon, Pierre, 8
Pulitzer, Joseph, 205
Pullman, Mrs. George, 116

Quay, Matt, 113
Queen Victoria, 1
Quinlan, Patrick, 84, 92
Quinn, James Aloysius "Hot Stove," 200
Quinn, Martin, 33

Ragen's Colts, 205, 248-49
Ragen, Frank, 212, 248-249
Ragen, James, 205-6, 209, 211-12
Ragtime, 135-36
Razzina, Frank, 134
Reagan, President Ronald, 204
Rector's Restaurant, 137
Reed, John, 222
Reeves, Professor, 223
Regnier, F., 110
Rehm, Jacob: resigns, 9, 16; appointed Chief, 15; grooms McGarigle, 45
Rehm, Jacob Jr., 28
Reilly, Colonel Henry, 220
Reno, Charles, 16
Revere House, 61, 69
Riccollet, Frances: suicide of, 169, 174-76; illustrated, 174
Risberg, Charles "Swede," 255
Robinson, Elisha, 55, 57
Roche, Mayor John, 41-42, 59
Rockefeller, John D., 187
Roe, Clifford, 130-32
Rogers, Alderman John, 178, 195
Ronayne, R.R., 246
Roosevelt, President Theodore, 103, 149, 152, 215
Rosencranz, Elihu, 192

Rosenfield, Sam, 22
Rosenwald, Julius, 145
Rowe, Louise Osborne, 242-43
Ruffo, Titto, 133
Runyon, Damon, 203
Russell, William, 104, 106-7
Russell, William F., 209
Ruth, George Herman "Babe," 254
Ryan, Frank "Chew Tobacco," 167
Ryan, Michael "White Alley": commands 22nd Street Detail, 150; quoted, 155; at Birns shooting, 157-58; payoff system, 159
Ryan, John, 179
Ryerson, Martin, 216

St. John, Fred, 67
St. John, Leonard: appears at jail, 61; career of, 62; role in escape, 63-65; ownership of the boat, 65; mentioned, 67, 73; indicted, 69
Scanlon, Judge Kickham, 153
Schaak, Captain Michael: promises Waller immunity, 22; profile of career, 26-28; accuses Eversold, 30; intrigues of, 31; criticizes Spies wedding, 36; attends execution, 38-39; mentioned, 40-41; scandal, 42-43; suspended, 43; death, 43
Schalk, Ray, 228, 255
Schlotter, Mrs. Lemuel (Leona Garrity): white slave case, 132-33
Schmidt, Frank, 30
Schneider, Nicholas: described, 54; mentioned, 57; testifies, 58
Schreiber, Belle, 146-47
Schubert, Detective Otto, 182, 185
Schubert, William, 157, 200
Schuettler, Herman: Haymarket involvement, 28, 31; illustrated, 33; mentioned, 160, 178; replaces Healey as Chief, 163; sends detail to *Traverse*, 185; builds wireless station, 186; gambling crackdown, 192-95; caricature, 193; removed from detail, 200
Schuettler, Mrs. Herman, 195

Schulkens, John, 14
Schwab, Michael: addresses meeting, 12; arrested, 30; leaves Haymarket, 33; mentioned, 39
Schwartz, Charles, 4
Schwimmer, Rosika, 219
Schwinn, Ignaz, 76
Scott, Anna, 170
Seavey, Valdous, 16
Seeberger, Louis, 181
Seliger, William, 30-31
Sennett, Mack, 243
Serritella, Daniel, 212
Serviss, Garrett, 115
Sewall, Arthur, 112
Sexton, Maria: suicide of, 169, 171-73, 176; illustrated, 172
Shannon, Nicholas, 24
Sharpe, May Churchill, 120
Sharpshooter's park (Riverview), 103
Shatz, Morris, 150
Shaw, George Bernard, 35, 169
Shaw, Victoria: mentioned, 137, 146; conspires to cover Moore death, 138; armed with revolver, 154; Friendly Friends, 161
Shea, Detective, 189
Shepard, Judge Henry, 57, 59, 70-71
Sherman, John, 113
Shippey, Chief George, 141, 148-49, 160, 171, 191-92
Shoemaker, William A., 98
Silver Ash Institute, 87, 92
Silver, George: loses Maxim license, 127; quoted, 128; saloon described, 128; mentioned, 165
Simmons, Rufus, 133
Simonson, Barton, 25
Sims, Edwin, 145
Slattery, James, 167
Sloop, John, 156
Smalley Cycling Club, 76
Smith, Charles "Social": mentioned, 179; sides with Bud White in war, 181; purchases *City of Traverse*, 185;

influences governor of Indiana, 187
Smith, Eugene, 93
Smith, Frank, 239
Smith, Henry, 24
Smith, Rodney "Gipsy": leads march, 143-44
Smithman, C.E., 231
Solomon, Moses, 33
Sousa, John Philip, 113, 136
South Side Clubs Association, 247
South Side Cycling Club, 77
Sowers, Baldy, 216
Speaker, Tris, 217
Spencer, Georgie, 161, 166
Spiegel, Jacob, 62
Spies, August: early life, 11; addresses rally, 12, 20; Revenge Circular, 21; mentioned, 21-22, 30, 33; arrives at Haymarket, 23; sentenced, 35; letter to Matson, 36; executed, 39
Spies, Christian, 30, 36
Stange, Gustave, 31
Stanton, Lieutenant James, 24
Starley, John Kemp, 76
Stauber, George, 244
Stead, William: inspects Chicago's moral condition, 120; mentioned, 143
Stefano, Rocco, 156
Steffens, Lincoln: article quoted, 121
Stelk, Judge, 251
Steunenberg, Governor Frank, 252
Stevens, Walter, 205
Stevenson, Vice-President Adlai, 75
Stevenson, Elliot, 220-21
Steward, LeRoy, 149
Stift, John, 28, 30
Stiles, Israel Newton, 58
Stillman, Mary, 176
Stokes, W.E.D., 166
Sullivan, Alexander, 61
Sullivan, John L., 251
Sullivan, Joseph "Sport," 255
Sullivan, Tim, 140
Sully, Bernard, 201

Index

Sumner, Dean Walter, 142, 145, 149
Swanson, Paul, 65
Swett, Leonard, 35
Swift, Gustav, 13
Sypher, Pearl, 132

Taft, William Howard, 133
Tait, George, 69
Teller, Henry, 105
Tennes, Helen, 209
Tennes, Jacob, 177
Tennes, Mont: early life, 177-78; remains aloof from gambler trust, 179; saloon raided, 181; expands interests, 182; gambling parlors, 184; influence of, 185; launches *John R. Sterling*, 186; Dearborn Pavillion, 187; house bombed, 191; Grand Jury investigation, 195-97; buys Payne Service, 198; extortion of, 199; *Daily News* Probe, quoted, 200-202; raided, 203; dealings with mob, 204; sells to Annenberg, 208-9; mentioned, 210-11; death, 212; will, 213
Tennes, Mont (Nephew), 208-9
Tennes, Peter, 181
Tennes, Willie, 201
Tetrazzini, Luisa, 133
Thaw, Evelyn Nesbit, 169-70
Thaw, Harry K., 170
Thielke, The Flossie, 65
Thistle Cycling Club, 76
Thompson, William Hale: wide open administration, 161-62; abolishes Morals Squad, 165-66; gambling influence, 203; arrives late at welcoming parade, 214; sues *Tribune*, 218; refuses to call National Guard, 245; calls up Guard, 246; manipulates Blacks, 247; revokes club's charter, 248
Thorsen, Albert, 101
Thrasher, Fredric, 247
Tillman, Ben "Pitchfork," 106
Tinee, Mae, 225

Tobey Furniture Company, 86
Torrio, Johnny: arrives in Chicago, 134; manages Colosimo saloon, 147, 153; quoted, 154; mentioned, 155; at hospital, 157; escapes to Indiana, 158; purchases Arrowhead, 163
Touhy, William, 212
Tracey, F.W., 201
Trostel, Fridrich, 116
Trude, Asa, 104
Trumbull, Lyman, 108
Tucker, Judge James, 219-20
Turpin, Tom, 136
Tuttle, Fred, 5
Twain, Mark, 93
Tyler, Billy, 50
Tyler, Harry, 78
Tyrrell, Frank, 24, 79

Union Club, 3
Union League Club, 3, 61

Van Bever, Julia, 130-32
Van Bever, Maurice: quoted, 130; white slave case, 130-32; mentioned, 133; at Birns shooting, 156
Van Dusen, Maude, 129
Van Pelt, John: arrested, 55; indicted, 60; convicted, 60; quoted, 70
Van Tassel, Emily, 88
Van Zandt, James, 36
Van Zandt, Rosnina (Mrs. August Spies), 35, 38, 61
Varnell, Harry, 53, 55, 60-61, 69
Venillo, Roxy, 155-56, 158-61
Verne, Jules, 115
Vesey, Lieutenant, 11
Vilas, William, 104, 106
Villano, Antonio, 165
Vogelsang's Restaurant, 215

Walderon, Carl, 150
Waller, Gottfried, 21-22
Walska, Ganna, 227
Walton, "Plunger," 5

Ward, Captain William: leads Haymarket detachment, 22; addresses Fielden, 23; contradicts testimony, 33; runs protection racket, 42; statue molded after, 44
Warner Glass Bending Company, 88
Washburn, Charles, 165
Washburn, Hempstead, 117
Washburne, Elmer, 16, 45
Washington, George, 223
Wasserman, Michael, 60, 69
Watson, Carrie, 120, 139
Watson, Thomas: career discussed, 112–13
Wayman, John: case against McCann, 149; mentioned, 150; illustrated, 151; career discussed, 151; vows to close Levee, 152; Levee raids, 153; death, 166; secures Enright conviction, 207
Weaver, Carl, 232
Weaver, George "Buck," 254
Webber, Jake, 198
Webster, Nina, 138
Weegham, Charles, 202, 252–54
Weeks, Harvey, 17, 47
Weinert, Albert, 41
Weismuller, Johnny, 213
Weiss, Ed, 125, 134–35, 147, 150, 163
Wentworth, Mayor John: Two o'clock purge, 15
West, James, 42
Whalen, Michael, 28, 30
Whalen, "Mockingbird," 51
Wheeler, John, 251
Whipple, Harold, 206
Whiskey Scandal, 16
White, Bud, 179–81, 185, 192
White, Stanford, 170

Wigmore, John, 234
Wilcox, Reverend, 97
Wilkinson, Berneice, 235
Wilkinson, Janet: murder of, 235–42; illustrated, 236
Wilkinson, Mrs., 239
Willard, Jess, 242, 251
Williams, Baldwin, 91
Williams, Reverend Charles, 68
Williams, Eugene, 244
Williams, Minnie: illustrated, 90; deeds property, 91; witness Holmes wedding, 92; mentioned, 94; finds personal belongings of, 96
Williams, Nannie: comes to Chicago, 91; murdered, 91
Wilson, President Woodrow, 215
Windle, Willie, 77
Wingfoot crash, 229–35
Wing, Frank, 125
Winter, Dale (Mrs. James Colosimo): marriage, 163–64; mentioned, 252
Wren, Dan, 55, 60
Wright, Nathan, 83
Wright, Orville, 227
Wrigley, William Jr., 200, 253

Yerkes, Charles Tyson, 75, 160, 168
Yoke, Georgianna (Mrs. H.H. Holmes): travels with Holmes, 91; marries Holmes, 92; mentioned, 93, 95, 97; testifies, 96
Young, William C., 232

Zeisler, Sigismund, 33
Zevertnick, Joseph, 171
Ziegfeld, Florenz, 164
Zimmerman, Arthur, 78